The Entrepreneurial Muse

THE ENTREPRENEURIAL MUSE

Inspiring Your Career in Classical Music

Jeffrey Nytch

Oxford University Press is a department of the University of Oxford. It furthers
the University's objective of excellence in research, scholarship, and education
by publishing worldwide. Oxford is a registered trade mark of Oxford University
Press in the UK and certain other countries.

Published in the United States of America by Oxford University Press
198 Madison Avenue, New York, NY 10016, United States of America.

Library of Congress Cataloging-in-Publication Data
Names: Nytch, Jeffrey, 1964– author.
Title: The entrepreneurial muse : inspiring your career in classical music / Jeffrey Nytch.
Description: New York, NY : Oxford University Press, [2018] |
Includes bibliographical references and index.
Identifiers: LCCN 2017027561 (print) | LCCN 2017027133 (ebook) |
ISBN 9780190630973 (cloth : alk. paper) | ISBN 9780190630980 (pbk. : alk. paper) |
ISBN 9780190630997 (updf) | ISBN 9780190631000 (epub)
Subjects: LCSH: Music—Vocational guidance. | Music entrepreneurship.
Classification: LCC ML3795 .N97 2018 (ebook) | LCC ML3795 (print) |
DDC 780.23—dc23
LC record available at https://lccn.loc.gov/2017027561

9 8 7 6 5 4 3 2 1

Paperback printed by Webcom Inc., Canada
Hardback printed by Bridgeport National Bindery, Inc., United States of America

To my parents, who taught me the value of hard work,

And to my husband, who taught me to enjoy the fruits of my labors.

CONTENTS

PREFACE

WHAT IS THE PURPOSE OF THIS BOOK?

The first conservatory in the United States was founded in 1857 at the Peabody Institute in Baltimore. The Oberlin Conservatory followed a few years later, and by the early twentieth century most of the great American conservatories had opened for business. Up until World War II, these small elite institutions turned out a highly select supply of musicians trained in the European classical tradition. Students worked as apprentices, with those deserving of careers receiving the necessary introductions from their teachers. Career paths were few, well known by all, and specific; training beyond mastery of the instrument was not even conceived of, much less required. It was a closed but relatively stable system in which the demand for concert musicians and teachers and the supply of conservatory graduates were more or less in equilibrium.

Then came the postwar era and the GI Bill. While it was undoubtedly one of the greatest contributors to our nation's economic and civic health over the last seventy-five years, the GI Bill produced some unintended consequences. The explosion of college enrollees led to enormous growth in higher education, especially public state universities. With each of these institutions wanting to offer a comprehensive education, departments of music multiplied exponentially—as did the number of music graduates. Many of these graduates stayed in school, pursuing graduate degrees they could then redeem for a teaching post in one of the growing number of music schools nationwide. Many others found work in numerous orchestras and chamber music groups that emerged to serve a burgeoning middle class. The result was a self-perpetuating system of music schools needing to fill their ranks with more and more students, requiring more and more teachers, which in turn drove continued expansion of music programs from the most selective conservatories to the most humble community colleges. In a few decades we went from graduating perhaps a few hundred classically trained musicians a year to graduating tens of thousands of them.

While the growth of music higher education in the decades following World War II has had many positive outcomes, the flip side is a situation in which the supply of music graduates has far outstripped the demand for their talents (at least in the traditional jobs of orchestral musician, soloist, chamber musician, and teacher). Meanwhile, the mainstream classical music world (symphonies, opera, chamber music) has been in more or less continuous state of crisis: audience numbers have declined sharply over the last two decades, public funding of the arts is smaller than ever, and the digital revolution has completely reshaped the ways audiences experience, interact with, and purchase musical content. Taken together, these trends present challenges to the aspiring professional musician that are both numerous and profound. How does today's musician distinguish himself or herself from thousands of others with essentially the same set of credentials? How does one create value for one's music when the market is already saturated with content? How can we remain relevant in, and engaged with, a field that is in a constant state of change?

The purpose of this book is to answer these questions by exploring the discipline of entrepreneurship. While career skills such as marketing, fundraising, and not-for-profit administration are now being taught in more and more music schools, they are insufficient to the task of creating—*and sustaining*—a fulfilling career. What's needed in addition to career skills is an integrated and flexible *strategy* to guide their deployment. Entrepreneurship provides the means for this by focusing on how value for one's work is created, and how that value is unlocked for costumer and entrepreneur alike. Entrepreneurship is also infinitely adaptable to both the unique gifts of the individual musician-entrepreneur and a virtually infinite number of contexts and situations. That's good news for musicians trying to thrive in the ever-changing and complex world of our modern culture. Entrepreneurship isn't a "magic bullet," but it provides the best mechanism music professionals can use to identify and build a unique and fulfilling niche in the twenty-first-century musical marketplace.

WHO IS THIS BOOK FOR?

If you are a music student, a recent graduate, or a working professional, I hope this book will give you the entrepreneurial tools you need to build and sustain your career. I also hope it will help you see a much broader and more diverse range of options that you can pursue, options that entrepreneurship can help you unlock.

If you are a music educator, this book will help you understand the principles of entrepreneurship and how those principles play out in artistic settings. It is my hope that this can inform and enlighten your classroom practice and that this book will complement the career skills resources you're already using.

Finally, this book is for anyone who is concerned that entrepreneurship and artistic integrity are incompatible. In fact, my hope is that the skeptical reader will find solace and encouragement in the stories and case studies I share within these pages. After all, whether the challenge is creating/performing a musical masterwork or filling a concert hall, the solution lies in creatively engaging the problem in new ways and from a new perspective. My hope is that readers will come to see how entrepreneurship can occupy a vibrant and positive place in their musical lives—that musicians from across the classical world will come to understand, and embrace, the entrepreneurial side of their muse.

I use three terms in this book that I would like to define. I use the phrase "classical music" in the common colloquial sense of the word, as opposed to referring to the historical period of classical music that existed in the latter half of the eighteenth century. My definition of "classical (lowercase) music" encompasses anything that is presented for the purpose of reflective listening, including symphonic, choral, chamber, solo music, and opera.

Any discussion of entrepreneurship requires talking about the entrepreneur's product(s). Throughout this book I use the word "product" in its broadest sense: something for which there is a market that values it. In this context, therefore, "product" can be a physical object (a trumpet mute), a service (music lessons), or an experience (a musical composition or performance). Purely for the sake of simplicity and clarity, I refer to all these things as "products," for, indeed, they are all things for which we seek value in the marketplace.

I also talk about a musician's "art," and I use the terms "musician" and "artist" interchangeably. I do so with great intention, and in order to underscore the universal artistic impulse within all creative endeavors. I also wish to continually remind you, the reader, that the "highest" aspect of your music making—the *art*—is never far away from the entrepreneurial process.

Throughout the book you will find various case studies and exercises designed to build understanding of entrepreneurial principles and illustrate how those principles operate in the context of classical music. These resources are distinct from the main narrative thread so that they can be easily extracted for classroom or individual use and so that you can revisit them as your entrepreneurial understanding and experience grow.

ACKNOWLEDGMENTS

The more I consider whom to acknowledge here, the more people come to mind. I think of my first grade teacher's aide, Miss Beja, who noted that I loved to write and gave me a blank book with the inscription "Keep writing! As you fill the pages of this book, may it help you in writing your first." Or my tenth grade English teacher, Ms. Diamond, who flunked me on my first essay (much to my offense) and took me aside after class with these words: "I gave you an F because I know you can do much better."

I think of my many undergraduate professors and mentors, who taught me how to think critically and communicate clearly, gave me the courage to explore the unknown, and instilled in me a lifelong love of learning: Courtney Adams, John Carbon, Bruce Gustafson, Roger Thomas, Bill Whitesell, Stan Mertzman, Ed Beutner, Brad Dewey, Dick Kneedler, and so many others. And, of course, Barb Brummett who believed in me and who taught me to love fiercely, to find sacred joy in the small things of life, and to "pick every grape from the vine."

The blessing of amazing teachers continued into grad school. My mentor, Paul Cooper, not only shaped my compositional life but also showed me what it meant to be a professional, while others, including Tom Jaber, Sam Jones, Larry Rachleff, Anne Schnoebelen, and Michael Hammond, opened my mind to the endless joys of learning, performing, exploring, and discovering the musical universe. These people forged the musician—and the man—I grew up to be, and their wisdom and inspiration are behind every word of this book.

I'm also blessed to live in one of the most entrepreneurship-friendly communities anywhere, Boulder, Colorado. The culture of entrepreneurial collaboration can be found in every corner of this city, and I'm particularly grateful for those local mentors who have taught me and encouraged me. Special thanks go to all the Boulder "Co-conspirators," especially Frank Moyes, Brad Bernthal, Erick Mueller, and Jason Mendelson: your friendship, generosity of spirit, and wealth of experience have been invaluable in shaping my thoughts on entrepreneurship, and your impact continues to have ripples throughout the burgeoning field of arts entrepreneurship. And to Joan Braun, colleague, sounding board, cheerleader, and cocktail buddy: ever since our first margarita at Cantina Laredo I knew we'd be the best of friends.

An enormous thank you goes to my graphic designer, Debbi Pace, who gave my charts and figures an artist's touch and designed the cover art for this book. A thousand thanks also to Val M. Cox, who assisted me with my citations, copy editing, and index. The generous encouragement and feedback of my University of Colorado colleagues Tom Riis and Elissa Guralnick was instrumental in moving me past "thinking about" this book and actually beginning work on it. And I owe a great debt of gratitude to the entire team at Oxford University Press, especially my editor, Norm Hirschy, who has been an indispensable guide throughout the process of writing this book. His gentle but clear feedback has been just what this first-time author has needed to both believe in his writing and persevere in making it better.

The life of the mind and of the artist requires constant stimulation, so it's the colleagues and friends of today whom I wish to both acknowledge and thank the most. To Kieren MacMillan, whose incredible gifts and steadfast encouragement continually inspire me to be a better composer; to Cory West, who has always reminded me to believe in my own worth, and to claim it; and to Kevin Noe, the most loyal of friends, who keeps me honest, keeps challenging me, and never, ever lets me settle for less than my very best: *Thank you, all.* You are the reason I'm where I am today. You're also the embodiment of the joy I feel each day as I continue this beautiful life in music.

Last, though certainly not least, thank you to my husband, Jeffrey. Whatever success I've enjoyed over the last decade, a big piece of it belongs to you. I couldn't have made it otherwise. The well of gratitude I have for you is deep beyond measure: you're my best friend, you never fail to make me laugh, and I know I can always depend on you. You are nothing short of my rock. Thank you for walking by my side as we take this journey together.

The Popcorn Epiphany

It all started with popcorn.

I can remember the moment quite clearly: that moment when you realize you have to change the way you've been thinking about things, change the way you've been approaching a problem. For me that moment occurred when I was working at a concession stand at the University of Texas Frank Erwin Center, scooping popcorn for patrons who hardly noticed me, much less cared about who I was or what my circumstances were. I was a food dispenser, and that was all.

The year was 2001, two months after 9/11. I was seven years out of my DMA in composition from Rice University and had already had my *Concerto for Clarinet and Orchestra* recorded by Richard Stoltzman and a chamber orchestra piece performed at Lincoln Center. I had been sure those milestones would soon open more doors, and I was confident my career was about to take off; it was only a matter of time before my name would be gracing concert programs from coast to coast.

Then I hit a wall. The commissions dried up, the performances slowed to a trickle, and I began to feel like I was losing my creative voice. A crisis ensued, one that was as much personal as professional.

By the time I had finished my degree program at Rice I had decided that an academic career was not for me. My teachers were appalled: after all, what does one do with a doctorate in music composition if not become a college professor? But I was adamant that I was going to make my living as a working musician: composing and performing were to be my sole activities, undiluted by teaching or any other institutional distractions.

My mentor at Rice, Paul Cooper, was dubious. The day I came to his office to announce my decision felt momentous to me, as if I were announcing a breakup or sharing a dread diagnosis. I delivered my speech, well-rehearsed. The room was quiet for some time while he sat there in his leather chair, puffing away on his cigarette, his icy blue eyes reflecting deep thought. Finally exhaling a cloud of smoke, he looked up at me and quietly said, "Well, Jeff, if anyone can do it you can."

So I jumped off the cliff . . . and seven years later here I was, scooping popcorn for basketball fans attending a game I couldn't even watch.

In that moment, I knew: something had to change. I could no longer tell myself that if I just continued to persevere, just stayed patient and "kept the faith," that things would somehow turn around. I'd been telling that to myself for the last two years, yet things just kept getting worse. How in the world had I ended up here? And how was I going to get myself out of this hole? I knew it was time to find answers to these questions, but I had no idea how to even begin going about it. I was financially, emotionally, and artistically lost.

This story is hardly unique; I'm sure many readers will be able to relate to their version of it. Sometimes it feels like we were set up: our education trained us to be the finest musicians we could be, but nothing else. Perhaps we were stars at our respective institutions, hailed by our teachers as one of the special talents who were destined for a prominent career, and this gave us a false sense of how easy it would be to win over the wider world. Perhaps the first few years after school bore out our teachers' predictions; buoyed by a competition win or a young artist grant, we enjoyed some early successes. But once that initial postgraduation boost was spent, a cold reality hit: we had no idea what to do next. If we were lucky, we'd taken a career skills class while we were in school, but now even our best social media efforts, our spiffiest demo, and our most earnest gig-hunting weren't getting the job done. At the end of the month, there was still a cavernous gap between the requirements of life and the realities of our bank accounts. Faced with no other alternative, we took day jobs that ate up our time and sapped our energy—making the whole enterprise of building a music career even more challenging. Discouragement, frustration, and bitterness followed. Many of us ended up leaving music altogether.

Sound familiar? If so, you're not alone.

So what's the missing piece? Why aren't the marketing, fundraising, and promotional skills we (hopefully) learned in school enough to create and sustain success? Well, in order for those skills to be effectively applied, they require an integrating strategy, one that is based on an understanding of what makes your music valuable and how to unlock that value for your patrons, your audience, and the public at large. Without this strategic understanding, career skills tools, like marketing or grant writing, are merely blunt instruments— when what we need in today's constantly evolving and ever more complex world is instruments that are both razor sharp and infinitely adaptable to changing circumstances. What we need is entrepreneurship.

Entrepreneurship. Few words are more misunderstood or bandied about in today's media and civic discourse. Elected officials and community leaders use it for political rhetoric. Educators use it to rebrand themselves or their institutions as "relevant." Members of the creative class debate whether or not entrepreneurship offers anything new or useful to those engaged in the age-old struggle of making a living by doing what they love. Despite the popularity of the term, however, the practice of entrepreneurship is rarely understood or explained. It's become such a loaded term that I've taken to calling it the "E-word."

While businesspeople and politicians embrace the "E-word," artists tend to approach the subject of entrepreneurship with suspicion, if not outright hostility. This wariness is understandable: the world artists and musicians inhabit often feels like one under siege. Traditional funding models are either drying up or disappearing; audience numbers are in decline on many fronts. Broad cultural trends underscore these challenges: the digital revolution has made artistic content far easier (and cheaper) to acquire—often at the expense of those who created it—while the commoditization of art in the commercial realm crowds out those artists who have little or no interest in selling to the broadest or most lucrative market. It's no wonder artists feel under siege!

Then along come the self-proclaimed entrepreneurs! They're full of promises: "Step right up! Just make your art a product and the money will start flowing in!" But from the artist's point of view, this looks an awful lot like something that devalues your artistic worth and places your work on a par with a kitchen appliance or a garden tool: a utilitarian object—mundane, infinitely reproducible, disposable. The accusations follow: entrepreneurship mandates a "dumbing down" of the art, it places commerce above creativity, and it commodifies artists and their work. At its core (so the thinking goes), the role of entrepreneurship is fundamentally at odds with the role of the artist. Entrepreneurship is motivated by profit, and the artist is motivated by, well, the *art.* At best the two are incompatible; at worst, entrepreneurship undermines artistic integrity and cheapens the work.

But none of these concerns, albeit real and sincerely expressed, captures the truth about entrepreneurship. While entrepreneurial thinking does require us to look at our art as a product, not all products are merely utilitarian. Some products are extremely precious, unique, and valuable, and few products are more precious and unique than artistic ones. The problem is most artists can't see how they can remain true to their best, highest, most uniquely personal artistic voice . . . and still pay the rent. Nobody has ever taught them such a thing. Within this limited mindset they therefore operate under a false choice: remain "true" but starve or compromise and pay their bills.

Your career need not be hamstrung in this way, however. While the mainstream media maintain a kind of mystique surrounding entrepreneurship, as if entrepreneurs possess some sort of magical insight hidden from the rest of us, the truth is that entrepreneurship consists of a few core principles that are easily defined. It embodies both a particular mindset—a way of approaching the problem of how to support the thing you're called to do—and a set of tools to implement that mindset within the real-world marketplace. A mindset can be developed; tools can be learned. There is no magic in entrepreneurship, but it does need to be clearly defined and understood.

In a nutshell, entrepreneurship is about unlocking the value of your creative gift. It also asks you to look at the relationship between your product and your audience in fundamentally different terms from those you may be used to. Rather than developing their products in a vacuum and then attempting to convince others to desire it, effective entrepreneurs start with the needs of their target market and devise creative ways to meet those needs. And entrepreneurship is never about "selling out." In fact, your artistic integrity is your most valuable asset—to compromise that makes no sense in an entrepreneurial context.

Entrepreneurship is about enabling art's deepest, most valuable purpose: connecting with people, creating community, challenging us to view the world from new and different perspectives, stirring the soul. It's about empowering artists with the tools they need to release the value of their work by connecting it with a market that desires it. And when it's done well, entrepreneurial action exists harmoniously within the artist's creative life, each side fueling creative insights for the other. Rather than being fundamentally at odds with each other, entrepreneurship and artistic expression can be mutually empowering forces that can unleash great things for both musicians and their audience. Rather than two disparate things, entrepreneurship and artistic expression can be two sides of the same precious coin.

In the end, selling popcorn helped me through a rough patch in my life. But it was not an activity I wanted to keep as part of my career portfolio—I'd much rather enjoy munching on the stuff after a productive day of work in the studio! But it shows just how entrenched we are when it comes to our career options and what it takes to develop them: I had to find myself in the middle of every musician's worst nightmare—doing something menial and completely divorced from one's training and passion just to survive—before I began to look at my artistic life through a new lens. Once I began to explore entrepreneurship, though, I didn't just discover a more diverse palette of potential career activities; I also discovered that it could open up new creative possibilities as well.

My hope for this book is that readers will overcome their unease with the "E-word," learn how it can operate within their own creative lives and, in turn, inspire them to build a career that is both artistically fulfilling and financially sustainable. Entrepreneurship is not an end in itself but a process by which artists can realize their core artistic purpose: creating content that makes a difference to people, that makes the world a better place. Entrepreneurship is a vibrant, creative, and stimulating endeavor that can be an extension of your artistic creativity. It can help you to reimagine your career by revealing a much broader canvas of professional and creative possibilities. It can both empower you and equip you to pursue your dreams and ambitions. It exists, in short, to serve you and your audience, and as such it will be what you make of it.

The chapters that follow explore all of these topics in depth. You'll study the core principles of entrepreneurship and see how they play out in a variety of settings. You'll work through exercises to help you develop your entrepreneurial perspective. And I'll share with you some real-world case studies that I hope will both inform your thinking and inspire your heart. After all, since both music making and entrepreneurship are driven by creativity, there's no reason why our muse can't also be an entrepreneur. Let's find out how.

CHAPTER 1
Artist or Entrepreneur?

Traits of Entrepreneurial Thinking

A few years ago I attended a career development conference sponsored by the Network of Music Career Development Officers ("Net-*MC*-Doh"), hosted at the Manhattan School of Music. This wonderful annual gathering—more a retreat and a forum for reflective thought than a typical conference—brings together educators from a broad spectrum of music programs, from conservatories to public universities, to discuss current challenges and trends in the field of professional development for students of the arts. This particular year, we spent some time in focus groups with students in order to learn more about their own needs and perspectives on the question of preparation for a career in music.

My group contained six students, and as we chatted I noted that their attitudes ran the same gamut I'd encountered in similar discussions with students across the country. Some students are enthusiastic, but a far greater percentage are ambivalent: they recognize the need but don't feel they have the time to add yet another thing to their already packed schedules. Finally, there are always a few who are actively hostile to the notion of anything pertaining to "the business side of things."

My focus group that day was no different, including one student who had been quiet throughout the conversation. I asked him what he thought about all this.

He shifted uncomfortably for a moment and then, without lifting his eyes, said, "I don't think we should study this stuff."

"Why not?" I asked.

"Because I just want to be able to make music and not worry about anything else. I didn't come here to study business, I'm here to study music."

I was suddenly aware that all the others in the circle—students and colleagues alike—were holding their breath, keenly listening to this exchange: we had engaged the elephant in the room, as it were.

"What would you like to do with your career?" I asked.

"I want to write and perform my own music."

"Okay, good!" I then made sure I asked this next question in as quiet and nonthreatening a way possible. "Have you given any thought to how you'll accomplish your goal?"

He scowled and said, "I shouldn't have to worry about that."

"Why is that?"

"Because then I'll be making music just to make a buck, and I'll end up having to sell out."

And there it was, the two most dreaded words in the music conservatory: *sell out*. When students use that phrase I press them to define what they mean by it, and after some digging we usually discover that they believe that the only way to have a successful career is to compromise their art, that the largest markets embody the least sophisticated tastes. In other words, there is no market for what they want to do, and therefore they must compromise and do something else if they are to sustain themselves financially.

In this case, however, no sooner had we gotten to this core issue than our moderator rang a bell and announced that the students were going to have to go to their next class. As we stood up and the students gathered their backpacks and instruments, I went up to this young man and said this: "Hi. I realize you don't know me from Adam, and I hope I didn't put you on the spot back there, but I want to suggest a different way of looking at this issue. What if you looked at your music and connecting that music to an audience as *one thing*? Rather than looking at 'artistic stuff' over here," I stretched out my right hand, "and 'business stuff' over here," I stretched out my left. "Why not look at *all* of it as a single creative endeavor?" I brought my hands together and interlinked my fingers. "What if building your career was just another creative challenge, instead of something that will work *against* the music you want to create? Building a career is just a creative extension of the art itself, not some opposing, corrupting force. I'd like to challenge you to think about that."

"Okay," he said, albeit a bit reluctantly.

"And please, if nothing else, always remember this: your artistic integrity, your best, most uniquely *you* work, is both your most valuable artistic asset *and* your most valuable business asset. Don't ever let anyone tell you otherwise. I hope you'll remember that."

"I will," he said.

"Good!" I clapped him on the shoulder and wished him luck.

This encounter stuck with me for days following the conference. If I believed this student was an outlier I might have had an easier time letting go of it, but I'd encountered this attitude countless times before. And it's understandable: college students of all stripes are rightly concerned about their career prospects in the face of an unpredictable economy and skyrocketing student debt. For aspiring musicians, the anxiety is ramped up further by the double whammy of entering a field with comparatively fewer jobs while carrying the belief that the only way to succeed is to compromise the thing they hold most dear.

As hard as it can be during school, the struggle to live one's artistic dream only gets harder once the student has graduated and is out in the world trying to make a living. Sadly, many run face-first into a very rude and painful reality: they are ill-equipped to "make it" as professional musicians—not because they lack talent but because they lack an understanding of the arts economy and the tools required to thrive in it. And in that moment of realization, they come to see that all the years of self-discipline, of tireless practice and devotion to their craft, is rendered powerless in the face of the harsh realities of the modern arts marketplace. Many recent music graduates feel caught between the proverbial rock and a hard place, trying desperately to hold on to practice time and regular performing while having to take whatever work they can find (often unrelated to music) in order to pay their bills. Some young professionals caught in this dilemma get creative with their careers and develop new opportunities for their skills to be put to work. Whether they realize it or not, these musicians are becoming entrepreneurs. Others take the opposite approach, becoming hostile toward a capitalist system that they believe requires artists to choose between practicing their art and making a living, that turns art into a commodity and artists into salespeople. For these individuals, entrepreneurship isn't a solution, it's part of the problem.

Contemplating this point of view reminds me of the swimming safety class I took as a kid at day camp. I remember learning how to tread water, how to do the dead-man's float, and how to assist someone who was drowning. We were shown how to throw or extend all manner of objects to the person in distress but were strongly cautioned not to jump in and try to save them unless we were trained lifeguards ourselves. Why? Because most people who are drowning are so panicked they will attack the person trying to save them, often resulting in both victim and rescuer going down.

This seems to me to be not much different from the vehement resistance of aspiring musicians, facing an uncertain future, to entrepreneurship. Having pondered what drives their hostility to the dreaded "E-word" for some time now, I'm convinced it's often driven by fear: fear that entrepreneurship's additional activities will rob them of practice time, fear that they are not suited to tasks like accounting or marketing or the schmoozing of patrons, fear of . . . *selling out*.

And sometimes the more we fear something, the more we resist the thing that could be our liberation. It's counterintuitive, but so is punching and kicking the person trying to rescue you as you slip beneath the water's surface.

Fear is visceral, and we respond in kind. In the case of musicians, the practice of our art is foundational to our very identity. Chances are we've spent the better share of our lives developing the skills required to perform at the highest level of excellence. Often we know nothing else; failure in music would represent a catastrophic failure to realize our deepest, most personal dreams and aspirations. Given what's at stake, fear is understandable. It's why many musicians build a wall around their art to keep it unsullied and "safe" from outside influences that threaten its integrity. The greater their fear, the greater the urge to defend their creative castle at all costs. In this mental construct, entrepreneurship and anything having to do with "business stuff" is seen as a threat. The problem, of course, is that it's highly unlikely they can connect with an audience and support themselves financially from within the confines of the walls they have constructed. These are the individuals most at risk of abandoning their careers out of bitterness and frustration, a sad (and often avoidable) end to their musical journey.

So what exactly does it mean to be an entrepreneur? Given the complex web of fear and misunderstanding surrounding the topic of entrepreneurship, it is necessary to define what it is—and what it isn't. At first glance, though, defining "entrepreneurship" can prove elusive. I like to joke that if you asked ten entrepreneurs to define what they do, you'd get twelve different answers. Even in the academy, where scholars thrive on codifying and defining things, there is no universally accepted definition for entrepreneurship. Is it a process? A mindset? A set of behaviors? Can it really be taught or is it an innate skill that some and not others are blessed with? Does "being entrepreneurial" consist of anything more than engaging in a set of business practices, of "selling ourselves"? Does it mandate a particular outcome? What role does innovation play, and is there any difference between entrepreneurship and, say, running a family-owned neighborhood business? And, perhaps most critically, is being an entrepreneur fundamentally incompatible with being an artist?

Answers to these questions vary widely, and reveal an enormous range of views on the subject of what entrepreneurship is and what it facilitates. Further adding to the confusion is the fact that "entrepreneurship" has become a buzzword in our civic and political discourse, something that communities and their leaders are encouraged to embrace—even when those touting it are vague about what exactly it is they're advocating.

Finally, "entrepreneurship" is a weird French word. I must type it one hundred times a day, and my fingers still get tangled up with it!

Rather than seeing the broad canvas of perspectives on entrepreneurship as a problem, however, we can view it as a core quality of entrepreneurship itself. While the entrepreneurial approach employs a specific set of principles, the particulars of how these play out are infinitely varied and can operate on any scale. Entrepreneurial "success" can mean an IPO worth billions of dollars or a small, community-based business. Some entrepreneurial ventures are designed to be "scalable" (that is, able to efficiently increase their capacity in order to accommodate a progressively larger market), and others are meant to remain at a fixed size. Entrepreneurial action can center around a new, unique, and innovative product or service, or it can be about delivering something established to a community or market that does not currently possess it. An entrepreneurial venture can be a business or organization with many employees, or it can be an individual looking to support her or his creative work; if you are an independent musician, *your career* can be an entrepreneurial venture!

And while it is often assumed that entrepreneurship must always, by definition, be motivated by profit (the larger the better), many entrepreneurial ventures are designed from the outset to operate outside the for-profit realm. The bottom line is that entrepreneurship can operate in any field and in any endeavor, in both the for-profit and not-for-profit realms, and with or without developing an innovative piece of technology or instituting a groundbreaking paradigm shift. For musicians, entrepreneurship can result in something as straightforward as devising a sustainable career with your art or as grand as creating a new business model for monetizing and distributing musical content on the web. In other words, entrepreneurial motivation and outcomes are limited only by the creative imagination and vision of the entrepreneur. While that can make it difficult to define, the virtually infinite range of potential outcomes is also freeing and empowering—especially for those of us in the arts, for whom creative activity is as necessary as breathing.

At its core, entrepreneurship is about unlocking value for a product by connecting it to a need in the marketplace. But how does one go about engaging in this process? And what qualities must one possess in order to be an effective entrepreneur? To get at the answers to these questions, let's begin by recognizing that entrepreneurship is both a mindset—a way of thinking and viewing the world around you—and a set of practices. This chapter explores the qualities of entrepreneurial *thinking*. How do entrepreneurs view the world? How do they identify opportunities? How do they evaluate their endeavors, and what do they do when they encounter "failure"? Chapter 2 dives into the characteristics of entrepreneurial *action*. How do entrepreneurs operate? What are common traits that successful entrepreneurs tend to share?

Defining these distinct groups is helpful in untangling the many different perspectives on entrepreneurship: rather than trying to determine whether entrepreneurship is a mindset, a set of attributes, or a process/practice, we can observe that it is *all* of these things. Entrepreneurship requires a mindset, a way of viewing the world and one's surroundings, but that's just the beginning. Entrepreneurial observation and the recognition of opportunities still require action if they are to result in a successful venture. Just as the entrepreneurial mindset has certain defining characteristics, entrepreneurial action also operates from a set of core principles that guide decision-making and implementation. Taken together, these characteristics and principles form the entrepreneurial process: a strategic guide for identifying opportunities, developing products/services, and finding value for them in the marketplace. What defines a venture as "entrepreneurial," then, has nothing to do with what the venture *does* and everything to do with *how* the entrepreneur views the world, develops ideas, and executes them in the marketplace. Let's begin exploring this more deeply by looking at key aspects to entrepreneurial thinking.

ENTREPRENEURIAL THINKING: STRATEGIC OBSERVATION AND THE ENTREPRENEURIAL MINDSET

One of the biggest misconceptions I've encountered regarding entrepreneurship is that entrepreneurs possess some sort of sixth sense for opportunities, that they are inherently able to see things that "normal people" can't. In all my research and experience, I've rarely found this to be the case. After all, anyone can have a "Eureka moment"—a flash of inspiration that, by all appearances, came out of nowhere. But entrepreneurs are not any more prone to such moments than anyone else. What sets entrepreneurs apart—and defines the entrepreneurial mindset—is their habit of observing the world around them in very particular ways. I call this habit one of "strategic observation," and it is the unifying impulse behind the entrepreneurial mindset. It might look as if seasoned entrepreneurs have some sort of magical ability to see opportunities, but the truth is they've simply developed a habit of viewing the world through a different set of lenses from the rest of us.

The entrepreneurial mindset can be characterized as embodying three components: opportunity recognition, customer focus, and flexibility/adaptability. Together, these thought patterns help entrepreneurs envision and develop their ideas—the first steps in creating something of value in the marketplace.

Opportunity Recognition

To illustrate this first entrepreneurial attribute, let's go bobsledding. Ever since the 1980 Winter Olympics in my native New York State, I've loved watching bobsledding. I love the speed and excitement, the precision with which the sleds must be steered to gain the most speed but also avoid disaster. I'm also fascinated by the tracks themselves: how are they made and maintained? And how did this thrilling (and dangerous) sport develop in the first place?

During the last Winter Olympics, I decided to find out more about bobsledding, and I uncovered a great example of opportunity recognition. It turns out that in the late nineteenth century in alpine resort towns of Switzerland, toboggans became very popular—so much so that they were a nuisance: folks were racing them, often careening through city streets, taking out pedestrians or colliding with carriages in the process. Clearly, something had to be done. The first solution was to design a steering mechanism, and while that helped avoid some mishaps, it made riding the sled even more exciting and popular. The calamity continued.

Then an enterprising hotel owner in St. Moritz named Caspar Badrutt had a thought: what if he built a special track for "bobsleighs" that would contain the sleds? This would both allow them to attain greater speeds and avoid their running over the townspeople. He went on to build the world's first halfpipe-style bobsled track. It was such a hit that not only did his hotel thrive but he built another resort nearby to accommodate the increased tourism. St. Moritz went on to become one of the great winter resorts in the world and host several Olympic games.

So what does all of this have to do with music entrepreneurship? Well, for starters, entrepreneurship of any kind hinges on being *willing to see things with new eyes*, to see something from a perspective that others aren't. For Caspar Badrutt, he didn't see bobsleds as either a civic nuisance or something that should simply be relocated to a less populated area. He saw an opportunity to capitalize on their popularity and the obvious desire for greater speed and competition. But it didn't end there. Entrepreneurship also embodies a process by which an idea is translated into a sustainable venture: if Caspar hadn't also figured out *how* to run a bobsled down the mountainside in a controlled way, he would not have had the breakthrough success he enjoyed. Entrepreneurship is identifying an unmet need—an opportunity—*and then* creating a way to meet that need effectively and efficiently.

For an example from the world of music, let's look at entrepreneur Bob Lord and the company he founded, PARMA Recordings. Bob already had a busy career as a performer, producer, agent, and composer, but in 2005, when he met William Thomas McKinley, the founder and owner of MMC Recordings, he began to wonder if there was a new opportunity emerging. He was struck by the "cognitive dissonance" in an enterprise that had issued recordings with a wide array of major artists—Grammy-winning clarinetist Richard Stoltzman, the London Symphony Orchestra, the New York Chamber Symphony, and many others—yet was operated out of "a century-old dilapidated house with a couple of run-down computers resting on bedroom doors pulled from their frames and laid atop wooden sawhorses, with piles of dust lingering in forgotten fireplaces." He believed that by overhauling MMC's operations, establishing new systems of production and delivery, forging fresh partnerships and lines of business, and creating infrastructure focused on attention to the artist and composer, he could turn things around. The initial opportunity recognition was borne out of encountering something that was broken and believing he could fix it.

While "fixing what's broken" can often be a valid and fruitful opportunity, in the case of MMC it proved not to be the case. In Lord's words, he "soon discovered that MMC's reach had far exceeded its grasp: angry letters and phone calls from clients who did not receive what they paid for, hundreds of unreleased masters stretching back as far as a decade in some cases, piles of unpaid bills and dozens of creditors, essentially no staff to fulfill obligations, the works. What upon first blush appeared to be a respectable and effective company revealed itself to be something quite different."

At this point in the story, Bob Lord engaged in a different kind of opportunity recognition: he understood how he could make a classical and jazz recording label a viable business, but he also understood that he was not going to be able to do so from within MMC. With this insight, he saw a new opportunity, an opportunity to do something quite a bit more challenging but also far more exciting: he bought out the unfulfilled contracts from MCC and launched his own label, one that would not just produce and distribute recordings but also build on his previous experience as an artist-manager and composer of music for commercials, television, and film. PARMA Recordings was launched in 2008, offering a full range of services, including project planning and development, contracting, studio production and recording, audio postproduction, graphic design, product manufacturing, distribution, marketing and publicity, publishing, licensing, rights management, and administration. The greatly diversified range of income streams produces a more financially stable company and allows the less lucrative jazz and classical recording divisions to maintain an integral role in the business. In this case, opportunity recognition was a multistepped, ongoing process—something that is extremely common among entrepreneurs and that I'll explore more fully shortly.

Customer Focus

You'll note that Caspar Badrutt's idea for the bobsled didn't begin with him looking for a way to expand his resort business. He began with observing what the people in St. Moritz were doing and pondering what he might do to better meet their needs. This is a critical piece of the entrepreneurial mindset, one this book will return to again and again: entrepreneurial ideas begin with an orientation toward the customer. What do they value? What is the dynamic of their interaction? What products do they use and why? Are there other ways (better, cheaper, etc.) to meet their needs? In other words: *What problem are you solving?*

Many would-be entrepreneurs skip over these essential questions. They begin with something *they* would like to do or sell, and proceed to try and convince customers to want it—without consideration of their desires or sensibilities. This is of course what most artists and arts organizations do vis-à-vis their own work and programming. And while this act of "convincing" is often labeled as "being entrepreneurial," it is, in fact, just the opposite: a true entrepreneur would never launch a venture without first having determined that there is a need or desire for it on the part of the customer.

At this point we come up against a truth that is hard for many of us in the arts to accept: we are not, as a rule, focused on our customers. We *assume* that they will be edified by our compositions and performances, because those things resonate so deeply in *us*. But that is a dangerous assumption to make, especially if we wish to learn how to think and act entrepreneurially. Once we make the shift toward our customers, however, we begin to look at our talents and offerings in terms of how they will meet the needs of the people whose support we seek. This is at the very core of what it means to "be entrepreneurial."

As I've mentioned, identifying needs is ultimately borne out of observation—viewed through the eyes of the customer, not your own. To illustrate this, I'll stick with the bobsled problem in St. Moritz. City leaders might have sought to address the issue by eliminating sledding within the town limits. The sledders themselves might have been willing to go elsewhere, but that would have upset the café owners who depended on customers coming inside and warming up over a cup of hot chocolate. Sled makers were happy with the status quo, since as long as people were sledding there was a market for their product. None of these perspectives resulted in an entrepreneurial opportunity, however. Why? Because each of the parties in question was thinking about the situation in terms of how it affected *them*. Caspar Badrutt, on the other hand, viewed the situation in terms of *need*: sledders wanted to sled, and the townspeople needed streets free of hurtling bobsleds. A self-contained track would solve both these problems—as well as create a new enterprise. The placing of said track at Badrutt's resort followed quite naturally. From that point on, the promotion of this new feature and, ultimately, the expansion of his properties was simply good business on his part. The entrepreneurial aspect of the story came in solving the problem to begin with.

The customer needs in the bobsled example are relatively easy to quantify. Identifying the needs of a musical audience is not nearly so easy. As chapter 3 will explore more fully, determining the needs of musical audiences is complicated by the fact that needs exist on many levels. First we have immediate, identifiable needs like accessible parking and adequate restrooms in the venue, needs that can often have a profound impact on whether or not an audience will return in the future (or even show up in the first place). Then there are, simultaneously, far more abstract needs, such as the deep-seated need for shared experience and emotional catharsis, the desire to experience something memorable and compelling.

At first glance, this complex constellation of customer needs might seem inscrutable: how can we focus on our customers' needs when they are so varied? The use of "design thinking" can help us untangle this mystery through the concept of "empathy." Developed at Stanford University in the 1980s and 1990s, design thinking began as a methodology for problem-solving in the realms of architecture, industrial design, and urban planning. Later, Rolf Faste developed its application into "a method of creative action" (which is, actually, a pretty good definition of "entrepreneurship" as well). A key element of this "creative action" is "empathy," a mindset oriented toward "user-centeredness"—that is, the needs and sensibilities of those who are consuming your product, rather than your own.

"Empathy" is a critical piece of the entrepreneurial mindset because it keeps the focus on those you are trying to reach with your product. Without in some way demonstrating awareness of their experiences and sensibilities, you cannot create something they will want to consume; you cannot generate *value* for what you do in the marketplace. In addition, for musicians seeking to connect with an audience, the term is perhaps preferable because it gets at the emotional/spiritual aspect of our music making. After all, the artistic experience consists of much more than the simple act of meeting a utilitarian need; its deepest impact—and the essence of why people value it—stems from its ability to stir our emotions and touch our souls. With this in mind, let's take a look at the entrepreneur's "customer focus" in terms of empathy for your audience, a concept that is wonderfully illustrated by the string quartet Brooklyn Rider.

Formed in 2004 as a way for four friends to simply get together and play music they enjoyed, Brooklyn Rider soon began to evolve into a significant part of the careers of members Johnny Gandelsman, Nicholas Cords, and brothers Eric and Colin Jacobsen. During this evolutionary period, the guys thought a lot about what kind of group they wanted to be. They cherished the established canon of string quartet literature, but they also believed that the very essence of that tradition was one of innovation, growth, and pushing of established boundaries. The result is a group that plays an eclectic range of traditional repertoire and new works, the latter consisting largely of works written especially for them, often in collaboration with artists working in other genres, like dance and visual art. What makes Brooklyn Rider a great example of empathy in action, however, is not the work they choose to present per se. They embody empathy in the very way they go about creating, organizing, and presenting each concert they perform. Each component is fashioned with one overarching goal: to create a compelling experience for their audience. Repertoire is chosen with an eye for bridging old and new (or old and old, or new and new) in order to establish connections between works that the audience might not have considered before. The repertoire Brooklyn Rider programs must possess connections far deeper than the obvious sorts of "themed" programs so often seen in today's concerts, however. Instead, pieces are chosen to work together in such a way that a deeper, more intuitive sense of unity is forged, resulting in a whole that is greater than the sum of the parts. In the quartet's words, their aim is for "the familiar to feel fresh and for the new to feel familiar." They also consider other aspects of the performance, such as the choice of venue and the use of whatever other media may or may not be employed, in light of how well they support the broader experience and conceptual goals of the concert. The result is a holistic approach to concert making that is designed, from beginning to end, to move and compel the audience.

"Music is always *about* something," says violist Nick Cords. "It speaks to every aspect of the human experience. So our goal is to inspire conversation through an experience that is unique and compelling."

How does one develop this empathy for one's audience? For the members of Brooklyn Rider, empathy begins with their own roles as members of the ensemble. "I don't think you can be just a player anymore," says Cords. "In order to really connect with people, you have to be a lot more well-rounded. For us, that begins with understanding the bigger picture of what's required behind the scenes to put a show together, so that by the time you're on stage you're already invested in the experience. The audience can sense that."

Once on stage, the musicians consciously adopt a personal and relaxed style, each person dressing as he pleases (and nobody in formal wear) and maintaining a presence that is individual and authentic. Once again inspired by tradition, the quartet consciously tries to create the intimacy and informality that marked the beginnings of chamber music—usually played in the private parlors of individuals. When speaking to the audience, remarks are fashioned to inspire thoughtful reflection rather than "the usual travelogue."

Brooklyn Rider also seeks to know and understand its audience in more direct ways. For instance, social media are used less as a promotional device and more as a way to interact with fans, to continue the conversation begun in performances. Members mingle with the audience after shows, asking questions of them and learning how the experience did (or did not) touch them.

Perhaps one of the most striking aspects of empathy that came out of my discussions with Brooklyn Rider was their sensitivity during the act of performing. "We talk a lot amongst ourselves about being aware of, and responsive to, the energy of an audience during a performance. It's all about breaking down that fourth wall so as to create a connection." The result is the ability to take more risks in performance and to approach even established classics in a fresh way.

"Ultimately, that bond of empathy creates trust on the part of our audience," says Cords. "And that trust gives us more artistic freedom to continue to push the envelope and try new things. Because our audience has come to trust us, they come to our shows because of who we are—because of the experience they know they'll have—not because of the repertoire we're playing."

Think about that last bit for a moment: *Brooklyn Rider's audience comes to their shows because they know they'll have a meaningful experience, not because of the repertoire they're playing.* This is the complete opposite of the traditional way classical music groups promote themselves, choosing repertoire based on their own desires and/or the assumed tastes of the audience (an assumption that is often wrong) and then promoting the event in terms of that repertoire and who's performing it. But Brooklyn Rider has demonstrated that if every aspect of your programming is about the customer *first and foremost,* then your marketing is simply an extension of the community you've built and the trust that binds that community together. Nobody needs to be *convinced* of anything. As one of the hottest groups in chamber music today, Brooklyn Rider illustrates the power of customer focus and how that can play out for those of us who are working in the world of twenty-first-century concert music. Customer focus certainly helps build an audience for what we do—an essential element to sustaining ourselves, and our art—but it goes beyond that as well. As Brooklyn Rider shows, placing the focus first and foremost on creating a compelling experience for the audience inspires an artistic vision, and helps keep the great tradition of concert music alive, vibrant, and relevant. Ultimately, it is this sense of connection and relevancy that will create value for the classical musician's art.

Flexibility/Adaptability

One of the things experienced entrepreneurs will tell you again and again is that their ideas almost never remain static. The finished product or the business that launches is likely to be different from the initial idea—sometimes *very* different. As a concept is developed, critical flaws might emerge. Additional market research might reveal that customers actually desire something else. Or sometimes pure serendipity opens up another possibility you hadn't considered before—one even better than the idea you started with. In short, the entrepreneurial path is almost never a straight line; skilled entrepreneurs learn to keep their eyes open for unanticipated curves and use them to their advantage.

For another wintry illustration of entrepreneurial thinking, let's leave Switzerland and head north to Sweden. Yngve Berqvist ran a summer river rafting business that started out of his simple desire to leave his unpleasant mining job and spend more time outdoors. And while his business grew into a thriving venture, Berqvist was limited by one unavoidable fact: the short duration of the Scandinavian summer. Once winter set in, the river he rafted on was frozen solid. Since his business depended largely on tourists, Yngve began to wonder what sorts of tourists he could attract during the long winter months. His quest led him to Japan, as he had heard of Japanese tourists who often traveled to Alaska to see the Northern Lights. While considering how to tap into this market, he met a Japanese ice sculptor. Soon the two men were planning a winter ice-sculpting workshop and exhibition in Sweden.

The morning of the exhibition started out with great promise: accomplished ice sculptors from around the world had assembled and created stunning works. They had received great coverage in the press, so there was a good crowd of tourists. It appeared that Berqvist and his partner were about to experience a great success.

Then, a catastrophe: a freak warm front moved in, and it started to rain. The delicate sculptures that people had flocked to see—and, with them, the entire event—were literally melting away into nothing. At that moment, it would have been understandable if Yngve Berqvist had just admitted defeat and gone back to work in the mine for nine months out of the year. Instead, contemplating the bitter irony of his melted venture inspired him to view the situation from a different angle: rather than look at the inherently temporary nature of ice sculptures as a weakness, a *flaw* in his idea, he wondered how that quality could be leveraged as an *asset*. Building on the relationships he had already established with the tourism industry in Japan and the knowledge he had acquired during the ice-sculpting workshop, he came up with the idea of the Ice Hotel. This winter-only venture would be both a beautiful and a unique attraction for tourists looking for something outside the norm. Furthermore, the transient nature of the Ice Hotel would underscore its novelty: each year's hotel would be a unique, one-of-a-kind creation. What had been a weakness became a key defining asset. A "bug" became a "feature."

Now more than twenty-five years old, the Ice Hotel franchise continues to grow. Each year new a new selection of world-class artists and designers come together to create that year's hotel. The brand has even expanded to include ice products made from genuine Torne River ice and a partnership with spirits manufacturer Absolut to create the IceBar, now in major cities around the world.

The Ice Hotel story illustrates flexibility and adaptability on a number of levels. Most obviously, Berqvist used the ice sculpture debacle to inspire a completely new idea. Rather than allowing a day of warm rain to defeat him, he got thinking about how the ephemeral nature of ice might be used to his advantage. The result was something not only very different from his original idea but also bigger and more successful than he had ever anticipated.

Flexibility and adaptability were in operation at other points in the story, too. Remember that Berqvist headed to Japan hoping to tap into the interest there in viewing the Northern Lights. His chance meeting with an ice sculptor had nothing to do with his agenda, but he decided to trust his gut and go with it just the same. Even before that, the raft business that started everything was itself an act of adaptation: Berqvist's interest in river rafting began simply as a fun hobby while he was still working in the mine. Only when tourists began asking him to guide them did he see a way to get out of a job he hated. He started to go down to the tourist office every morning and soon had more customers than he could handle. In other words, Berqvist kept a mind that was open to possibilities and changes in course and open to the notion that his previous agenda might not be the best one.

Of course, this doesn't mean that entrepreneurs are blown to and fro by every shift in the wind. In fact, many entrepreneurs must struggle to persevere with their venture in the face of serious obstacles and sometimes even outright derision from others. This is especially true for musicians! But while they are forging ahead with their vision and persevering in the midst of struggle, entrepreneurs are also constantly observing and evaluating as objectively as possible. They maintain an open mind as circumstances unfold and are willing to consider a change in tactics, or even a major shift of direction, *if* the evidence points that way. Rather than looking at something that didn't work as a dead end, entrepreneurs look at those situations as opportunities to learn, adapt, and improve. In fact, countless entrepreneurial successes—perhaps even a majority of them—have been built on the remains of previous failed ideas. To the entrepreneur, a "failure" is an opportunity to either improve on your idea or, as in the case of the Ice Hotel, uncover an even better one.

This different view of failure is particularly important to musicians. So much of our musical life revolves around a binary understanding of success and failure. You either missed that note or you nailed it. You were either in tune or you were flat. You won the audition, landed the gig, got the job . . . or you didn't. Furthermore, our music education system tends to reinforce the notion that "success" in the classical music world encompasses a narrow range of options: soloist, orchestra performer, chamber musician, teacher. This makes it particularly difficult for conservatory-trained musicians to open up the aperture of their career lens and pursue new, unconventional paths—not to mention remaining nimble enough to adapt to changing circumstances and capitalize on setbacks. But for the would-be musician-entrepreneur, this flexibility is critical.

A great musical example of the entrepreneurial trait of flexibility and adaptability is percussionist, writer, and educator Jennie Dorris. When Jennie was in school, she was faced with a dilemma that many musicians encounter: trying to choose between music and some other discipline they also love. In Jennie's case the loves competing with music were writing and journalism, but unlike most folks with disparate interests, she decided to look for ways that each could support the other. Initially this simply meant maintaining a more or less divided career, with writing and editing jobs supplementing her freelance work as a percussionist. Soon, though, she began to wonder if there was some way to fuse her two passions such that each would be enriched and so create a more fulfilling creative life for herself as well.

The result of this was Telling Stories, a monthly concert series featuring original essays read aloud by their authors and paired with live classical chamber music, all curated and grouped around a given theme. Venues included nontraditional spaces like coffee shops, cafés, breweries, and art galleries, which in turn attracted audiences far younger and more diverse than that of a traditional classical music concert. When Colorado Public Radio caught wind of the series, they approached Jennie about broadcasting the events as a weekend show to complement the likes of *A Prairie Home Companion* and *This American Life*. It would seem that national syndication was surely just around the corner!

But it was not meant to be. As the financial crisis hit in 2008, funding dried up. While creating a nonprofit structure seemed like the right way to go initially, managing it became more and more of a challenge. When Jennie's husband was offered a job in Boston, she decided it was time to shutter Telling Stories and move on.

Except that's not where the story ends. In fact, this was only the first chapter. Jennie knew that the Telling Stories experience was a powerful one. She'd seen her following grow and talked with audience members who raved about the uniqueness of the show. If supporting it as a performing outlet wasn't financially sustainable, though, what other form might it take? And here is where you can see the entrepreneurial quality of flexibility and adaptability at work. A few years earlier Jennie had started a program at the Denver School of the Arts where students were using the Telling Stories format to develop their own creative voices through words and music. Perhaps this was where Telling Stories really belonged? Rather than a performance model, perhaps it was destined to be an educational one?

Fast-forward nearly a decade, and we see that Jennie has developed and implemented a whole range of educational and engagement programs both in Boston and now Pittsburgh. She's created programs for cancer patients, single moms, and other groups, and she's using the relationships she's built to develop new and fulfilling ways to continue to perform as well. What started as a different kind of concert experience has become a vehicle for social change, cultural understanding, self-actualization, and personal healing.

Jennie has built a diverse and fulfilling career that is "successful" by any measure, but it wouldn't have happened if she hadn't maintained an open mind about how her gifts could be used and what her career might look like. As is often the case with entrepreneurs, her first venture—Telling Stories the performing group—didn't make it. But the entrepreneurial mindset requires us to evaluate not just why the venture failed but whether the core concept behind it—in Jennie's case, personal expression through the intersection of music and creative writing—is worth deploying in a different way. Just as Yngve Berqvist pivoted from ice sculptures to an ice hotel, Jennie saw that her initial concept for Telling Stories was not as powerful or financially sustainable as what could emerge next. In true entrepreneurial fashion, she redirected her vision and energy to something that has proven to be more sustainable—and rewarding—than what she first envisioned.

The principle of flexibility and adaptability is particularly important for musicians, for whom career paths are rarely straight. Even those who end up in a "standard" career, such as playing in a full-time orchestra, probably didn't step into those jobs fresh out of school. Far more commonly, musicians will end up someplace unforeseen, doing something they never would have imagined doing the day they graduated from college. What an entrepreneurial mindset does for you is equip you with a set of evaluative tools that can help you make more effective, strategic decisions each time you arrive at a career crossroads. And the more flexible and adaptable you are, the more likely it is that you'll discover some new paths you never imagined existed.

DEVELOPING THE ENTREPRENEURIAL HABIT

Having considered the key traits and characteristics of entrepreneurial thinking, how can you begin developing these habits in yourself? You're probably not used to the kind of "strategic observation" that folks like Caspar Badrutt exhibited in the bobsled story. Or perhaps you have a hard time seeing yourself coming up with a solution to a problem once you've identified it. That's to be expected with something that is new and unfamiliar. So before leaving this discussion of the entrepreneurial mindset, I'll suggest some strategies you can employ that will help you develop and strengthen your entrepreneurial perspective. Like any habit, you'll soon find that the more you practice it, the easier and more natural it will become.

Observe, Observe, Observe

When asked in a student Q and A about where he got his ideas, a Boulder entrepreneur once quipped, "I take notice of what pisses me off." Many entrepreneurial ideas are borne out of just such an observation. If we have a problem—"something that pisses us off"—then chances are that others have that same problem. And in that moment of observation an unmet need has been revealed, and an opportunity might be waiting to be realized. This is what I mean by "strategic observation": you observe your situations and your surroundings with a particular purpose: to identify unmet needs and potential solutions.

To demystify this a bit, you can use your own experience as a musician to get familiar with "strategic observation." For example, ask a string player what their top two or three irritations are with their instrument or equipment, and they will have some pretty quick answers for you: they're living with these problems every day! No doubt you have similar gripes about whatever it is you do as a musician. (For instance, as a composer, it's best that you don't get me started on the many shortcomings of music notation software!) These gripes are problems in need of solutions, and remember that solving problems/meeting needs is how you create value in the marketplace for your product. "Strategic observation" means that rather than taking these problems for granted, accepting them as a given, or using them to fuel an epic rant on social media, you instead take note of them . . . and ponder what the solution might be.

Once you've built the habit of strategically observing your own familiar corner of the world, you're ready to broaden your scope of observation. One way to do this is through what musician and educator Gretchen Amussen calls "knowledge of contexts." Amussen identifies five contexts in which entrepreneurial observation takes place: cultural, geographic, social, economic, and political. Observing your surroundings in these contexts reorients your thinking and, hopefully, opens up novel and creative possibilities you might not have considered before. For instance, evaluating the potential for your teaching studio in a geographic context might reveal that while the market is saturated in your current location, smaller communities a few counties over are underserved. Perhaps there is some cultural movement you're interested in or a current event of civic importance that might present an opportunity for a collaboration, partnership, or project funding. Being aware of and considering these different contexts helps you focus your strategic observation, which in turn helps you to define better the nature of the potential solution.

In addition, as you work to develop your observational habits, make sure not to limit your perspective to just your area of musical practice. Often our other interests, passions, associations, and life experiences are the keys to opening doors of opportunity for our music. (Check out appendix 1, where I discuss an example from my own creative life.) What sorts of things are the people around you doing (or not doing)? What things do they value, and how do they put those values into action? What are some defining characteristics of your community? Are there iconic places or signature events that you might be a part of or tap into in some way? Then ask yourself which Amussen context(s) are in operation. The more you begin to observe your surroundings in this way, the more potential opportunities you'll begin to identify. Some of them will be trivial, others will turn out to be impractical, and still others might simply reside outside your own circle of interests. But every great entrepreneurial venture begins with an idea—usually borne out of observing people and their needs or sensibilities. The more you develop the habit of observation, the more you begin to see that you are surrounded by unmet needs and potential opportunities. You begin to see your world as one of abundance as opposed to scarcity. It's a process that not only serves to continually stir the pot of our creativity but also can be quite fun!

Walk a Mile in Your Customers' Shoes

Every one of us is a customer. We are all consumers of things from the trivial to the profound, from the daily coffee to a once-in-a-lifetime trip. In fact, most of us are so used to the purchasing experience that we hardly notice it—unless something during the transaction goes either inordinately well or inordinately wrong. Once we're in the position of trying to get people to consume *our thing*, however, we often forget what it's like to be a customer. We're so invested in what we're offering that we lose our objectivity, our ability to see our product through the eyes of someone who's never encountered it before. A key part of entrepreneurial thinking is to not make that mistake.

As with the practice of strategic observation, one of the best ways to begin developing your habit of customer focus is to observe your surroundings. The next time you are entering into a transaction, whether it's at a local business, an online merchant, or a concert venue, pay very close attention to the details of the experience. How welcomed do you feel? How easy is it to complete the transaction? What is it about the experience of the product or service—both during and after the purchase—that you liked or disliked? What went well and what didn't—and why? Do you feel valued as an individual or just as a source of income for the seller? Then, start observing your fellow customers: how do they appear to be experiencing the product? Do they appear to be having a good time, or are they irritated and impatient? Are they engaged or checked out? Be sure to pay attention to details: sometimes it's the little things that show the customer that you're thinking about them and want their experience to be a good one.

One exercise I give my students, designed by an entrepreneurial mentor of mine, Frank Moyes, is "Lurk and Listen." The assignment asks students to go into the retail establishment of their choice and simply observe the proceedings for an hour. It's remarkable how much you notice when you're a passive observer, watching how customers are treated, whether or not the employees appear engaged and committed to providing a good experience, and so forth. Try a dry run of this at someplace simple like a coffee shop. Then spend some time going to different types of concerts or other cultural venues and observe the behavior of *their* customers and staff. Once you're intentional in your observations from the perspective of a customer, you'll begin to see how your own interactions with customers might be changed—or even reimagined altogether!

In using our observations to help develop a keener understanding of what's required to create a positive customer (or audience) experience, we return to the concept of empathy. In order for your customers to value your product, you need to be able to see how what you're offering benefits your customers, your audience, your patrons. You need to be empathetic to their needs and sensibilities, and that empathy in turn helps you shape the development and delivery of your product.

In addition to observation and your own experiences as a customer, the best way to understand your customers is simply to talk to them. If you're developing an idea, ask folks for honest feedback on it: What do they like about it? What do they dislike? How much would they be willing to pay for this product or service, and how often would they pay it? This can be scary, of course, because you might find that the overwhelming consensus is that your idea is a bad one, or it's overpriced, or you need to redesign the delivery of it. Just as in your music-making, it takes courage to put yourself out there and be vulnerable to the criticism of others. But it's absolutely critical to entrepreneurial success—and better to find out your product's shortcomings during the development stage than later!

If you're already up and running, feedback from your existing customers (as well as potential new customers) is valuable, too: it can provide incredibly valuable information about how to improve what you do, reach more customers, and possibly expand your activities into new areas. Soliciting this feedback can be done formally, as in an audience survey or focus group, or informally, by chatting with your audience, conversing on social media, or taking a valued patron to lunch. In fact, the more avenues for soliciting and receiving feedback you utilize, the more solid and useful that information will be. And once you've gathered this information, treat it like the gold it is: *hear* what your customers are telling you, and *respond*.

Do Your Research

When a particular observation catches your attention or piques your curiosity, the next step is to gather more information. Information can prevent you from going too far down the rabbit hole before discovering that your idea isn't feasible or someone else is already doing it. It can also reveal new, better ideas. In the early stages of considering an idea, it's likely that you understand only some of the cultural, geographic, social, economic, and political contexts Amussen identifies. Or perhaps, as just discussed, you're not sure anybody out there would actually purchase your product. Maybe you only understand one aspect of the idea you're considering (the attributes of a good clarinet reed) and lack related technical knowledge required to develop your product (how to modify the machinery that makes them). So the process of research is critical to fleshing out your observations.

One other critical part of your research is simply expanding your knowledge. Do not begin your research with a predetermined outcome in mind. After all, when exploring a new area of knowledge, you don't know what you don't know. Focusing your research too tightly on a specific thing may cause you to miss valuable, necessary information. It can also obscure tangential issues that might turn out to be more interesting to you or more fruitful as a venture. Casting a wide net with your initial research will help you understand more intimately what exactly is going on in your particular field. It will also take your idea out of an isolated vacuum and place it in a broader context. This understanding will play a crucial role in determining whether or not there is an opportunity with your idea and will inform how you go about developing it. Even if you think you know everything about the product or market you're considering entering, do your research anyway: you might be surprised, and even inspired, by what you find.

Remember What the "Box" Is

The cliché "think outside the box" has become so ubiquitous as to be an irritation, yet it continues to be used because it gets at something very important: try as we might, most of our brainstorming still results in pretty conventional ideas. And so we are exhorted to "think outside the box"—to consider the unconventional. This is easier said than done, of course: if we could simply *will* ourselves to think less conventionally, we probably would. To help resolve this dilemma, let's begin with a question: what exactly is this "box" outside of which we're supposed to think?

Well, to be blunt, the box is *you*.

The "box" consists of all our assumptions and preconceptions, the things that limit our point of view and prevent us from seeing solutions outside what is familiar and comfortable. While the realm of the familiar is a good place to start developing the habit of strategic observation, the next step, identifying an opportunity, requires more from us. To develop an opportunity into a successful idea, you may be forced to challenge your assumptions, find out what knowledge you lack, put yourself in the shoes of your customers—in short, get outside the box of your own perspective and scope of understanding. The "box" limits us to what we already know; often the best opportunities reside beyond those limitations.

Understanding the nature of "the box" is particularly important for musicians. Our musical training tends to focus on a very specific set of skills: technical mastery, historical context, analytical insights, and standard performance practice. If you're lucky, your teacher will also give you some tools for finding your own artistic voice, but even those tools are likely confined to a fairly strict range of acceptable practice. Unless we're studying jazz (or composition), we're not likely to be encouraged on a regular basis to improvise, experiment, or break down the barriers of standard practice.

The same can be said of the career options we're taught to consider. Year after year, my first-day-of-school survey of students' career goals yields the same results: performers hope to be university or studio teachers, orchestral performers, or soloists; composers want to write for film (or video games); education majors want to teach K–12; musicologists and theorists assume they're bound for graduate school and, eventually, academia. There is nothing wrong with any of these career paths, of course. But limiting your options to such a short list closes out all manner of other possibilities and, given the enormous competition for jobs in those fields, can ultimately prove to be self-defeating. For musicians, the standard career "box" can be particularly constrictive and counterproductive. Therefore, your efforts to develop the habit of using opportunity recognition, flexibility/adaptability, and customer focus are seriously hampered if you don't also develop strategies to get out of your "box."

The first step of getting "outside the box" is accepting that there is a vast and varied array of career possibilities beyond the traditional paths defined by previous generations. This step is fairly easy: after all, in today's digital, globally connected, quickly evolving world, the virtually endless variety of possible career activities is readily apparent (even if you don't yet see what those might be for you personally). On the other hand, developing *ideas* that are "outside the box"—learning to think beyond your current knowledge, understanding, and frame of reference—is harder. But like almost any other kind of skill, thinking "outside the box" is something you can develop over time. And there are tools to help us out.

If you go online or browse the self-help and business sections of your local bookstore, you'll find lots of books and exercises designed to encourage "outside the box" thinking. Most of these exist under the "brainstorming" rubric, and though many have their merits, brainstorming exercises by themselves aren't likely to get you beyond the limits of your own experience and perspective. Moreover, I suspect that anything that is staged in that way is not likely to stimulate creative thoughts. (It might, perhaps, even stifle them.) After all, are you more likely to be struck by a cool idea while in the shower, working in the garden, taking your morning jog . . . or while in a meeting at work when your boss says, "Okay, we're going to solve this problem in the next hour"? The reason for this is that creative thinking has a mind of its own. Your muse does not like to be forced or commanded to reveal its secrets. Creativity requires time for reflection and rumination. Likely as not, the idea emerges in its own time and place, and there's precious little we can do to change that.

Being aware of the dynamic of your muse, though, can help you solve the "box" problem. Start with exploring, and then actively creating, the conditions under which your best ideas tend to emerge. It might be as simple as making the time to take a walk by yourself for at least thirty minutes every day. Maybe it's yoga. Meditation. Working out. Cooking. Whatever it might be for you, find a way to nourish your muse, to provide the conditions under which it best speaks and can be heard. Give yourself the time and mental space to free-associate—and break yourself of the habit of rejecting things out of hand as "too stupid" or telling yourself "That would never work." Learn how to let your mind wander, and see which ideas stick with you.

Then, share your ideas with others. The "box" can also be a wall, an insular force that protects you from criticism or feedback that might challenge (or even derail) your idea. So be intentional about getting feedback from people you can trust to provide honest, constructive, thoughtful observations—and listen carefully to what they tell you. In the early stages of your idea, this feedback will likely be in a more personal and informal setting—the people with whom you share certain interests and sensibilities and whom you trust. As one of my entrepreneur friends likes to say, "It's three of my best friends and a couple six-packs of beer." Later on, this outside feedback may come in a more structured way, through things like customer surveys or interviews with professional colleagues.

The success of each of these strategies for developing the entrepreneurial mindset hinges on us getting past our existing limitations, on getting "outside the box." As long as you remember what your personal "box" is, and how it limits you, you can be intentional about getting out of it as much as possible.

Having explored the characteristics of the entrepreneurial mindset and how to develop it, we come back to the question that opened this chapter: is it possible to be both an entrepreneur and a musician? The answer very much lies in how we define entrepreneurship. If we insist on a narrow definition— that which results in a scalable, for-profit business—then most musicians will probably dismiss the entrepreneurial path: "I'm a musician, not an entrepreneur." Furthermore, choosing a narrow definition of "entrepreneur" implicitly relegates music to a secondary role in the venture (at best), another non-starter for most of us.

But what if we view entrepreneurship in much broader terms? Rather than seeing it as limited to specific outcomes, what if we view it as opening up a far wider range of outcomes than we have been traditionally taught are possible? What if we view it as a guiding strategic approach to our professional life, based on a mindset of identifying and pursuing opportunities to create value for our work? What if you were to make a distinction between viewing an entrepreneurial venture as a business or organization (a formal entity that can be a for-profit business or a not-for-profit organization) and viewing your creative life *itself* as an entrepreneurial venture? When we begin to ponder these broader definitions, the question of whether or not we apply the "entrepreneur" label to ourselves is irrelevant: we remain musicians first and foremost, only now we are armed with a potent strategy for realizing our reimagined careers. If the title "entrepreneur" still bothers you, then don't use it—just don't allow your discomfort to force a rejection of entrepreneurial principles. They exist to open you up, not shut you down.

When we look at entrepreneurship this way, we can see how "selling out" is precisely the *opposite* of behaving entrepreneurially: why would we compromise our most valuable asset? The key to creating a sustainable venture in the arts is not to water down the product but rather figure out how to connect that product to a market that values it. Rather than limiting options or forcing artistic compromise, entrepreneurship reveals new (dare I say infinite) possibilities for shared value of the thing we cherish the most.

Once we understand how entrepreneurship can be the extension and application of our artistic work as musicians, we can see how the "artist or entrepreneur" question is a false dichotomy. My identity as an entrepreneur is shaped by my identity as an artist, and my identity as an artist has been shaped in incredibly powerful and positive ways by my identity as an entrepreneur. The two constitute a contiguous set of creative acts. While the specifics of those creative actions will be different for each musician, ensemble, or organization, the process by which those actions are unified is the same. Regardless of the particulars of a given enterprise, entrepreneurship is about empowering and enabling individuals (and/or organizations) to create new connections between the things they are passionate about and the markets they seek. For musicians, that means creating new connections between your music and your audience. These connections in turn open up new ways for your work to be valued by audiences and their communities. And when you create value for what you do, you have laid the foundation for a sustainable career. Rather than resisting entrepreneurship as something that takes us away from our core purpose as musicians, we can embrace it as enabling the thing we most want: for our art to sustain us and to make a difference in the world.

Furthermore, the more we can view entrepreneurship as a way of viewing the world around us, a way of solving problems, and a strategy for effective deployment of our career skills, the more we can see that an entrepreneurial orientation is in perfect harmony with a musician's sensibilities. Entrepreneurial traits like creativity, learning from failure, discipline, analytical skills, and many others are already integral parts of a musician's profile. As artists we are seeking ways to make an impact with our work and a difference in our communities. Identifying ways to do that is opportunity recognition. Musical careers rarely unfold in a straight line, and often opportunities come from unexpected places. Being open to that and willing to capitalize on the unexpected demonstrates flexibility/adaptability. Connecting with an audience and creating a compelling experience for them is something every musician hopes for, and focusing on our customer helps us achieve that. For these reasons, I believe that musicians have the capacity to be excellent entrepreneurs: we already possess the traits and abilities required, and the kinds of outcomes generated by entrepreneurial action are precisely what today's classical music world needs the most. I do not need to choose between being a musician or an entrepreneur any more than I need to choose between being a composer or an educator: they go together, complement each other, and in the best of circumstances, inspire and energize each other. And it's my muse—my creative soul—that is the common link to all of these things, the shared point of contact for all my endeavors. Regardless of whether I'm composing, teaching, writing, consulting, or performing, my muse is at the center of it, inspiring, empowering, and energizing me every step of the way.

EXERCISE: CREATE A BUG LIST

In order to develop the habit of observing your surroundings with an eye for opportunity, entrepreneurial mentor Frank Moyes suggests keeping a "bug list" of things you encounter on a regular basis that irritate or annoy you (for instance, my quest as a composer for a decent mechanical pencil that has very specific properties). But rather than turning these things into a rant you post on social media, start looking at these "bug items" in terms of whether or not there's a solution that either nobody has tried or has not been executed well. If we regularly engage in this kind of strategic observation and reflective thought, we'll soon find that we're viewing the world around us in a fundamentally different way: we're starting to view the world in terms of potential opportunities, and that's the entrepreneurial view.

Activity

Start keeping a "bug list," either in a journal or digitally, and try to come up with at least one interesting idea every week that might address those items. Don't worry about the feasibility of your proposed solution—the point of this activity is to train you to look at the world around you as one of infinite possibilities and creative opportunities. If an idea piques your interest or keeps nagging at you, take a closer look at it and consider its viability as a potential product, service, or delivery system.

EXERCISE: KNOWLEDGE OF CONTEXTS

Gretchen Amussen identifies five contexts in which entrepreneurial observation takes place: cultural, geographic, social, economic, and political. Get together with a few close friends in the relaxed setting of your choice and spend some time with the following. First, identify some key characteristics for each of Amussen's contexts in your own community. Second, identify possible opportunities you and your friends could potentially pursue in each of these. As with the bug list, feasibility is less the issue here than just getting your creative juices flowing.

Activity

This work-through of each of the five entrepreneurial contexts, using my home of Boulder, Colorado, as an example, will suggest ways you can identify unique characteristics and opportunities in your own community.

CULTURAL

Characteristics: Eclectic; music—pop/indie dominate, but also a strong classical and world music scene; small city feel but with international profile due to the university; a number of prominent festivals and events throughout the year; artisanal, locally produced art, crafts, and food are all greatly valued.

Possible opportunities: "Home Grown Colorado" music series featuring local artists, local food, and local microbrews and distilleries.

GEOGRAPHICAL

Characteristics: Front Range of Colorado—linear north/south (rural, agricultural plains to the east, mountain wilderness and resorts to the west); transit up and down the Front Range corridor is relatively easy; east-west less so, especially on the few corridors into the mountains on weekends.

Possible opportunities: Use the ease of north-south transit to explore gigs along the length of the Front Range corridor: Greeley, Fort Collins, Loveland, Boulder, Denver, Castle Rock, Colorado Springs. Or perhaps take advantage of east-west traffic bottlenecks on weekends to create some sort of "musical rest stop" to ease the annoyance of the trip.

SOCIAL

Characteristics: Distinct subcommunities: students, longtime Boulder residents, new arrivals (young professionals); highly fitness oriented—especially outdoors (biking, hiking, rock climbing, etc.); foodie; feels like a very "youthful" place but also has many retirees. "Boulder Bubble" phenomenon—folks don't see the need to venture outside it, unless it's to the mountains.

Possible opportunities: Find a niche that speaks to you or you're already involved with and find out what those folks are interested in. Maybe you love working with seniors: affluent retirement communities already have a lot of music going on, but what about lower-income shut-ins? Or perhaps there's something you could do with your rock-climbing club at an outdoor venue? Your neighborhood community garden? Busk with your brass quintet at the launching point for tubing on Boulder Creek and call it "The Joy of Tubing" (get it?). Lots of possibilities here!

ECONOMIC
Characteristics: Prosperous, growing; large gulf between working/service-class people (mostly students and minorities) and a much more affluent professional class; enormous commuter population (i.e., many more people work in Boulder than live there); economy driven by the university, several national labs, and a thriving entrepreneurial community (mostly tech, biotech, and renewable/sustainable energy).

Possible opportunities: Rush-hour concerts for commuters? Education and outreach to the "other" Boulder (working-class, mostly minority populations who are mostly invisible here)? Emerging ventures like edgy, new things: project underwriting possibilities?

POLITICAL
Characteristics: Very liberal; high degree of civic discourse on local issues; dedicated sales tax for arts and culture reveals strong civic support.

Possible opportunities: Identify local issues you and your friends care about and do some themed performances to highlight the issues, raise awareness, and so on.

INTEGRATION
Now start thinking of how these contexts might work together. Take the "Home-Grown Colorado" idea: perhaps you perform up and down the Front Range urban corridor (geographic), build audience via local garden groups (social), get sponsorship from restaurants and distilleries (economic), and seek branding and underwriting through the city and local arts council (political). *What sorts of things can YOU brainstorm for your community? Have fun with it—you might be surprised what you come up with!*

CHAPTER 2
Walk Like an Entrepreneur

Traits of Entrepreneurial Action

"I'm not much of a pianist."

Graduate school had just begun, and as a composition student I was required to embark on two years of piano study. I was nervous. I hadn't played seriously for several years, and even at my best my playing was never more than passable.

"Who told you that?" my teacher Bill asked.

"Well, my piano teacher growing up. Plus, I have these weird joints in my thumb that don't bend. They make scales and passage work really hard."

Bill grabbed my hand and examined my misshapen fingers for a moment before releasing them dismissively. "Your fingers are fine. Why don't you play something for me?"

So I played something slow—one of the easier Chopin preludes—and then something faster. (Scarlatti? I don't remember.) I clammed all over the place, and when I was done I turned to him with a sheepish smile on my face, bracing for his withering criticism.

"You have all the makings of a fine pianist," said Bill, to my shock. "You play very expressively and have a wonderful sense of touch and phrasing. What I'm guessing, though, is that you never learned how to practice."

I wanted to blurt out "You mean there's a practice for practicing?!" As a composer (with voice being my primary instrument), I'd never delved as deeply into instrumental practice as my colleagues, yet the idea that I'd missed out on such a basic aspect of musicianship still knocked me for an emotional loop.

So I spent the next six months learning how to practice. I learned how to break down a passage into its component parts, master each chunk, and put it back together again. I learned how to instill good muscle memory through things like working with a metronome at slow speeds and gradually working back up to tempo. And I discovered that by loosening up my arms and using the whole length of them to navigate the keyboard, my frozen thumbs became a nonissue. The more I practiced practicing, the more surprising it was to me that I'd managed to advance at all in my prior years! Consequently, I improved more in that first year of study than I had in years of study as a kid. And while I had no desire to be a professional pianist, I was able to put to rest something I'd internalized and held on to for years: that I had no "talent" as a pianist.

Talent. It's such a complicated concept, isn't it? We assume that everybody who is good at something must have It—"It" being an innate ability to master the thing in question. The more talent you possess, the easier mastery becomes. But it remains intangible and difficult to define, and as such we imbue it with a kind of mystical quality. You don't know where it comes from, and the lack of it becomes a convenient scapegoat for your failure to master something.

As musicians we know it's more complex than that. There are, of course, "naturals" at any pursuit you can name. In music, these "naturals" appear to master technique with ease, while the rest of us mere mortals must toil away at it. The "naturals" don't seem to need much practice, and we never see them laboring over meaning or expression. Music just flows out of them, seemingly without effort: they're the Mozart types. We look on them with a mix of admiration and jealousy—before returning to the practice room for another few hours of humble woodshedding.

In the world of entrepreneurship, the question of "natural talent" is a controversial one. Scholars, businesspeople, and entrepreneurs alike all wonder: are entrepreneurs born, or can they be made? Some entrepreneurs appear to be "naturals": ideas flow out of them easily, and they seem to have an uncanny ability to anticipate what markets will want. How do they do it? Can anyone learn how to act entrepreneurially, or is there some mysterious set of proclivities that is present in successful entrepreneurs, some X factor, that the rest of us lack? While the habits of observation, perspective, and attitude I've discussed can certainly be learned and developed, are those enough to make us successful entrepreneurs? Is there such a thing as a "natural" entrepreneur, and if there is, then should the rest of us even bother? For the musician, looking from a considerable distance at the unfamiliar landscape of entrepreneurship and wanting, first and foremost, to *remain* a musician, this question needs an answer.

To get at that answer, let's step into the kitchen for a moment. My husband is a "natural" cook: he can open up the refrigerator and whip up an incredible meal with whatever he finds inside (no matter how random); he simply follows his innate instincts regarding what will work. That doesn't mean he hasn't had to learn the proper techniques to realize his culinary instincts, but his facility in the kitchen makes the process appear effortless to the casual observer. In contrast, I generally start with a recipe, plan my shopping, and after a few runs by the (cook)book, start to improvise from there. There is a great deal of trial and error in my cooking (emphasis on the latter), and it is not something that comes easily to me. Still, while I'm not a "natural" by any means, family and friends consider me an excellent cook. But reaching that point has involved more than a few culinary disasters.

I'm an artist, not an entrepreneur . . .
I don't think that way . . .
I don't possess that talent . . .

These are things I hear musicians say all the time, but the truth is that such statements are not any more true than my assertion that I lacked talent as a pianist, or my concluding that I'm a terrible cook because I make a lot of mistakes and still can't consistently crack an egg without making a mess. What *is* true is that I haven't *mastered* the piano (or the cracking of an egg), but that's a very different thing from being inherently *unable* to. Insisting that you lack the ability to do something with which you are unfamiliar is a self-fulfilling (and ultimately self-defeating) prophecy.

I went rock climbing once and got left in the dust by everyone. Clearly, I'm no rock climber.

Well, you're not a rock climber *yet*. And maybe you don't want to be; that's fine. But until you get instruction, have the proper tools, and practice to develop your skills, you'll never know what truly stands between you and mastery. As I found with the piano, once I had the proper tools to work with I excelled farther than I ever imagined was possible.

Mastering entrepreneurship is no different. The entrepreneurial mindset discussed in chapter 1 might not come naturally to us. It might feel foreign or even uncomfortable at first. And yes, just as with those "natural" musicians, some folks will master entrepreneurship more quickly and easily than others. Just as the habits of entrepreneurial observation and problem-solving can absolutely be developed, the same thing applies to the principles of entrepreneurial action I'll discuss next. It might be intimidating and challenging, but cultivating an entrepreneurial mindset and learning how to act entrepreneurially are things we can indeed master.

This is an important point for musicians to recognize. After all, there are few folks better at mastering difficult things than musicians: when it comes to such challenges, we're in our element. Just think about what it felt like when you were first learning an instrument. None of us started out as masters; we didn't just pick up our fiddles and toss off some Paganini! It was a process, one that required time, discipline, hard work, and struggling to overcome what at times felt like an insurmountable challenge. And just because you might not have the capacity to become the next Yo-Yo Ma or Luciano Pavarotti, you needn't give up altogether: you become the best musician you can be, and you find your own patch in the wonderfully diverse quilt of music.

"But what if I just don't *want* to be an entrepreneur?" Quite often, this sentiment is what's *really* behind the statement "I'm an artist, not an entrepreneur." To many, the need to master *one more thing* feels overwhelming—particularly when that thing is so new and feels so completely divorced from their life's focus. Such feelings are understandable: mastering one's music is challenge enough! But I would argue that if you feel you don't "want" to be an entrepreneur, it may be because you're still clinging to the notion that being an entrepreneur means moving away from your music or pursuing a business that doesn't interest you. But entrepreneurship doesn't mandate any particular outcome: a thriving teaching studio in a small town can be just as successful an entrepreneurial venture as a startup company that explodes to multibillion-dollar stardom. The definition of entrepreneurial success is something *you* get to determine for *yourself*. Entrepreneurship is a means to an end that *you* get to define. And so each of us gets to define for himself the degree to which entrepreneurship operates in his or her professional life. For some, it will be the central, driving force. For others, it will enable more modest goals. So what if you don't aspire to become the next Steve Jobs—neither do I! What's important to remember is that entrepreneurial principles are infinitely scalable, from guiding the formation of a private studio to reinventing the modern classical concert. Learn those principles, and decide for yourself how best to deploy them in your career.

With that in mind, I'll proceed with explaining entrepreneurial action. And remember: we get better by doing. Understanding entrepreneurial tools guides our actions and helps us excel, just as good practice techniques help us excel with our instruments. Mastery comes with diligence and time.

ENTREPRENEURIAL ACTION: PUTTING IDEAS INTO MOTION

Chapter 1 explained that the entrepreneurial mindset embodies "opportunity recognition" through strategic observation, focusing on the needs and sensibilities of others ("customer focus/empathy"), and being "flexible and adaptable" in the face of failure or changing circumstances. But an entrepreneurial mindset by itself does not necessarily result in a successful entrepreneurial venture. Identifying opportunities, focusing on your customers, and being flexible/adaptable are just the first steps. Entrepreneurial thinking must be followed by entrepreneurial action.

There are three core qualities of entrepreneurial action that any venture, large or small, needs to embrace: risk assessment, resourcefulness, and storytelling. I'll explore each of these individually and give some examples of these principles at work in the world of music.

Risk Assessment

When I poll students on how much tolerance for risk they think entrepreneurs possess, most say "a great deal." After all, anybody who launches a business from scratch or attempts to create something new and innovative must be pretty impervious to the potential to fall flat on their face—particularly when we know that about eight out of every ten new businesses fail within their first eighteen months. Once you understand the entrepreneurial mindset, though, you begin to see that entrepreneurs have no more tolerance for risk than the average person. In fact, they sometimes have even *less*. This is because, in addition to understanding failure in a more positive way, entrepreneurs do their homework, ask lots of questions, and don't proceed until they have a reasonably good handle on what the risks are and how to mitigate them. For the entrepreneur, *risk tolerance* is not to be confused with *initiative*. Entrepreneurs possess initiative in spades—risk tolerance, not so much.

A survey of the literature on why new businesses tend to fail reveals a few common mistakes, most of which could be avoided by doing the kind of homework entrepreneurs engage in. While things outside one's control, like strife with a business partner or downturns in the economy, contribute to many business closures, other common causes include not accounting for the competition, not pricing the product appropriately for the market, failure to adapt to changing circumstances, and not paying attention to customer feedback. And these are precisely the sorts of issues an entrepreneurial approach encourages one to research and consider carefully before launching a venture (and, once the venture is launched, continually evaluate). In addition to the customer-oriented observations just mentioned, entrepreneurs ask a *lot* of questions. Who is this product for? How much will they pay for it? Who else is already in this market and how can I differentiate myself from them? What's the best way for me to find out what this market wants, and how can I deploy my gifts and skills to satisfy those wants?

The more data that can be gathered to answer these questions, the more knowledge of the field and connection to customers the entrepreneur has, and the better he can assess the potential viability—the risk—of a venture. The best entrepreneurs are the ones who are able to gather and assess data in a clearheaded and objective way, with the end goal being to understand their risk—and, where possible, mitigate it.

For musicians, an objective assessment of one's market may not come naturally. We tend to assume that once our audience truly understands what we have to offer, they will enthusiastically embrace it. And so we commence with *convincing* without having any real understanding of what the people on the receiving end of those efforts really *want*. Given this approach, it's no wonder so many arts organizations are left scratching their heads after an expensive marketing campaign fails to significantly increase their attendance: such a campaign of *convincing* is focused on exactly the wrong thing.

Another equally dangerous mindset takes us to the opposite extreme where we assume that demographic X or population Y is just never going to "get" what we do—so there's no point in even trying to reach them. Classical musicians and organizations are frequently guilty of this, gearing their promotional efforts only to those people they have assumed—a priori—will like what they do (for instance, those of a certain socioeconomic class or level of education). The entrepreneurial approach, however, mandates that we jettison our assumptions, remain as objective as we can in our observations, and keep an open mind as we gather our data. If their research disappoints them or points them in an unexpected direction, entrepreneurs are willing to see where that information leads. And when they appear to have reached a dead end, entrepreneurs continue to contemplate the information they've gathered in the hope of finding a new approach, a new angle, an unmet need, that will allow them to successfully deliver their product to the market. While the new approach to a problem might look risky on the surface, the careful consideration of information that leads there ensures that much of the potential risk is, in fact, removed. That doesn't mean that every entrepreneurial venture succeeds—far from it—but it does considerably improve the chances for success. Mitigating risk through careful research and asking the right questions is therefore a critical part of entrepreneurial action.

One common (and remarkably simple) way of assessing risk is the analysis of strengths, weaknesses, opportunities, and threats (SWOT). Strengths and weaknesses are internal to your venture: what you possess (or don't), what you having going for you (or don't), and so forth. Opportunities and threats are external: how big is the market you're entering? Are there related markets you might expand into or potential partnerships that will help you grow? And on the flip side, how easy is it for a competitor to swoop in and steal your business? What will happen to you if a key piece of technology changes or market sensibilities shift? The internal pieces of the SWOT analysis are things you have the power to change. External pieces are out of your control but can still have a profound impact on your success (or lack thereof); being aware of what they are is critically important.

Ventures that have many strengths and opportunities and few weaknesses and threats are viewed as relatively low risk. Conversely, ventures with many weaknesses and significant threats are considered very risky. A risky venture might still be worth pursuing, but first the entrepreneur needs to see if there are ways to reduce that risk, and whether or not the potential payoff is worth it. You'll note that, once again, the entrepreneur has the freedom to implement the process however she or he sees fit. For some entrepreneurs, a SWOT analysis that reveals moderate risk will dissuade them from pursuing the venture. Others might feel the potential payoff is sufficiently promising that it's worth the risk. Tools such as the SWOT analysis help define and clarify potential risks, but you still have to make a personal decision regarding how you feel about them and what action is appropriate in response.

A great way to both expose potential risks and mitigate them is to perform a "premortem," a tool advocated by research psychologist Gary Klein. In this exercise, you imagine that your venture has failed and then list every possible reason you can think of for why it happened. Looking at it from this perspective will likely expose things you hadn't considered, since your first impulse when contemplating a new venture is to let your excitement over the idea drive an overly optimistic view of things. The premortem will also, therefore, provide a list of issues you need to fix/address (thus mitigating your risk)—or, if an issue can't be fixed, expose a fatal flaw in your idea while it's still on the drawing board.

We should also understand that risk can take several different forms. In addition to the sorts of things already discussed—market considerations, your own inventory of skills, and so on—the next two examples show that addressing risks can manifest in ways beyond simply determining the chances of success.

When Taylor Welsheimer had a stroke at age twenty-three, the beginnings of a promising career as an oboist took a back seat to her recovery. And while extensive therapy helped her regain most of her function, she found that processing speech remained difficult. She soon discovered a gap in the continuum of care from acute trauma to being released from medical care: she had done all the work she could with a speech therapist but still needed to find some kind of endeavor that would help her to process and deliver her speech more fluently. Quite by accident, she found that singing was incredibly beneficial. And with that discovery, an idea began to take shape in her mind.

Fast-forward to my entrepreneurship class at the University of Colorado, where Taylor undertook an opportunity assessment of her idea. Stroke of Mozart would be a service for stroke survivors who had completed their formal medical care but still needed that last bit of polish to resume 100 percent normal function. She would teach singing to these patients and offer support and networking for the stroke community—especially that relatively rare and poorly understood population of otherwise healthy people who suffer strokes at a very young age.

Taylor had identified an unmet need, defined her market, devised a product that addressed the need in question, and formulated a business model that was simple and realistic. At first it would seem that this idea had all the makings of a viable entrepreneurial venture. But then the SWOT analysis came along, and things started to change.

The first realization came out of a classic entrepreneurial question: *How is my product different from what else is already out there?* Taylor's idea was, to a great extent, simply a continuation of formal speech therapy treatment. It went past the point where formal medical treatment was still required (and therefore past the point where insurance would pay for it) but nevertheless was still practicing a kind of voice/occupational therapy. Moreover, she soon recognized that the only realistic way to assemble a sufficiently large client base was to partner with existing medical and/or social service entities— entities that would not risk the legal liability of conducting such a program without trained and licensed personnel. So in this case, the risk was less about the idea itself and more about potential legal exposure for an entrepreneur lacking any formal training or credentials in speech, music, or occupational therapy. Taylor was forced to conclude that, while she might someday form a private support group for young stroke survivors who get together to sing, implementing the idea as a *business* venture was probably not viable. Said another way, the idea was valid; the business was not.

Another kind of risk assessment is more personal. When Bob Lord initially arrived at MMC Recordings in 2005, he believed he could turn the struggling company around. He soon discovered the task was far greater than he initially realized. Moreover, he began to see firsthand the depth of animus many customers felt, something he described as the "radioactive reputation" of the company. In this case, "risk" hinged on more than whether or not it was even possible to turn things at MMC around: Lord also had to assess the risk to his own professional reputation. If he failed to reboot the company, what would that mean for his career?

In the end, Lord concluded that the risks were too great. He had spent too long building a reputation as an ethical and honest broker to risk damaging that by working for a company that was on the verge of collapse. In deciding to buy out the outstanding MMC contracts and establish his own label from scratch, he both preserved his own integrity and was able to build a company on his own terms from the ground up. PARMA Recordings has been thriving ever since.

The personal aspect of Bob Lord's risk assessment of the MMC venture leads us to the last aspect of risk. When measuring the risk associated with a potential venture, we also have to ask ourselves what pursuing the venture will force us to *give up*. Perhaps launching your venture will be extremely time-intensive. If you're a performer, how many gigs will you have to forgo to free up that time? What kind of impact will that have on your finances? Let's say you decide to take on a part-time adjunct position at a local university. How many fewer private lessons will you be able to give if you're now at school two days a week? The assessment of what you *lose* by pursuing another opportunity is called the opportunity cost, and it's an important consideration for musician-entrepreneurs. Some opportunity costs can be temporary (once things are up and running smoothly you may be able to return to your previous gig schedule). Others can be permanent (when an ensemble member decides to take on the role of the group's executive director, that member may have to accept that she or he just can't practice and perform as much as before). If the opportunity cost is small, that's one less risk your venture entails. If it's very large, then the potential payoff had better be very large, too—otherwise, perhaps it's not a risk worth taking. Once again you can see how entrepreneurial principles give you the flexibility to implement them as you see fit, in a way that is in harmony with your own sensibilities and needs. Coming to terms with risk is an important business consideration, but it has a personal and subjective side to it as well. Having a protocol for risk assessment helps us sort through what can be a frightening and confusing phase in developing an entrepreneurial venture.

Resourcefulness

A few years back I had a student in my class with an idea that was quite grand in scope. It had many components and was being envisioned, right out of the box, as a large corporation. While I listened to the passion with which the student explained his idea, I wondered how I could bring him back down to earth without squelching his enthusiasm. When he was finished, I was quiet for a moment and then said, "Okay . . . you've got a great vision for this company. Let's take a step back for a minute, though, and figure out how we get there. Can you imagine how this would get started? What's the very first step?"

Without missing a beat, this exuberant young man declared, "All I need is ten million dollars."

I tried to contain the raising of my eyebrows, but he caught my expression nonetheless.

"Okay," he said, undeterred. "Maybe only five."

"Do you know someone who will give you five million dollars?"

"No, but I'll find investors."

"Well, first of all, investors aren't easy to find—particularly without a lot more information and data than you have at this point. But even if you could find some, their money comes at a high price—often, a controlling interest and the ability to fire you if they don't think you're doing a good enough job.

So rather than pinning your hopes on the equivalent of winning the lottery, let's look at how this could begin on a smaller scale and with a more realistic view of what resources you can access."

After a number of weeks of working with this student to answer the question "What can I do *right now?*" he decided that his idea wasn't practical and discarded it altogether. I simply couldn't convince him that the entrepreneurial process usually unfolds one step at a time, using available resources, evaluating, refining, and then taking the next step. Even the behemoth Microsoft started in a garage! In addition, and more often than not, entrepreneurial ventures that receive a load of venture capital at the outset flame out once the money is gone. Easy money allows young companies to avoid hard questions. Moreover, media coverage of those few companies that rocket out of nowhere into multibillion dollar enterprises tends to paint a false picture of ease by glossing over the hard work, missteps, and sacrifices of the early years. Finally, most entrepreneurial megasuccess stories didn't start out with a vision to conquer the world; they usually began with solving a problem at hand, and greatness followed. After all, when Mark Zuckerberg started Facebook, he wasn't trying to create a platform to connect the world's population; he was just trying to improve his social life. The growth, and then the global vision, came later—informed by those aspects of his original idea that were resonating in the broader marketplace.

The gap between having an idea, perhaps even a rather grand vision, and identifying the first step required to realize it is one of the biggest sticking points for novice entrepreneurs. In part, this is due to our natural tendency, particularly as creatives, to envision the end product first. We can picture the cool venue we'd like to create; we can see ourselves traveling the country with the unique workshop we're going to develop; we can imagine how our new record label will change the recording industry with its innovative business model. But for all the inspiration fueling these ideas—some of which might be really good ones—we're still no closer to taking that *first step*. Part of this uncertainty might be due simply to lack of familiarity with basic business practices or the particularities of a given industry: stepping into the unknown can be scary! But business practices can be researched and learned; uncertainty about the market or what potential customers might want can be researched. These are not insurmountable problems.

There's another problem that may be harder to solve, however: what are the resources required to realize my vision? Once again, our tendency to see the end product first gets in the way of answering this question because we calculate what's needed based on the idea that, if we only had the money, we could launch a fully realized venture right out of the box. "All I need is ten million dollars."

It hardly ever works that way. (Though I confess to once in a while enjoying a nice daydream about the things I'll do when I win the Powerball!)

For entrepreneurs, even those in money-soaked environs like Silicon Valley, money from investors is not easy to come by. Investors want to see a "proof of concept"—a prototype, beta version, or other proof that the idea in question both is workable and will appeal to the market. And even if investors were willing to fund you at the very outset, it might not be an attractive proposition in the long run. You must remember that investors are not in the business of helping you; they're in the business of making money off your idea. And their money will come at a high price, often in the form of a controlling interest in your venture. In the shark tank world of venture capital, you could see your idea taken away and reshaped in ways you never intended or wanted. Once you begin to look at it more closely, the idea of an outside investor swooping in and giving you a blank check might not look so appealing.

Besides, for those of us in the world of classical music, Silicon Valley–style investment is so far divorced from our world that it might as well be from another planet. Whether your venture is for-profit or not-for-profit, arts patrons are still most likely motivated by the work you're creating, the impact you're having on your community, or the prestige that accompanies the tradition of fine arts patronage. A solid business model is still required, but the driving force behind someone supporting an arts-based venture is likely to be something other than the desire for riches. After all, institutional investors seeking a robust return on their investments have far more fertile fields to explore than classical music.

So where do we find the resources we need to get started? The difficulty of attracting investors in an artistic context means that we have to find other means to get our ventures off the ground. This is what I'm terming "resourcefulness." While we usually think of resourcefulness as a personality trait—"She's a resourceful person"—it has a specific meaning in an entrepreneurial context. Rather than focusing on what they don't have (and therefore can't do), resourceful entrepreneurs look at what they *do* have—and what they *can* do today. They find ways to stretch the resources they already have at hand to the maximum extent. And they devise cheap (or free) ways to gain access to resources they otherwise could not afford. Through resourcefulness, the first phases of an entrepreneurial venture can be implemented sooner rather than later. This is called the "lean startup" approach to entrepreneurship, and it is by far the most common way new ventures get off the ground. And while the first iteration of your idea in a lean startup scenario is likely to be a far cry from your vision for the finished product, this approach has significant benefits. The forced smallness of a lean startup allows the entrepreneur to refine, tweak, and improve the venture without putting a lot on the line. This reduces the financial risk of the startup and, perhaps even more important, increases the chance of ultimate success by keeping the initial phase nimble and adaptable. Think of it like a theatrical preview or a dress rehearsal for a concert: you have a chance to work out the last kinks of the show before it goes in front of your audience.

A good place to begin planning for a lean startup is to take an inventory of what you already have. Do you have any money saved up? Are there supportive family, friends, or patrons who already believe in you and can help? Are there partnerships you can enter into that might both support your venture and benefit your partner? Is there some unused space in your house that can be converted into a makeshift office or studio? Do you have anything you can barter for needed services? This inventory should go beyond mere physical resources: what skills and talents do you possess that you can utilize in your venture? Are there things you can learn, DIY resources you can avail yourself of that will help you avoid having to hire someone or make an expensive purchase? How can you leverage your resources such that you can stretch them as far as possible?

The element of resourcefulness in the entrepreneurial mindset is especially germane for musicians, who tend to start out with nothing more than their instruments and a lot of passion. You might have an inspiring vision to create a new kind of theater or a multimedia concert hall, but unless you happen to have a very wealthy patron in your vest pocket, you'll probably have to figure out a more modest way to get started. Resourcefulness means you take stock of your own assets, your relationships and connections, the underutilized and underengaged resources in your community, and you find a way to get started *today*. Hopefully you'll get to that new concert hall someday, but most likely you'll get there by effectively leveraging what you've already got at each step of the way and pursuing your vision step by step.

One of my favorite examples of resourcefulness is the story of the Round Top Festival Institute. Though it is now a stunning campus and a major year-round institution for performance and study, it had humble beginnings. The initial impulse came from pianist James Dick's desire to create a summer haven where he could teach, practice, and enjoy a respite from the stress and bustle of his touring career. He chose the town of Round Top, Texas, the smallest incorporated town in the state, situated in the scenic rolling hills of east-central Texas. Round Top was more than a quaint town, though: it was strategically located, roughly equidistant from the three of the state's largest cities—Houston, Dallas, and San Antonio—and less than an hour away from its booming capital, Austin.

Originally the Institute was a two-week festival with ten piano students. The first concerts were open-air affairs in the town square that utilized a portable stage built from a repurposed flatbed truck. Dick's extensive network of teachers and recitalists allowed him to bring internationally known artists to his festival, and audiences quickly began to make the drive to Round Top to hear them. Plus, the bucolic surroundings offered a perfect day trip away from the bustle of Texas's major population centers.

After a few seasons, the festival was expanding to include other instruments of study, more concerts, and an extended schedule. It was soon time to look for a permanent home, and in 1973 Dick chose a few acres just outside town. He could not have chosen a more unlikely plot of land: the new site of the Round Top Festival, rechristened "Festival Hill," was on the grounds of the former town dump.

Dick and his partners soon got to work transforming the property. In a few years, a decaying school building had been fixed up to house the first classrooms and rehearsal space. When a historic house in a nearby town was set for demolition, Dick negotiated for the building to be moved to Festival Hill and provide much-needed additional space. It was a critical turning point for his venture, coinciding with the emerging trend of historic preservation and the birth regionally of interest in antiques and the artisans who restore them. Soon Dick was building his festival grounds with historic buildings (mostly houses) from the surrounding countryside that were in danger of demolition. He partnered with local artisans and established an apprentice program that not only provided affordable labor but also ensured that skilled craftsmen were overseeing the restoration of the buildings that would become offices, artist housing, rehearsal space, and performance venues. Other than an initial loan of $2,000, the Institute has never borrowed money. Instead, new projects are only undertaken when money has been raised and is in the bank. In addition to ticket sales from concerts, the Institute generates income throughout the rest of the year by renting out its facilities for conferences and meetings; the restored living quarters operate as a bed and breakfast. Finally, the focus on historic preservation has opened up funding sources that a venture focused solely on music would not otherwise have had access to.

It's taken more than thirty years, and the property continues to evolve, but the result has been a spectacular and unique gem, a historically significant campus that was assembled at a fraction of the cost of building such a place from scratch. While Dick and his partners probably don't view their approach as such, they were exhibiting one of the quintessential traits of entrepreneurial action: working with what you have, and taking advantage of latent opportunities around you to accomplish your goals. From the ruins of the town dump, the founders of the Round Top Festival Institute have created a venue of international stature—one bit at a time.

Storytelling

One of the most important aspects of entrepreneurial thinking is communicating effectively about your product, why it's valuable, and how it's an authentic reflection of your artistry. This is what I call "storytelling," and without it, it is incredibly difficult to create a connection between your customer and your product or service—the very connection that's required to motivate a customer to buy what you're selling. Storytelling may not involve a narrative tale in the traditional sense of the word (though it can); nor is it simply an argument for your product or idea. It translates that argument into human terms, through words and images that demonstrate why the product in question is valuable *to people*. Done well, storytelling conveys the essence of our artistic selves: what motivates us, what we are seeking to accomplish, and why we are passionate about it.

Entrepreneurial storytelling plays out in three distinct contexts: as a marketing tool, as a way of pitching your product or idea to potential supporters, and as an expression of artistic ideas. The easiest one to see is how it operates in the context of marketing. Every successful marketing campaign is designed to communicate a message about a product or service through images, text, and various media. To shape that message, however, a "story" must be told. That is, the elements utilized must add up to a message that will compel the would-be consumer to see the value of the product *for them*. There are countless examples of this, but one campaign I'm particularly fond of in this regard was the "I'm a Mac/I'm a PC" campaign from the late 2000s. In this campaign, a young hipster personifies Apple's Mac computer while an older, frumpy, and rather awkward guy personifies the PC. The message is clear: "PCs are behind the times, lacking in style, and decidedly *not cool*. Macs are modern, hip, and the very *essence* of cool. Which would you rather be?" The marketing team at Apple used actors who were evocative of a very specific set of values and associations, values they successfully linked to their product. The "story" being told in this campaign was so potent that numerous iterations of it played out for months, and parodies were spawned; the Mac guy and the PC guy entered the popular lexicon.

The use of storytelling as a marketing device only begins to get at its power, however. Whether you're writing a grant proposal, seeking support from a patron, or pitching your idea to a prospective client, the more clearly you can articulate the value of your product in terms of how it personally benefits individuals—the more compelling the story you tell about your product—the more effective your efforts will be. Moreover, funders, patrons, and customers alike want to support those who are passionate about what they do, who act out of a sense of purpose and in service to something larger than themselves. Storytelling helps us convey these things.

I witnessed a great aspect of storytelling in the context of a pitch during the University of Colorado's New Venture Challenge a few years back. I'd been working with senior voice major Brooke Murray's pitch for "Sing It Forward," a voice studio for underserved youth, for weeks. Yet we still hadn't unlocked the secret to conveying the powerful potential of her venture—why it *mattered*. We hadn't yet found the right story to tell.

A few hours before the competition was to begin, I received a voice message from Brooke: "I've completely re-done my pitch, but I'm really excited. See you tonight!" As Brooke's turn to pitch approached, I experienced some professorial nerves: she was about to stand up in front of Boulder's entire entrepreneurial community with a pitch I had not yet seen or approved.

I needn't have worried, though. Brooke started by telling an actual story: how when she was a child she was mauled by a dog and underwent months of surgery to repair her disfigured face. She was regularly mocked and bullied by her classmates and ostracized by her friends. "But music saved me. It was my salvation. I honestly don't know what I would have done if I hadn't had music. And now I have a chance to pass along that gift to a new generation of young people." All the people in the room were on the edges of their seats: they saw the power of what she was offering before she even revealed her product.

If you doubt the power of having an actual story to express the value of your product, consider what happened after the competition was over. Judge and Boulder entrepreneur Jason Mendelson came to the microphone to announce the winner; "but first I want to say something. Brooke, I was really moved by your story. You see, when I was a kid I was in an automobile accident, and I spent a year in a wheelchair. And I was bullied and ostracized. And I can totally relate to what you were saying because music was *my* salvation, too. So you didn't win. But I'm going to pledge $5,000 in seed money to help you get your venture off the ground."

The place erupted. Another angel investor came forward and matched Jason's gift. An attorney offered Brooke his legal services in setting up her organization. And that's storytelling: communicating value in human terms, in terms that move people to *act*. You might not have a powerful personal story related to your product, but if you can't find some authentic, compelling reasons for why anyone should care about what you're offering, spend some time developing some before you go any further. After all, if you can't articulate the value of your product to yourself, how can you expect someone else to see the value in it?

Moreover, effective storytelling doesn't exist in a vacuum—it can be part of a broader narrative you develop regarding your venture, its purpose, and your vision for it. For instance, the "I'm a Mac/I'm a PC" campaign was really just a reflection of a corporate narrative that Apple was developing at the time, one that said that the company was transforming mere technology into a lifestyle choice—a narrative that has guided every aspect of how Apple has developed its products, shaped its brand, and communicated with its market for over a decade.

The final sort of storytelling serves as a vehicle for composers and performers to connect with their audiences. Survey after survey has revealed that many people perceive the classical music concert as boring, stuffy, and anachronistic. Even those who like the experience will often say that the music is merely "relaxing." These characterizations of classical music grieve us, of course, because anybody who truly knows this music sees how much action, tension, energy, and emotions it embodies. Clearly, then, somewhere along the line there is a disconnect between performers/presenters and the broader audience: only the most devoted fans seem to be able to access the true treasures of the music we perform. There are many reasons for this, and discussing them fully is a book unto itself, but I think part of the responsibility for this lack of connection between the power of our music and our audiences lies with musicians' own inability to tell a compelling story about—and *through*—their music. I'm not just talking about program notes or delivering some engaging remarks from the stage (although we tend to fail miserably at these things, too). I'm talking about the very way we conceive our concerts and their purpose. I'm talking about our stage demeanor and how effectively we communicate through our body language, our facial expressions, and the very nature of our playing. Are we just performing the repertoire we'd like to perform? Is our performance so self-absorbed that it has no regard for who is hearing it or how it's perceived? Or is our *primary goal* to create a compelling experience for our audiences, to reach them, move them, and communicate something to them? If it's the latter, then we must be cognizant of the narrative—the story line— we are trying to convey through our music, and we must consider how best to embody and communicate that narrative to our audiences in *every aspect* of the concerts we are putting together.

The quartet Brooklyn Rider carefully designs every program to convey some sort of narrative by bridging apparently disparate pieces and genres. Such narratives need not be literal, like that of an opera or a programmatic symphony. A narrative thread can be defined by an intentional emotional journey or unifying components that reveal connections between works that wouldn't otherwise be seen. But whatever shape this form of storytelling takes, it's about creating a sense of experience, and it requires that each element of that experience has an intentional role to play in the greater whole. Once we determine what it is we want the audience to experience— the journey we're asking them to take with us—we must think long and hard about the best way to convey that. We must think about every aspect of the audience experience: the repertoire, the order of the program, the venue, and how best to provide some kind of dramatic framework, some kind of context in which to understand what's going on. At its heart, storytelling is about drawing our audiences—our customers—*into* the value of the experience we are offering.

So if you're opening up a private teaching studio, storytelling helps you communicate why you teach and what makes your studio special. If you've decided to create an after-school program for at-risk youth, storytelling can help you illustrate why these kids need your program and the impact it has on their lives. Articulating the story behind what you do can help clarify your sense of mission and purpose, which in turn strengthens your case for others to support you.

And finally, having a clear and compelling story to tell is at the heart of developing your brand and sharing that brand in the marketplace. It is a critical element of every press release, poster, grant application, biography, cover letter, headshot, donor pitch, season brochure, set of preconcert remarks, website design, social media strategy, and choice of venue, clothing, and presentational style. Your story is at the very center of expressing the value of what you're offering; make sure you tell that story every day and in everything you do.

As you can see from these examples, storytelling is both a way to express the value in your work *and* a potential artistic catalyst. It can help you articulate why an existing artistic product matters to your customers, and it can help you conceive how best to communicate an artistic message you wish to share. In both cases, storytelling is about connecting your artistic product with the needs and sensibilities of potential customers. And that's at the very heart of what it means to be an entrepreneur.

LEARNING TO ACT: ATTRIBUTES OF SUCCESSFUL ENTREPRENEURS

In addition to traits like hard work and discipline, which are useful in any number of pursuits, are there specific traits entrepreneurs tend to share? I believe there are. These traits fall into a handy acronym that occurred to me one afternoon while working in the garden (another pursuit at which I am far from a "natural" but have gotten pretty good at and which is an important activity for nurturing my muse). Entrepreneurs *ACT*: they are *authentic, creative*, and *tenacious*.

Let's look at each of these in turn and spend some time reflecting on how these three attributes of successful entrepreneurs inform, and are informed by, the action qualities of assessing risk, resourcefulness, and storytelling. I'll also show why these attributes are particularly important for artist-entrepreneurs to incorporate into their practice.

Authentic

Remaining true to your passions, true to your best artistic self, is of the utmost importance to entrepreneurial success—especially in the arts. I can't think of a single entrepreneurial success (artistic or otherwise) that didn't have somebody's passion at the center of it. Even so-called serial entrepreneurs, who have no particular field or pursuit they're committed to, are nevertheless driven by their passion for starting things and connecting with the needs of their customers. No matter what form it takes, passion—a sincere belief in what you're doing and a personal ownership of it—is essential to entrepreneurial success.

When it comes to music, the power of authenticity is even more critical. After all, how can we expect to move our audiences if we are not moved ourselves? How can we expect to convey something to a listener if we don't have anything within us worth conveying? And in a culture where commercial media designed for mass consumption saturates people's lives, where image and extravagance trump content and subtlety, the need for authentic, meaningful, compelling experiences is more profound than ever. Who better to deliver such experiences than those of us in the performing arts?

That said, many musicians—particularly instrumentalists—struggle with this notion of finding one's personal artistic "voice." This is partly the fault of our music education system, which often stresses technical mastery over individual expression, and partly due simply to the fact that when one is still developing as a musician the focus is understandably on developing craft and facility. The problem, however, is that worrying about developing an artistic voice "later" often results in a musician leaving school and embarking on a career with exceptional ability on an instrument but having little to say with it. Addressing this challenge is essential for the musician-entrepreneur, because your unique voice is the primary mode through which you differentiate yourself from your competition. It's also essential to creating a compelling experience for your audience. Your artistic authenticity isn't just conveying somebody else's version of passion or pathos, it's conveying *your* understanding of those things. In the words of my friend and fellow composer Kieren MacMillan, it is self-expression "without artifice."

Your "artistic voice" certainly begins with your personal performing style and interpretive approach, but it can go much farther than these. For soloists or conductors, it might include specific repertoire in which they specialize, or the incorporation of other media into the experience. A composer's artistic voice goes beyond musical style to include the kinds of projects and collaborations she undertakes or the way she links her work to entities in her community. A chamber ensemble might define its artistic voice by the kinds of venues where it plays, its unique blend of repertoire, the way its members interact with the audience, or simply the genuine, personal way they interact with *each other* during the act of making music together. Indeed, the most compelling performers have probably cultivated more than one of these differentiators as they developed their unique artistic voices. Even orchestral players—where individuality may be contrary to the needs of the ensemble—might find ways to make their own unique contribution through their exemplary collaborative styles, education and outreach events, or other performances outside the orchestra. The point is, your artistic voice encompasses many things beyond musical interpretation: it's the sum total of your artistic identity. By broadening your definition of "artistic voice," you are more likely to find a way to distinguish yourself from all the other talented musicians out there. This not only opens up more professional options for you, it also serves your personal need for artistic fulfillment and staying fresh.

Artistic authenticity, in whatever form (or forms) it takes, is therefore the core, essential requirement for connecting with an audience. Without authenticity, meaningful connection and communication is impossible. I am continually amazed at how quickly an audience can sense whether or not the performers are personally invested in the experience, whether or not they are enjoying making music and genuinely want to communicate to the audience. As performers and composers, we too can sense the energy of an audience: we know when we're reaching them—that is, if we're tuned into them and paying attention. The self-reinforcing circle of performer-and-audience energy creates a powerful bond, one that edifies everyone involved and contributes to an experience that audiences want to revisit and support. Thus, authenticity is essential to creating value. In an entrepreneurial context, this means that your most authentic artistic voice becomes more than an expression of your artistic integrity. It is your most valuable business asset as well.

Creative

The binding thread woven throughout this book is creativity. When Yngve Berqvist turned a freakishly warm day into an enduring tourist phenomenon, creativity helped him see how to turn a disaster into an opportunity. The members of Brooklyn Rider look at every aspect of their performance as a creative opportunity, from the choice of venue and repertoire to the artists they choose to collaborate with and the avenues they employ to connect with their audience. When James Dick needed more space for his growing festival, he found the answer in the surrounding countryside—a creative insight that transformed his venture into something far more than a music venue, all on the remains of the town dump. When entrepreneurs look at what everyone else sees as an obstacle, it is their creativity that allows them to turn that bug into a feature. When entrepreneurs' research and data point to some unexpected conclusions, it is trust in their creativity that allows them to go down the untrodden path to something completely new.

Of course, "creativity" is one of those words that is casually bandied about but difficult to define. Like entrepreneurship itself, creativity can lead to an infinite number of disparate outcomes—making it hard to identify the common impulses driving it. And while a full exploration of what makes up creativity would be a book unto itself, the way it plays out in an entrepreneurial context is somewhat more specific.

The scholar Thomas Ward has identified two powerful mechanisms driving the development of creative ideas. The first is what he calls "conceptual combination," the bringing together of two apparently disparate things to create something new. With conceptual combination, the final result reveals "emergent properties"—new and unique traits that were not present in either of the constituent components. That's what Yngve Berqvist was doing when he combined the notions of a hotel and an ice sculpture. Each of the elements was clearly defined in and of itself, but their combination created a new and unique thing nobody had envisioned before.

The second creative mechanism Ward has identified is "analogy." This process applies a known and familiar domain to a less familiar or unknown one. One use of analogy is as a way to explain an idea to an audience that may lack the particular knowledge or vocabulary required to understand it. (This makes analogy an excellent tool for storytelling.) For instance, Ernest Rutherford employed analogy when he used our knowledge of the form of the solar system to explain and illustrate the structure of a hydrogen atom. Another great example is depicting the entire history of the Earth as a twenty-four-hour clock, with humans appearing on the scene at 23:59:40. This analogy helps us understand our place in the vastness of geologic time in a way we could not otherwise fathom. As these examples demonstrate, analogy is particularly useful in the areas of science and technology, but it can be useful in music as well—and for some of the same reasons. The technical qualities of the musical experience, and its complexity, make it difficult to talk about with laypeople; using analogies can help us convey important musical events or concepts while avoiding insiders' jargon. One of the most common mistakes musicians make when speaking to an audience is to embark on a technical explanation of what it will hear: how a motive is transformed, how the form will unfold, or how musical building blocks are deployed. The problem with this approach is that the few people in the audience who can follow such an explanation don't need to hear it, and the rest don't care. Analogy, however, can help a lay audience relate to the experience by giving them familiar images and concepts to apply to their listening.

The other way analogy can be used is for the development of new ideas, by placing known and familiar aspects of something in a new context. The excellent example Ward gives is the musical *West Side Story*, which used the process of analogy to reshape and reapply the story of *Romeo and Juliet*. The basic structure and archetypal themes of the original are retained, but they are deployed in a completely different way so as to create an experience that is simultaneously familiar and new.

Ideas borne out of analogy are common throughout the arts and may be especially useful to musician-entrepreneurs seeking to develop new ways to present and contextualize their art. Consider, for example, (Le) Poisson Rouge, in New York City, where the familiar notion of a live-music nightclub is brought into the classical music realm. Another example would be the Theatre of Music idea employed by the new music group Pittsburgh New

Music Ensemble. In the Theatre of Music, principles of dramatic focus from the world of theatre and of continuity from the world of film are employed in the shaping and structuring of contemporary chamber music concerts. (More on this ensemble in a later chapter.)

Ward's research is of vital importance to the entrepreneur, because it repudiates the common notion of creativity as "making something out of nothing." In fact, creative ideas nearly always draw, either directly or indirectly, from an existing paradigm or point of knowledge. Creative ideas are a combination of the novel and the familiar, where the ratio between the two exists on a continuum. An idea can be mostly familiar, in which case the "creativity factor" would be fairly low, or it can be mostly novel, in which case the idea might be considered quite groundbreaking and "out there." Artistic ideas may consciously build or expand on existing techniques or styles, or they can intentionally rebel against and confound established norms. In either case, though, creative ideas don't just come out of the blue—even when our experiences of "brainstorms" might feel otherwise. So, once again, you find out that an attribute you might all too quickly assume you lack—the creative impulse—is, in fact, something that exists in all of us.

This note about creativity and the entrepreneur comes back to "the box." The techniques discussed in chapter 1 for getting yourself outside the limitations of your own personal "box" are ultimately about freeing up your creativity, about finding new ways to address old problems. For instance, maybe you decide that even the most well-crafted set of remarks, using excellent analogies, still don't really communicate what you want to say about the piece you're about to perform, or perhaps they break up the flow of the program in a way that detracts from the experience. You're now presented with a choice: do you compromise the integrity of the program by going ahead and speaking anyway? Do you leave the audience in the dark by providing no frame of reference whatsoever? For the musician-entrepreneur, this problem is simply another a creative challenge, one that will be worked over and explored until a solution emerges. Perhaps you employ a new mode of expression—a short film, monologue, or poem? Or perhaps you must change or adjust some other aspect of the concert in order for your original spoken remarks to fit more organically into the experience. Perhaps you reshuffle or revise your repertoire so that the thematic thread you wish to convey is more clearly illuminated and further explanation is redundant. Whatever you decide, the process of tackling the issue is, at its core, a creative one.

What's important here is that creativity can (and should) reach every aspect of our musical lives, whether we are performers, teachers, composers, scholars, or presenters. Each field has its own set of problems and challenges, and that means that each field needs our creative engagement. The process of creative problem-solving and developing new ideas will be fed by observation and data, driven by our innate creative impulse to combine known things in unknown ways and to place the archetypal truths of our culture in new and novel contexts. If classical music is to reestablish itself as a central force in our society's cultural life, these kinds of creativity will have to play a significant role.

Tenacious

A good friend of mine recounted the time that Wynton Marsalis came to her school to give a talk to music students. The trumpet great had a tough message for these aspiring professionals: most music students, he said, were not truly willing to put in the hard work necessary for success in their field. As a result, most would fail.

My friend freely admits that she was "totally not in the space to hear that at age 19." But over time, she came to realize just how accurate Wynton's assessment was. Making it in the music business is tough: it requires enormous commitment, and many fail in their attempts. Those of us in the business of helping musicians launch and sustain their careers do a disservice to our students when we pretend otherwise. Acknowledging the challenges is not about discouraging aspiring professionals, though. On the contrary, an effective career plan must recognize those challenges and their nature in order to increase the odds of overcoming them.

While tenacity certainly embodies hard work and commitment, it's also more than these things. The trajectory of a musician's career is almost never a straight line from school to dream job to retirement party. Instead, there is often a long period of struggle and piecemeal work, experiences that, over time, coalesce into a sustainable and fulfilling career. In addition, early career experiences often open up unforeseen options or take musicians down paths they never conceived of previously. It's important to recognize this, because when we're facing those moments of decision, evaluating the fork in the road, it can be easy for us to feel confused and discouraged. After all, embracing a new opportunity often requires letting go of an old one, and this can force us to face disappointed expectations, reevaluate our goals, and even struggle with our self-esteem and sense of worth. Tenacity is what will help us continue to move forward.

History is not a very good teacher with regard to identifying the need for tenacity—or at least, our *telling* of history isn't. When we open up a concert program and read the bio of that night's featured soloist, for instance, we are reading a sanitized version of that career in which the successes are highlighted and the low points left out. This gives the reader—particularly if that reader is a young or aspiring professional—a very skewed notion of what a "successful" career looks like. If you've internalized this image of successful careers proceeding in an orderly fashion, from prestigious school to competition prizes to lucky break to international fame, it's very likely you'll compare that image to your twisty, bumpy path and conclude "Surely, I don't have what it takes."

In his wonderful book *88x50*, pianist Adam Tendler illustrates this beautifully. If you were to visit Adam's website and look at his bio today, it would read like a fairly traditional combination of awards, high-profile engagements, praise from the press, and a note about his training. You would read the bio and conclude, "Wow—here's somebody who has 'made it,'" without consideration of what it took to get there. The story told in *88x50*, though, provides a much more complete and complicated picture, one of prolonged personal and artistic struggle. It's important for musicians to hear such stories because they are much more the norm, much closer to the reality of our careers than the sort of straight-line-to-glory account that tends to get fed to us in concert programs and promotional materials, social media, and even history books. Stories like Adam Tendler's are much closer to the kind of real-life scenarios most musicians face. Our path is long, bumpy, and filled with blind curves and unexpected barriers. There is often a personal price to be paid in the form of strained (or failed) relationships, financial burdens, and personal stress. (Not to mention the extremely limited cuisine options of someone living day-to-day: I ate a *lot* of red beans and rice when I was starting out!)

The hardships of getting started as a professional musician have some positive benefits, though. For one, there's nothing like a little deprivation to force you to decide what you really want from your career! In the case of musicians, not everybody is cut out for such a life, and there's no shame in recognizing that you might be just as happy and fulfilled doing something else. But those of us who simply *must* follow the call of the muse will have to discover those things we can rely on when we're tired and discouraged. When we fall flat on our faces, we'll have to learn how to stand back up and keep walking. We have to create our own support systems—because we're sure to need them. We have to develop our own methods of building and practicing tenacity.

Successful entrepreneurs can teach us something about tenacity. I have never met a group of people more proud of their "failures" than entrepreneurs. I remember speaking with one serial entrepreneur who cheerily stated, "Oh yeah: I've started four companies so far. With the first few, I had no idea what I was doing; one was a complete disaster. The next one made me a millionaire. We'll have to see about the one I'm in now; so far I'm feeling pretty good about it." Entrepreneurs are not only hard-working, energetic, and focused, they are also completely undeterred by what anyone else would call failure. It's not that they don't get frustrated or discouraged, and it's not that their ventures always succeed. Some ventures crash and burn—spectacularly. But entrepreneurs look at *every* outcome as just another step in an ongoing journey of learning and improvement. The more enormous the setback, the greater the potential lessons. This is a key element to this question of tenacity, because it recasts failure as something positive, as a valuable experience that is going to help you reach your ultimate goal. This perspective helps us see entrepreneurial tenacity as more than mere determination, and it's certainly not equivalent to bullheaded stubbornness. In an entrepreneurial context, tenacity is an attitude of constant forward progress, where "failure" is just an opportunity to do better next time. Adam Tendler's story illustrates this, too: despite being personally and artistically lost, he pressed on, driven by his unrelenting desire to touch people through music, to make a difference with his art, and to somehow support himself while he was at it. When a recital was a disaster, he tried to figure out what went wrong and how to fix it next time. When the concert venue was virtually empty or made up of people who had no real context for understanding his music, he pushed through the inevitable discouragement of such moments and tried to use the experience to learn more about himself, his playing, and his audience. In the rocky early days of his quest to play recitals in all fifty states, there were many opportunities to stamp "FAILURE" all over his endeavor. Instead of succumbing to that—or perhaps, in spite of it—he pressed on, learning what he could at every step of the way.

This brings us to the second benefit that often stems from the early struggles of an aspiring professional musician, and it's a benefit that might not reveal itself for a long time. The postscript to Adam Tendler's biography—and the bios of so many others like him—could talk about how one of his most compelling traits isn't just his mastery of the piano but his uncanny ability to connect with his listeners, to talk in compelling ways about the music he performs and to project an intimacy of presence, even inside a large concert hall. These are all traits that Adam developed during his years of playing small venues that were off the beaten track and not frequented by classical music aficionados. Rather than becoming bitter and frustrated by the seemingly dead-end trajectory of his career, Adam used his experience as an opportunity to learn how to connect with audiences of all types, sizes, and sensibilities. And in so doing, he developed the very qualities that would distinguish him and propel his career forward once he started to get some breaks. Without his long path of personal struggle, Tendler would have never had the career he enjoys now; he would have turned out to be just another talented pianist—with nothing compelling to say. His tenacity—that combination of determination, persistence, and a forward, growth-oriented outlook—did more than carry him to the point of having a "career." It shaped the very artistic voice that makes that career a successful one.

These first two chapters have shown that entrepreneurship plays out in incredibly diverse ways. They've also revealed that the overlap between entrepreneurial thinking and action is considerable—so much so that one could look at them as two sides of the same coin. The arts entrepreneurship scholar Linda Essig expresses this in terms of entrepreneurial outcomes existing along a continuum, with "habits of mind" at one end of the scale and "new venture creation" at the other. In other words, you can apply entrepreneurial thinking to what you're already doing—your performing career, for instance—or you can use the entrepreneurial process to create a new business venture from scratch. I call these two end points "applied entrepreneurship" (employing entrepreneurial habits of mind to standard career activities) and "direct entrepreneurship" (creating a new venture based on market observation and creative problem-solving). I'll discuss this more in later chapters, but the take-away for now is that entrepreneurship exists both as a mindset and as a type of action, the two acting in concert with each other, and it is not bound by any preconceived or prescribed outcomes. It's designed to take you where you want to go, to be an expression of your uniqueness as an artist and as a person.

One more thing about entrepreneurial action: you've heard the declaration "Go big or go home." It's meant to inspire, of course, to motivate us and encourage us to reach for our most ambitious dreams. And that's a good thing. But not everybody is cut out to "go big" right off the bat. Some are not ready to take such a big leap, particularly as their first foray into entrepreneurship.

And that's okay.

Time and again I've heard students ask established entrepreneurs the question on every beginner's mind: *how do I get started?* And the answer is always the same: once you've done your homework, once you've asked and answered the many questions posed in this chapter and coming chapters, just take what you've got . . . and *start*. It'll be messy, you'll make mistakes, and you'll learn some lessons the hard way. But eventually there's nothing for it but to take the plunge. You won't be realizing your ultimate vision right away, and the place where you start will likely look quite different from the place where you end up. That's okay, too: as I've said, sometimes the new and unforeseen path turns out to be a better one. So if "Go big or go home" is a bit too much for you to face all at once, try this: *Start small and keep going.*

EXERCISE: CONCEPTUAL COMBINATION GAME

Creative ideas reside in a mix of the known and the new: the more novel something is, the higher the ratio of "new" to "known." Conversely, the more conventional something is, the higher the ratio of "known" to "new." The most successful innovations tend to have a fairly even balance between these two poles, lest they be either so novel that nobody understands them or so conventional that they fail to add anything new to the issue being addressed.

Activity

As Ward pointed out in his research, combining two apparently disparate things to create something new results in "emergent properties"—qualities that didn't exist previously in either of the two components. To develop your understanding of how "cognitive combination" works in the development of innovative ideas, pick two nouns at random from a dictionary and spend some time envisioning a product or service that would encompass these things. Depending on the words chosen, some possibilities might present themselves fairly quickly; this is fine, but don't be satisfied with easy success. Try to push beyond the obvious and let your creativity run wild. See what kinds of truly novel things you can cook up! To ensure complete objectivity, have a friend pick out the words for you—and no matter how bizarre the combination might be, force yourself to contemplate the possibilities. This is particularly fun if you're in a small group (four people, max), so you can riff off each other and see where your collective creativity takes you. You might be surprised at some of the stuff you come up with!

EXERCISE: STORYTELLING

Percussionist, educator, and music entrepreneur Jennie Dorris has developed some excellent exercises to help you improve your ability to talk about yourself. Almost all people have a difficult time talking in an authentic way about their gifts, attributes, and abilities. Artists of all kinds may have an even harder time, given the extremely personal nature of their work. In order to help you get more comfortable with this, Dorris suggests bringing some trusted colleagues into the mix: they will help ensure that you neither puff yourself up too much or sell yourself short; they may also see things about you and your work that you don't see yourself. The goal is to become comfortable and fluent in telling the "story" of your music: what it means to you and why you'd like to share it with others.

Activity

Step 1: Get others to help you
Find three colleagues who have known you at different points in your musical life. Ask them to describe your music making at that time in specific terms: "How would you describe my performance of *Piece X*?" "In what ways was I different from your other students?" And so forth. Conclude your questions with "What else should I have asked you that I didn't?" As Dorris says, "This is when people get honest."

Step 2: Start talking

Jennie's words are the best ones here: "Using whatever recording device you would like, try to describe yourself as an artist or the artistic product you want to share with the world. You might find—as I always do—that this is a hard exercise to start with, and that you want to say just a few words and trail off in nervous laughter. Keep going. Record it all, and then write it down. Getting off the paper initially can help us stay natural and organic, rather than reverting to clichés or things we think we 'should' say."

Step 3: Find the right words

Now it's time to start aggregating the verbiage you've acquired through the first two steps, the goal being to clearly and concisely describe who you are, what you do, and why it's important to your audience/customer. Be sure to avoid broad but ultimately meaningless statements such as "Her music appeals to audiences of all ages" (Really? Does *any* music appeal to *everyone*?) or "He is a versatile performer" (Versatile in what way? Do you play jazz and classical? Baroque and modern instruments? Bluegrass and rock?). In other words, don't assert that you're "versatile" or "multifaceted." Tell me *how* you are those things in the most specific terms possible.

Step 4: Share it with others

Once you've done your wordsmithing and have something you think might work, share it with some friends who know you well and ask for honest feedback. Some of these folks should probably not be musicians, since avoiding technical jargon is also important to keep in mind. Ask them how the tone strikes them, if the descriptions are truly accurate and specific, and if you've avoided the use of clichés. Go back and refine your text as needed.

Step 5: Practice!

I would add to Jennie Dorris's excellent process the importance of repeating it again and again. As with anything else, it's in practicing our ability to talk about ourselves and our work that we get good at it. The four steps above can apply equally well to describing your work as an artist generally or to speaking about a particular piece you're about to present. It can apply to a venture you're looking to launch or a group with whom you perform. And you must not limit this to the written word: as often as not, musicians need to speak out loud to audiences, patrons, and colleagues. So in addition to working through the language as described in steps 1–4, you have to practice delivering that language verbally. Practice by yourself, in front of the mirror, in the shower, to your cat, or whatever else creates a context of *presentation*. Then try it in front of your friends: there's no substitute for having other people listening to your words, and you must get comfortable with this new form of performing (for this is most definitely a kind of performance). I suggest gathering a few musical colleagues and trading off as presenter and observer, giving feedback to each other, in a safe and encouraging space. Speaking aloud, whether you're talking about yourself, the piece you're about to play, or your new venture idea, is not easy—particularly at the beginning. But the more you do it, the better you get at it. Eventually, it becomes second nature to you—but that will only happen after you've spent time becoming familiar with strong, descriptive language and getting comfortable with vocalizing that language out loud. Just don't let the initial awkwardness get the better of you: keep practicing, and you'll develop an incredibly important skill that will serve you anywhere your career takes you.

CHAPTER 3

Products, Markets, Needs, and Value

Unpacking the Entrepreneur's Maxim

For some reason, the image that sticks in my head is the dashboard.

There I was, sitting in my car, parked in an office complex garage, staring at my dashboard while tears streamed down my face. What on earth was I doing here? How on earth had I ended up at this place? I can still see the gauges on the dashboard, staring blankly back at me and then blurring as the tears flowed harder.

It was August 2001, and I had decided it was time to walk away from a career in music. My creative voice had seemingly left me—for good, I thought—and I was completely lost. When my personal life also fell apart that summer, I decided I needed to completely reboot my life: I would move to Austin and I would start a new career, one that I knew I could succeed in.

I was going to become an investment advisor.

You see, I was the kid who could never figure out what he wanted to be when he grew up. I had been involved in music for as long as I could remember, but it was not anything I'd considered for a career until much later. In elementary school I fancied myself a writer, probably due to the huge crush I had on John Boy, the sensitive writer at the center of that 1970s TV classic *The Waltons*. Then in junior high I discovered business and investments—and became enthralled. I went from identifying with the gentle spirit of John Boy to becoming the very embodiment of Alex P. Keaton, the mogul-in-the-making character from *Family Ties*. (I suppose it's a sign of my generation that our role models growing up were often television characters!)

I was so obsessed with business and the stock market that I saved every penny I earned working for my father in his veterinary clinic. My first venture, at age thirteen, was to open a bank in order to take advantage of my older siblings constantly borrowing money from me. That got shut down pretty quick by the Feds (i.e., Mom), with this exchange:

"You don't charge members of your family interest!" she admonished.

"Well, why not?" I shot back.

So that was the end of the bank.

My hunger for financial success continued anyway, and I soon began to invest my saved dollars in the stocks I had researched. Every Sunday morning I sat down with the newspaper, charted the weekly activity of stocks I was following, and used the patterns I noted to time the purchase and sale of my portfolio. I was so into it that I preferred to stay in on Friday nights to watch *Wall Street Week* to going out with my friends. (Yeah, I was that much of a nerd.)

Soon I had a decent little nest egg accumulated. And I had discovered that I had a genuine knack for picking winners and playing the peaks and valleys of the market to my advantage. As I left home for college my plan was to get a degree in economics, go to Wall Street, and become a millionaire by the age of thirty.

Of course, that's not how things turned out. One measure of a good college education is the degree to which it transforms your view of the world, and by that yardstick my education was a very good one indeed. I entered as an economics major and graduated with a dual major in music and geology. But my fascination with all things economic and financial endured, and I never lost that sense that someday down the road my experience with the markets would come back to serve me.

Fast-forward to the summer of 2001. My life was in a free fall. In the space of a single week I lost my relationship, my home, and my day job. I hated the city I was in. My creative life had been stalled for several years, and the last composition I had attempted had been, in my view anyway, an enormous failure. So I decided that was it. I was done.

Then I figured that if I was going to deprive myself of a musical career, I might as well console myself with money. So I decided to return to my Alex P. Keaton days and get into investments again. After all, I knew I could do that well. Time to grow up, I told myself, and do something "useful."

Six weeks of interviews and mock presentations later, the regional manager of a major financial services firm shook my hand and said, "Congratulations, Jeff. We'd like you join our team and would be happy to house you here in our Austin office. Do you have any questions about our starting package?"

"No sir, I'm good," I said. "I'd like the night to think it over, if that's okay."

"Absolutely. I'll look forward to a phone call in the morning."

"Thank you very much."

We shook hands again, and I went out into the lobby to wait for the elevator. There were two other young men standing there, talking. They were obviously new hires themselves, still in the training program and desperately trying to find clients to supplement the meager income trainees received. I suddenly realized that this job wasn't about researching investments and offering carefully considered investment strategies to my clients; it was, at its heart, a job in *sales*. As we traveled down the elevator I continued to eavesdrop, and everything about the conversation made my skin crawl: their "frat-bro" banter, the lack of regard for their customers as individuals, the utter lack of joy for any aspect of what they were doing. Advancement was predicated on how many accounts they opened, not the difference they made in their clients' lives. This job was just a way to pay for their weekends, their customers nothing more than a meal ticket. This was the culture I was about to enter.

When I exited the elevator I walked to the parking garage in a daze. I got in my car and just sat there. I couldn't do anything except stare at that dashboard. Then the tears began.

Finally, I said aloud, "I can't do this. I can't . . . I *won't*. I don't know what comes next, but by God, I'm never going to do anything that doesn't have music in there somewhere. Not. Ever. *Somehow*, I will find a way."

I might as well have been Scarlett O'Hara on her hands and knees in her muddy garden, raising her fist to the heavens and vowing, "As God is my witness, I'll never be hungry again!" I chuckle about that comparison now, but it captures the intensity of that moment. It was the lowest I'd ever been.

But it was also a turning point, the point at which I came to terms with who I was and what I needed to figure out about my life. It's important that we recognize that many creative folks—perhaps even most—have similar moments, moments when they have to reckon with just how badly they want a career in the arts. Once again we can note that the common narrative around successful artists is that their careers are the inevitable result of a desire that has burned since childhood and has only required time and hard work to turn out well.

Yet there I was, seven years out of grad school, with some impressive early successes, and I was back to professional square one. I had not lacked for hard work, discipline, and patience; yet in the end those things had not yielded anything sustainable. The narrative I'd been taught was completely wrong. And if that was the case, then what was the answer? What was I missing?

THE ENTREPRENEUR'S MAXIM

The most common misconception about entrepreneurship is that it is simply the equivalent of the proverbial "pounding the pavement," "pressing the flesh," or "marketing yourself." We've all heard these phrases; they describe a person with hustle and drive, someone who has his or her professional toolkit in order and is "out on the street," aggressively pursuing opportunities. This is what "being entrepreneurial" is usually assumed to mean. I had assumed this as well, and only when hustle and drive and "pounding the pavement" failed to keep my career moving did I begin to wonder what else might be needed.

It's important to again remind ourselves that the skills in the artist's toolbox—"pavement-pounding" skills like marketing, handling your finances, booking gigs, managing your social media, and so on—are *prescriptive* in nature. That is, they are designed to generate a particular outcome. For example, a press release is designed to inform presenters and the media about something that has happened or is about to happen. Done well, A + B = C. These are critically important skills, but they do not constitute entrepreneurial thinking or action. They can be, however, extremely important tools for the *implementation* of entrepreneurial initiative.

Conversely, entrepreneurship is *strategic*, not prescriptive. Entrepreneurship helps frame and guide the *deployment* of those "pavement-pounding" tools, turning blunt tools into far more precise instruments. It took hitting my personal low point to begin to discover this, however. (Nor was my insight immediate: it was two weeks after that scene in the parking garage that I was at the point where this book begins, serving popcorn at the University of Texas basketball games and wondering just how much lower I could go.)

Having explored the nature of entrepreneurial thinking and action, then, it's now time to look at the principles that underpin them. However we choose to define it, and whatever the particular outcomes, the ultimate purpose of entrepreneurship is the same: *entrepreneurship unlocks value for a product or service by fulfilling a need in the marketplace*. While this concept of how value is generated is a given in the business world, it requires some difficult paradigm shifts for those of us in the musical realm. Whether they are the original creators of content (composers and arrangers) or those responsible for delivering that content (performers and presenting entities), musicians are used to assuming that the value of their artistic product is self-evident to others. In that worldview, the only thing that is required to deliver your musical product is to convince an audience to come and hear it. Moreover, classical musicians tend to consider their product in a vacuum: the music exists in an immutable, "pure" realm, fundamentally separate from those experiencing it. For many, the size of the audience is almost irrelevant; what matters most is the art itself.

Entrepreneurship turns this concept on its head, however, by directing the primary focus toward the needs of the marketplace (the audience). Value is not assumed, nor is it determined by the desires and sensibilities of those delivering the product (the musician and/or presenter).

This is the point where many artists start to get uncomfortable. If artists are beholden to market forces, then doesn't that mean putting our artistic integrity aside? Doesn't it mean allowing artistic decisions to be determined by (gulp) the *market*? (And, by extension, doesn't "the market" mean the lowest common denominator?) In the realm of classical music (so the argument goes), the music's inherent complexity and duration render the market for it quite small. It follows, therefore, that the only way to grow the audience for classical music is to present only the least challenging and most "audience-friendly" works. This is the "dumbing down" argument, and it lies at the heart of the concern that entrepreneurship requires us to "sell out."

This common concern is rooted in confusion about the nature of artistic value versus entrepreneurial value. Artistic value is *intrinsic*. This value is inherent in the work itself, and that value exists as an intangible value to society, to individuals, to the nourishing of our collective sensibilities, and so forth. Art's intrinsic value is not influenced by or contingent on popularity, the cost of a ticket to experience it, or the price a work of art fetches at auction. A work's intrinsic value is determined only by itself.

Value in the marketplace is *extrinsic*: determined by *external* factors. This kind of value is expressed by popularity, monetary value, demand in the marketplace, and so forth.

Moreover, intrinsic value is *intangible* and *subjective*—beauty is in the eye of the beholder, after all. Extrinsic value is *tangible* and *objective*: it can be quantified and measured, and it creates a tangible return (whether that be money, "likes" on Facebook, bartered goods, or some other form of exchange).

These two types of value are not mutually exclusive. Just as the intrinsic value of a work of art is not contingent on any external value, the extrinsic value of a work does not express anything other than the market's response to it. These two types of value coexist in a fluid relationship, while also remaining separate from each other.

Now we can see how the concern that entrepreneurship requires us to "dumb down" our music or "sell out" our artistic integrity is likely based on a conflation of intrinsic and extrinsic value. Furthermore, it helps us see that the goal of entrepreneurship is to deliver the intrinsic value of art to a market that will express extrinsic value for a particular artistic product.

How, then, is artistic value transformed into market value? The answer lies in what I call the *entrepreneur's maxim*, the title and subject of the next section.

A MARKET WILL VALUE THE PRODUCT THAT MEETS ITS NEED(S)

Let's spend some time picking apart the entrepreneur's maxim to better understand its implications, starting with the notion of "products."

Art Music as Product

When I lecture on the entrepreneur's maxim, I begin the discussion of artistic products with a slide of a toilet factory. I do this because it forces us to address what exactly it means for something to be a "product." Our usual understanding of the term centers around a utilitarian object, something that is mass-produced, disposable, easily replaced, and without value beyond its function—for instance, a toilet.

But the definition of "product" is far broader. Simply put, a product is anything for which there is a market (that is, a body of consumers who value something sufficiently to pay for it). Many products are indeed mass-produced, utilitarian, and disposable. And when that's our view of what a product is, it's understandable that referring to art as a "product" can make folks uneasy. But utilitarian products are just one kind of product; many others are precious, unique, and irreplaceable. Some products are inexpensive to produce and carry a small price tag, while others are extremely expensive to produce and cost much more. Still others are one-of-a-kind items, sometimes priceless. The point is we are not demeaning our art by referring to it as a product. All we're saying is that it is something of sufficient value that somebody will (we hope) want to pay for it; this in turn gives us a rubric for understanding the relationship between the work of art and the marketplace. This is the first hurdle that a would-be musician-entrepreneur must clear: music is a product of great value, but it is a product just the same.

The range of musical products is vast, and encompasses everything from solo to orchestra performances (not to mention the products represented in each individual member of the group), from music written for professionals to beginning school ensembles, from music education for preschoolers to advanced graduate students, from conducting a wind ensemble to a church choir, and from performances on the accordion to the zither. Then there are what I call "ancillary" musical products—those that are adjacent to, or in support of, the primary products being offered. In music these include things like instrument manufacture and repair, countless accessories (music stands, cases, etc.), the recording arts, artist management, arts administration, and many more. The music industry is so enormous and multifaceted that there is almost no end to the musical products one can create, perform, manufacture, manage, or sell.

While some musical products are no different from other kinds of products (a piece of music software is, in entrepreneurial and economic terms, no different from any other kind of software), in the case of musical *performance*, the question of product is a little more complicated. Exactly what is the product our customers are consuming? Is it the music itself, or is it the performance of that music? Does the answer to that question depend on the medium of the experience (live versus recorded performance), the performers in question ("I prefer Christopher Hogwood's Beethoven to Herbert von Karajan's"), or other nonmusical factors such as the venue and the communal-social aspects of a concert? The truth is that the musical performance product encompasses all these things, and which factor reigns supreme in the minds of consumers varies from situation to situation and individual to individual. Nevertheless, no matter how complex and multifaceted the range of musical products is, every musical product has the same fundamental quality: it is something offered to the marketplace and for which the market (in some form or fashion) pays.

These examples also underscore another important aspect of "products": they can be concrete (a musical score), virtual (the music embodied by that score), or experiential (listening to that music being performed). Concrete products tend to be functional in nature (an oboe reed exists to aid in producing sound), whereas the purposes of virtual and experiential products can be a little more difficult to define. More on this point shortly, but for now simply keep in mind that the blanket term "product" encompasses all manner of concrete, virtual, and experiential products and services. *A product is anything for which there is a market.*

With so many musical products, and with so many layers to them, how on earth can you decide which musical products are the "right" ones for you to pursue? The answer to this question will come, but for now let's focus on the fundamental principles of this first part of the entrepreneur's maxim in terms of classical music:

1. Classical music is a product.
2. The classical music industry has an enormous and diverse range of products.
3. Musical products can be concrete, virtual, or experiential.

Sound complicated? Don't despair: we've only begun to unpack the entrepreneurial bundle.

The Audience for Classical Music—Its Market

Students planning their first concert outside school often visit me to discuss how to promote their event. My first question is always "Who is this concert for?" Usually after some thought they will kind of shrug and hesitantly answer, "Everyone?" This fundamental question usually stumps students because most likely they've never been asked to answer it. Traditional musical education trains students to play at the highest level of proficiency; getting an audience to show up to hear them is frequently viewed as someone else's concern. Further obscuring the answer to "Who is this for?" is the long-held bias among classical musicians and institutions that classical music, as the "highest" form of musical expression in Western culture, is meant for "everyone."

Herein lies the second challenge entrepreneurship presents to the arts: there isn't a product out there that serves *everybody*, and the more specialized and unique the product is, the more that is true. While the democratic notion behind the statement "our music is for everyone" has a noble appeal, even the most famous pop star on the planet only appeals to a certain segment of the population; we can be sure that the audience for something as rarefied as classical music will be smaller still. That's not to say that the market is too small to be worth the bother or that it is too small to present opportunities for budding professionals. It just means that we have to have a very clear understanding of who embodies the market for our particular product. Hard as it might be to accept, concert music is not for "everybody."

While that might sound elitist, it's not. Elitism in classical music—and it's certainly there—assigns a higher value to classical music based on the assumption that it is inherently superior to other genres and styles. The entrepreneur, however, does not make such judgments; she or he is only interested in understanding who desires a given product and why. Recognizing that your product isn't for "everybody" is simply accepting a reality that applies to *every* product and its corresponding market, and it's the first step in determining who it *is* for.

Before answering the question of who makes up the market for classical music, though, a little bit more about markets themselves. First of all, markets are made up of people—consumers—who share a similar sensibility and/ or need. This is why I will use the terms "market" and "audience" interchangeably: at their heart they are the same thing. Markets (and audiences) come in many sizes and types, and can be very broad and diverse in their product desires or quite narrow and specific. They may appear to be quite diverse on the outside or quite homogenous, but outward appearances like demographics or class are not what define a market/audience: what brings them together is that they have a shared desire/need for the product in question.

Generally speaking, the larger the market is for something, the more diverse it is (both in terms of the range of products offered within it and the demographics of those buying them). This is what's called a "broad" market. One very broad market we're all familiar with is the market for automobiles. Millions of customers purchase new cars every year, with many million more cars already in circulation. In fact, the market is so broad that it has a dizzying array of submarkets, each with its own brands and customer profile and defined by a specific constellation of needs and sensibilities. (The market for luxury sedans is quite a bit different from the market for hybrid minicars, for example.) By and large, the broader the overall market for something is, the more submarkets there will be. This phenomenon is called "market segmentation." The term refers to the fact that broad markets are not generally singular and monolithic in their character; they tend to be made up of multiple, more specified segments.

Moreover, just as there are ancillary products, there are ancillary markets. In the case of automobiles, their manufacture taps into markets for parts, raw materials, and so forth, and owners require service and repair, sound systems, all manner of accessories, and, of course, fuel. Contemplating the enormous reach and complexity of the automobile market helps us see why it is such an important part of the global economy.

To understand the relationship between a given market as a whole, its various segments, and its ancillary markets, think of it as a pyramid: the overall market, at its broadest, is at the top (the automobile market overall) with increasingly diverse market segments, encompassing more and smaller ancillary markets, as you move down the pyramid (fig. 3.1).

This pyramid illustrates two very important things to keep in mind when it comes to identifying markets. The first is that with very large, broad markets it's pretty much pointless to look at the top of the pyramid and try to draw any consistent conclusions about it: it just contains too much diversity of products, market segments, demographics, and trends. To illustrate this, consider the fact that when high gas prices cause sales of SUVs to plummet, sales of hybrids go through the roof. They're all part of the broad market for automobiles, but a single market force has the opposite effect on two different segments of it. Therefore, the further down the pyramid you go, the more likely you are to find insights into what is happening and where opportunities might reside. Why? Because the more specific the market segment, the more the needs and sensibilities of consumers begin to come into focus: the market for pickup trucks is vast and varied; the market for high-tonnage towing accessories is much narrower and easy to define because only certain individuals with very specific needs want them.

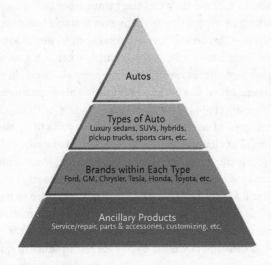

Figure 3.1 Market segmentation pyramid

A related point illustrated by the pyramid of markets is that market segments themselves become more and more diverse as we move down the pyramid. At the bottom of the automobile pyramid, for example, we have both a diversity of segment types (the vast range of services and accessories associated with all types of automobile) *and* diversity in a particular segment (those who get their car serviced at the general mechanic on the corner versus those who only service their Audis at the shop specializing in German cars).

With broad markets occupying one end of the market spectrum, "niche" markets occupy the other. Niche markets are limited by either geography or the narrow specificity of the need (or, sometimes, both). Niche markets are not segmented, though they may still have a sizeable number of consumers. The example I like to cite is the very real niche market for humane prairie dog eradication in Boulder, Colorado. Prairie dogs live all along the Rocky Mountain foothills and in the high plains to the east, and they are a sufficient nuisance that there is considerable demand to get rid of them. However, only in the ultraliberal "bubble" of Boulder is there a population of folks sufficiently concerned about the critters' welfare that there is a market for their humane eradication. So this niche market is limited by both geography (prairie dogs only live in some areas) *and* sensibility (most ranchers in the high plains don't much care how they get rid of their prairie dogs as long as it's successful). Other sorts of niche markets—highly specialized components for a specific machine, or something like high-quality cane for double reeds—might have customers scattered throughout the world but are still limited by the specific nature of the need and the specialized nature of the product that addresses it.

When you put the automobile market next to the market for humane prairie dog eradication, you can get a sense of the enormous diversity and complexity of markets and how they run the gamut from being major movers of the world economy to supporting perhaps only a single business in a particular locality. Moreover, broad and niche markets often coexist at opposite ends of a continuum. In other words, if the broad market is big enough it might become so segmented that some of those segments become, in essence, their own niche markets. Music is a perfect example of this phenomenon: the totality of the music market—surely one of the broadest of them all—has a virtually infinite degree of segmentation, all the way down to the unique fan base of a local band or chamber group or the patrons of a particular composer. This is an incredibly important concept for artists and institutions looking to support their unique creative work: even in the enormously broad market of music, there is still a place for your particular musical voice to be heard.

While broad markets are far more complex and multifaceted than niche markets, *all* markets—regardless of size or type—exist for the same reason: there are enough consumers willing to pay for the product in question that a sustainable business is possible. It's nice to know that in all these market sizes and types there is a core principle operating, isn't it?

Given this huge range of market sizes and types, where are the best opportunities likely to reside? At first glance you might look to the broad markets as having the most potential for success. After all, broad markets are made up of large numbers of consumers who, taken together, rack up large sales. If you can tap into such a market, you've tapped into a deep pool of wealth indeed! The problem is broad markets feed large *industries*, and the upper levels of a broad market pyramid are likely to already be serviced by big companies with deep pockets, established brands, and economies of scale that generate their products with great efficiency. Launching a venture in the face of that may not be realistic for the startup entrepreneur with few resources at hand. For instance, the development of Tesla, the high-end electric car company, required hundreds of millions of dollars, and it had to support years of operating losses before it became a viable business. Entering a large market with an established industry of competitors is an enormously risky and resource-intensive proposition. It is not for the faint of heart (or the shallow of pockets).

In contrast, the highly specialized segments at the lowest level of the market pyramid—and their close cousins, the niche markets—can present unique and often lucrative opportunities. Often these markets can be entered with relatively low risk and few resources; due to their specialization and smaller size, they may not attract much competition, either. Often, the "sleeper" opportunity—the one nobody has noticed—resides in a niche market, right under our noses in our communities or particular fields of expertise. And while ventures that start serving narrow or niche markets can sometimes really catch on and "make it big," many others stay more or less the same size and serve a stable, often local, market. These are the "lifestyle" ventures; that is, they are successful enough to support the entrepreneur while neither exploding to international stardom nor barely subsisting. So, once again, we see that entrepreneurial outcomes vary widely, and the entrepreneur has a high degree of choice in determining which path a venture goes down. While business students entering the entrepreneurial fray often seek "the next big thing" and an IPO to make them rich, for many artist entrepreneurs a lifestyle venture that provides a good living practicing their art is more than sufficient!

So how should we characterize the market for music? Just as the automobile pyramid contains millions of consumers buying a huge range of products, the music market encompasses an even larger range of genres, subgenres, and styles, each with its own body of consumers (fig. 3.2). Then there are countless performers and groups in each genre (each with its own fan base). Finally, just as in the market for automobiles, the classical music market encompasses a huge diversity of ancillary markets for things like supplies and equipment, sheet music, software, educational materials, music teachers, instrument manufacture and repair, and on and on. Clearly, the music market writ large is one very big pyramid of markets!

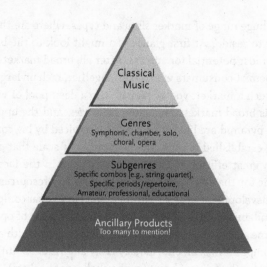

Figure 3.2 Musical markets pyramid

Since this book focuses primarily on classical music, let's consider the various components of that market. Let's start with the audiences for symphony orchestras, chamber orchestras, chamber ensembles of all sizes, choral groups, opera, and soloists. A huge number of market segments resides in each of these. For example, even the fairly specific segment of orchestral music has distinct market segments: for professional orchestras, volunteer community orchestras, and orchestras at educational institutions. While there is likely some overlap in these markets, there are distinct segments in them just the same: the aficionado of the professional orchestra may not be interested in the less polished performances of the community volunteers; many of those who support their local college or high school orchestra may do so out of institutional spirit or because their friends and children are in the ensemble and care far less about the polish of the performance (and even less about the repertoire being performed).

Then there are all the different types of chamber ensemble (string quartets, trios, etc.), soloist (a trumpeter versus an organist), and specialty of performer/group (a particular period or repertoire, such as early music, contemporary music, etc.).

Just this cursory look at a few of the many market segments in classical music performance reveals the fallacy in thinking that classical music audiences are largely homogeneous. While they may represent a fairly homogeneous demographic vis-à-vis the society as a whole, in the many segments of the market there is a wide range of tastes and desires: folks who never miss their local early music consort might not be caught dead at a program of contemporary chamber music. The highbrow aficionado of opera is not any more likely to visit the local high school production of *Hair* than parents with three young kids are going to risk a disturbance in the hallowed airs of Symphony Hall. We would be well advised not to paint the classical music audience—or any market for that matter—with too broad a brush.

But notice what unites each market: a shared taste and sensibility. A shared *need*. This means that we must look as closely as possible at our customers (and would-be customers) and determine not just who they are but what they want. If they are existing customers, why do they support you? (The answer might not be what you think.) If you're trying to attract new customers to your product, what might motivate them to try you out? (Again: don't assume you know the answer without asking them!) Whether it's current or prospective customers, understanding the needs and sensibilities of your market is the first step in devising ways to engage them.

And while the musical market is a textbook example of a broad market with a high degree of market segmentation, there is an important difference between the market for functional objects (like automobiles) and the market for music. In the case of something like the automobile market, the big industries at the top of the pyramid are the only ones producing the core product (the vehicle itself), as well as many of the upper-level segments (the different kinds of vehicle); despite the broadness of the automobile market, only a relatively few corporations produce all those vehicles. As a result, all of the ancillary and niche markets further down the pyramid are dependent on, and therefore to a high degree controlled by, the corporate entities at the top of the pyramid.

The same can't be said for the musical market, as enormously broad as it is. Yes, there are big entertainment companies at the top of the music market pyramid, but when one or more of them go belly-up, that may have little or no impact on your neighborhood piano teacher or symphony player. The nature of market segmentation in music is therefore different from that of, say, automobiles, and the difference lies in the nature of the products being consumed. While design and status are certainly factors in purchasing something like a car, the *primary* purpose of that vehicle is still utilitarian (transportation). And the many segments of the market are still, in large part, defined by utilitarian differences: pickup trucks, SUVs, sedans, and sports cars embody different types of transportation need.

In the case of music, however, the primary purpose of the product is *artistic* and *aesthetic*. (I'm including entertainment in the artistic/aesthetic rubric.) And since each piece of music is a unique entity, the music market becomes almost infinitely segmented in a way that even the largest markets for utilitarian objects do not. We can get a better handle on what this means by looking at a specific type of market that economists call a "long-tail" market.

The "long-tail" concept started as a way to describe a particular kind of business, one where a small number of high-volume products makes up the bulk of sales while a large number of small-volume products makes up the rest. Why would someone run such a business? Why wouldn't they just sell the top-selling products and cut the rest loose? Well, a big part of the value of a long-tail business is the very fact that it makes available those many products that do not sell as well. Your local independent bookstore provides a great example. While the store relies on bestsellers to produce most of the income it needs to survive, nobody would shop there if that was all that was available: the lure of an independent bookseller lies in the more obscure or specialized books you can't find at the big box retailer at the mall. For the independent bookstore, the presence of all those books that do not sell as well is a key component of the value consumers see in the business overall, even if no single one of those books makes the store much (if any) money.

If we apply the long-tail concept to markets (rather than businesses), we discover some interesting implications—especially for markets of aesthetic products like music. In a long-tail market, the top sellers dominate and are pervasive in their reach, but the many smaller players of the long tail are able to survive because the overall market is so large that it encompasses a wide variety of consumer traits and desires. In a long-tail market, even the most exotic tastes, the smallest market segments, probably have enough devotees to support a niche product. In other words, the long tail helps us better understand one way highly segmented markets can still thrive.

A simple example of a long-tail market is that for carbonated beverages. Coke, Pepsi, Mountain Dew, Sprite, and Dr. Pepper (along with their diet counterparts) encompass nine of the ten top-selling sodas in the United States, with Coke alone capturing upward of 40 percent. Behind these brands is a wide array of still-popular brands that do not sell as well. And as we move down the sales chart, we encounter progressively more specialized products, most of which most folks probably haven't even heard of: regional brands, artisanal sodas, bizarre flavors, and so forth. These smaller market segments are able to support viable businesses because the overall market for soda is so large that even a tiny market share contains a sufficient number of customers. They're also viable because most consumers of carbonated beverages often drink more than one variety: all but the most devoted Coke drinkers probably consume other flavors from time to time.

All of these products are defined by "differentiation"—the thing that makes a given product different from its competition. Highly segmented markets lead to a high degree of differentiation in the products that serve them. (The highly segmented carbonated beverage market has a wide range of different products serving those segments.)

When it comes to long-tail markets that are defined by aesthetic taste, differentiation is a key feature. This is because aesthetic taste is highly subjective and individualized; a product that appeals to some individuals won't appeal to others. But since long-tail markets are also large ones, there may still be enough consumers to support even the most unusual and highly differentiated of products. Moreover, as in the soda example, highly differentiated markets aren't a zero-sum game: the consumer of Coke may also enjoy some Dr. Brown's Black Cherry soda from time to time.

Diversity in aesthetic markets is more than merely *possible*, however; the long-tail nature of aesthetic markets exists precisely because *diversity is what the market demands*. If you like to read, for example, you're not going to be happy reading one book over and over again for the rest of your life. You want a steady supply of books, each one a unique creation. When it comes to clothes, one type and color of garment won't do (for most folks, anyway). So while the most popular clothing brands or the bestselling authors make up the bulk of sales in their respective markets, those markets are big and diverse enough in their tastes that there are still a lot of consumers who want something different and more unique—sometimes in addition to the mainstream product, sometimes instead of it. The more a market is driven primarily by aesthetic considerations, the more this is true and the more product differentiation is possible.

How does the long tail work in music? In the music performance market overall, a few genres like pop, country, indie rock, and hip-hop are by far the largest segments. Further down the sales chart is an incredibly large and diverse number of progressively more specialized segments like folk, jazz, world music, classical, and so on: a textbook example of a long tail. But in the infinitely varied markets for aesthetic objects (like music), long tails can exist *within* long tails, too: country music was the top-selling genre of music in the United States in 2013, but that segment contains a small number of big stars who can fill a stadium and a long tail of progressively less-known performers—all the way down to the local band that fills the neighborhood bar once a week. And the bigger a fan you are of country music, the more the diversity of the long tail is itself something of value to you: as much as you love your favorite two or three artists, you crave the variety of the others mixed in as well: you visit both the stadium *and* the local bar.

Classical music is another great example of layered long tails: while it may reside fairly far down the tail of the overall music market, the market for classical music performance has a long tail of its own, with the top soloists, largest ensembles (in terms of audience), and most popular composers making up the bulk of the market activity. Behind them is an extremely large group of progressively less-known performers and composers who, taken together, are a large chunk of the market but for whom the individual market segments of the tail are relatively small. There are Bach, Beethoven, and Brahms . . . and then there are Bax, Busoni, and Biber.

The extremely long and layered tail of classical music is good news for its practitioners, because it means that even if they lack the fame of a major solo-ist, the good fortune to land their dream orchestral job, or a compositional style that appeals to large numbers of listeners, there likely is still a place for them in the musical marketplace. This is because the diversity of the musical marketplace—its long tail—is a big part of what makes the marketplace as a whole a vibrant and prosperous place. Consumers of classical music enjoy a wide range of repertoire and performers, with each artistic offering constitut-ing a distinct product.

To illustrate this, let's take an extreme example: imagine what would hap-pen if the entirety of orchestral programming consisted of only three pieces, and every orchestra rendered an identical performance of those pieces. The market would, of course, collapse—and pretty quickly, too: once you've gone and heard orchestra A perform those three pieces, why would you ever go back to that orchestra or any other orchestra? In other words (and contrary to the self-defeating programming philosophy of many orchestras), it is the diversity of programming and performance *itself* that draws the mar-ket for classical music together. With this in mind, aspiring musicians need not conclude that the improbability of having a major solo career means their career prospects are bleak. On the contrary, the long tails of the classi-cal music market provide an almost infinite range of career possibilities for the musician-entrepreneur. The key is finding a market that will value your unique musical product.

One more thing about markets before moving on. As demonstrated throughout the discussion so far, you can't talk about a market without talk-ing about products: the two are inextricably linked to each other. Likewise, you can't talk about products and markets without also talking about indus-tries. These three things are so closely related that the terms "product," "mar-ket," and "industry" are often used interchangeably. But there is an important distinction: Industries are made up of entities; markets are made up of people. Industries *produce* things—products or services. Markets (that is, the indi-viduals who constitute them) *consume* things.

A few simple examples of the product-industry-market intersection will help to better understand the distinction between the three. Take clarinet reeds: there is the product itself (the reed), the industry (woodwind instru-ments and accessories), and the market (clarinet players). Another example would be something like choral sheet music: the product is the actual piece ("All Hail the Great Spaghetti Monster," by G. P. Q. Schmidt), the industry is the choral music publishing industry, and the market consists of those choral groups for whom the piece in question is appropriate. (I'm not sure I want to consider what sort of choir would program "All Hail the Great Spaghetti Monster," but you never know. Maybe G. P. Q. Schmidt is an undiscovered master!)

Let's recap this section on markets with a few bottom-line concepts:

1. Industries create products; markets are made up of people who consume products.
2. A market exists when there is a sufficient number of consumers with similar needs, tastes, and characteristics to support an ongoing business.
3. Markets can be very broad or very narrow. Broad markets feed large industries, and generally have a large number of segments (submarkets) and ancillary (related) markets; "niche" markets are specific and limited.
4. Long-tail markets are particularly common where personal, individualized tastes drive consumer decisions. This is good news for classical musicians because it increases the opportunity for finding (or creating) a market for your own unique artistic product.

How are markets defined? Said another way, how does a would-be entrepreneur identify the market for her product and identify whether that market is a segment of a large market or a niche market? To answer these questions, we must talk about the critical, central component in the entrepreneur's maxim: *need*.

What Is the Need?

Since the classical music industry encompasses products that include the music itself, the experience of that music, the teaching of it, and all the ancillary and support components of its performance, presentation, and distribution, you must consider a wide range of potential market needs in order to unlock the value you seek for your particular product. Furthermore, since we are talking about an aesthetic product, the question of "need" becomes a little harder to pin down. Fortunately, in an entrepreneurial context "need" is the same as "want": do I *need* that particular cut of suit? No, but it appeals to my sensibilities; I like it. And so I will pay for it (so long as I tell myself I can afford it), just as I will pay for the food and shelter I need to stay alive. As far as markets, industries, and products are concerned, there's no distinction between needs, desires, and sensibilities: they are all the same for the entrepreneur.

Identifying the needs and sensibilities of a market involves a dynamic combination of research, observation, experience, and, sometimes, pure inspiration. But it always boils down to answering the same basic question: *what do the individuals in the market get from what I have to offer?*

In the musical marketplace, the needs fulfilled by musical products are as vast and far-reaching as the products themselves and can range from the very broad to the very specific. How can we sort them out? Perhaps it's useful to start with the most basic, underlying human needs that are filled by music: without these, the driving force behind all musical endeavors disappears. After all, music has been around for millennia and has existed in every culture, past and present. Surely music meets deep needs that are tied into the very fabric of humanity. Some examples of these are our need for cathartic release, empathy, journeying into the mystical and subconscious realms of the soul, our need to transcend our experience of time, our need for shared rituals (such as celebration, mourning, worship, etc.), our need for diversion from the mundane, and so forth. These needs are at the core of what continues to motivate people to experience art in all its forms, and perhaps music most of all: music facilitates our experience of things we cannot access by ourselves; we require some external vehicle to lead the way. These needs are more or less universal and constant, and all those who choose to engage with the musical realm (writ large) will likely find something there to stir them. This is why music is perhaps the most culturally transcendent of all the arts. While differences in culture, history, genres, and style may not make it a "universal language," music is surely a universal *vehicle* for human expression. (And as neuroscience continues to discover more and more about how music operates within the human brain, we are beginning to see that we humans appear to be hardwired to experience and express music.) This universality is also why music is among the most widely consumed products on the planet, perhaps ranking behind only food, clothing, and shelter. In terms of "needs" it doesn't get more basic or primal than these!

In addition, once we start to go deeper into individual genres, styles, composers, and singular works, we slowly begin to incorporate a greater and greater degree of personal taste in the question of "need": our universal need for musical experience is met for each of us through a highly individualized set of preferences. That is, the need for music might be universal, but each individual understands that need in a unique way. This is analogous to the pyramid of markets: at the top is the universal need for music, at the bottom are the infinitely varied sensibilities of the individual.

Acknowledging the deep-seated, universal, and emotional/aesthetic needs met by music only begins to scratch the surface of the entrepreneurial question of "need," however: one must still figure out how the universal need for music translates into need for *your particular* musical product. For starters, needs exist on many levels beyond the emotional, spiritual, and existential realms; they can also be very concrete and specific: a young child needs a piano teacher, adults would like to find sophisticated entertainment, a bride requires music for her wedding. Moreover, needs can come from within the ranks of musicians themselves: a bassoonist needs good cane to make reeds, a music school needs teachers, a composer needs a reliable copy shop to print scores, and so on. And even when we're talking about our own creative products—our compositions and performances—the infinitely long tail of the music market means that there is likely a niche somewhere for our unique contribution.

When individual needs coalesce into groups of people with the same or similar needs, a market is born. Remember: markets are created for a product through a *shared need* of individuals. What entrepreneurs do is identify those needs, develop products to fulfill them, and deliver those products to those individuals who need or desire that product (the market).

Some product-need relationships are very clear-cut and singular: if you need to assemble something with nails, a hammer is the product for the job. And since lots of people use nails, at least once in a while, there is a market for hammers. (In my case the market for hammers also drives the market for pain relievers, but that's a topic for another day.)

The product-need relationship is usually much more complex than the hammer example, though. In fact, most products fulfill multiple needs simultaneously. To go back to the example of the car: the primary need for an automobile is transportation, but a host of other needs and desires are tied in to that product as well: comfort and design preferences, how the car handles in wintry conditions, and perhaps more abstract things like the status of driving a particular brand or the personal statement made by driving a sports car or an oversized pickup. The existence of multiple needs regarding a single product is extremely important, because it facilitates one of the most important aspects of entrepreneurial action (one already introduced): *product differentiation*.

Entrepreneurs can develop products in one of two directions. They can create something completely new (the first electric toaster) or they can create an improved or specialized version of something that already exists (a toaster with elongated slots for nonstandard slices of bread or an assembly-line toaster for restaurants that accommodates dozens of slices at a time). The larger the market, the greater the degree of product differentiation we tend to see. The reason for this differentiation is that the more individuals a product reaches, the more diverse a range of needs, tastes, and preferences likely exists: some folks would like a wider toaster slot to toast bagels while others require a flat toasting surface to heat Danishes. Still others may care more about the color or style of their toaster (bright pink to match everything else in the kitchen or a retro look to match that refurbished 1934 stove). This diversity of needs and desires, in turn, drives more products in the market, each one catering to a particular need. The larger the market, the more likely it is that a sufficiently large number of consumers will exist to support products designed to meet very specific needs. To illustrate this, just take a trip to the housewares department of your local department store: you'll soon see just how large—and differentiated—the market for toasting devices is! Take the exercise one step further and see if you can identify the specific needs each model and type of toaster meets. You'll soon begin to understand more clearly the intimate relationship between market needs/tastes/preferences and product development.

In this dynamic of multiple needs driving product differentiation, where does music fit in? What needs—beyond the deep, human needs noted above—are met through a musical experience? There are many! Recorded music may serve to motivate people while working out at the gym, provide a medium for careful study through repeated listening, or simply help people relax after a stressful day. A live musical performance may meet a need for entertainment, for shared/communal experience, as a venue for date night, or perhaps simply for the opportunity to "see and be seen" at a prestigious cultural venue. In another example, let's say that your product is a wedding band. The needs you meet begin with music for the ceremony but then quickly grow to include the need for fun, entertaining, and interactive leadership of the festivities. The wedding band that doesn't meet these additional, extramusical needs will not likely get many gigs no matter how well they play.

The enormous range of needs, aesthetics, and tastes in the musical marketplace means that there are tremendous opportunities for differentiation. The wedding band offers a great example of this: some couples want 1980s covers, some want klezmer, others want Greek folk music, and still others want a mix! And that's just the first level: there is another layer of infinite diversity within each of these genres, as dictated by the unique artistic approach of the group performing them, the manner and humor of the emcee or DJ, and perhaps things like ploys to get people dancing or a commemorative CD of the playlist. Because the market for wedding music is so large and the needs/sensibilities are so diverse, there is a correspondingly large capacity for differentiation.

In the case of concert music, how do we find the intersection between the infinite range of music that can be programmed (or composed) and the equally diverse range of tastes among the audience? Is the "need" for Beethoven's Symphony No. 2 different from the need for his Symphony No. 4? If one is programmed instead of the other, will it likely affect attendance? Performing arts organizations have been grappling with these questions for decades, and if you look at a broad swath of programming among orchestras, opera houses, ballets, chamber groups, and so forth, you might see what appears to be a lot of conflicting data. On the one hand, Orchestra A sees attendance spike when the standards are played, while Orchestra B is thriving with much more diverse and adventurous programming. For Orchestra A, there may be no difference between programming Beethoven's Second versus his Fourth, but there probably *is* a difference between programming his Second versus his Fifth. Conversely, Orchestra B, with its focus on the "roads less traveled," might actually attract a lot of attention for the relatively less-known Symphony No. 2.

Or think about a chamber group with a strong following of devoted fans: the repertoire probably has very little influence on attendance. (If you're a diehard fan of the Takács Quartet you're going to go hear them regardless of what's on the program.) In cases like these, the needs and desires being met are not primarily framed by the music being performed; they encompass other factors, such as the performers' virtuosity and the magnetism of their stage presence.

This is where the question of need takes an interesting turn, and it's a critically important one: while the ways we choose to meet our universal need for music differ according to personal tastes and sensibilities, the decision to consume a given musical *product* often hinges on factors unrelated to the music itself. Of course we make our choices of genre, style, and performer based on the music and its performance, but after that the mode and frequency of our *consumption* has little if anything to do with the art itself. We use earbuds and smartphones at the gym because they provide the music we like during our workouts. Sometimes we'll go see the Metropolitan Opera in the movie theater because we like to watch opera in our sweatpants and with a big tub of popcorn (extra butter, please) or simply because we can't make the trip to New York to see it live. We may choose not to attend a concert because the traffic that night is atrocious, the weather just turned bad, or the babysitter canceled. Whatever the particulars, an enormous range of individual and personal issues clouds the question of how, when, and where we consume musical products, and more often than not they have nothing to do with the music.

Research supports the notion that needs unrelated to the music itself—let's call them "extramusical needs"—often drive our formulation of need vis-à-vis a particular product. In his article "How Symphonies Grew Strong Audiences by Killing the Myth of the Average Consumer," Adrian Slywotzky writes about research undertaken by a consortium of orchestras trying to understand the behavior of their audiences. One issue in particular was the question of why first-time attendees weren't coming back. The participants expected that the surveys would confirm their assumptions about audience tastes: that audiences wanted only certain repertoire or that ticket prices were too high or that they only came for a particular "name" soloist. These are the same assumptions that many (if not most) classical music programmers make when formulating their seasons, and it's why so many classical music seasons look so strikingly alike—even when attendance and funding is drying up coast to coast.

But surveys conducted with thousands of first-time attendees revealed something quite startling. It wasn't the repertoire, the soloist, the ticket price, or the quality of the orchestra that kept newbies from coming back. The top reason, by far? Parking. This was at the top of every orchestra's list, but it was particularly acute for the Boston Symphony—which is hardly surprising if you've ever driven in that city. Longtime attendees there know the drill and have probably resigned themselves to just dealing with it come concert night. They may have even found certain tricks and shortcuts to make the trip a little easier. But for the first-timer? The hassle was *just enough* to discourage them from bothering to come back.

The idea that the artistic experience wasn't enough to transcend all other considerations might be a bitter pill for us to swallow, but it's the reality for the vast majority of concert audiences. There will always be the hardcore, diehard fans, the ones who would traverse the Yukon via dogsled if it meant they got to hear their favorite piece or performer. But the die-hards do not constitute a large enough market to sustain our musical organizations. Why? Because the classical musical product itself doesn't meet enough individuals' needs to create the critical mass necessary for the market to be sustained. That means that we have to look at *other* needs—those extramusical needs like parking—in order to create a critical mass of market size to sustain what we do.

As I'll talk about more deeply in chapter 4, extramusical needs can be extremely diverse and will likely vary from community to community. For Boston, the issue might be parking and the difficulty of getting downtown; for New Orleans, it might be something else altogether. So, once again, we see how the entrepreneurial approach helps us crack the mystery of our market's needs: observation, customer focus, and creative problem-solving can help us develop novel and effective methods to gather our audience and differentiate ourselves from the competition. Because these methods will be borne out of our own creative personalities, they will be authentic extensions of our artistic voices; because these methods are in response to the needs of our audiences, they will be effective in bringing them to hear us.

Parking might seem like an awfully mundane thing to worry about—an awfully *unartistic* thing—but just imagine the buzz you'd create if you found a really fun, unique, and perhaps a little whacky way to address that problem? Imagine that your clever and novel way to get people to your concert becomes part of your "brand," part of the thing that makes your group unique and desirable to others. All of a sudden you're not just dealing with the mundane, you're building your audience and creating a bond with them *through* your art. Isn't that what we're all about anyway?

This brings us to a critical point in our discussion of how entrepreneurial thinking operates in an artistic setting. You'll recall that entrepreneurship can follow one of two paths: "direct" entrepreneurship, where product development is driven by market needs, and "applied" entrepreneurship, where you bring entrepreneurial strategies to bear on an existing product. While this distinction can exist in any entrepreneurial context, it may be most important in the arts. This is because when the product is artistic content—a work that either already exists or is created in response to artistic impulse—direct entrepreneurship probably does not apply (though it can). So how does applied entrepreneurship play out when the core product is the art itself? Well, as the research of Slywotzky and others demonstrates, the product being consumed in arts settings (whatever the genre) goes beyond the work of art itself—it embodies the entirety of the *experience* of that work. In music, this broader experience—encompasing venue, access, and a host of other factors operating before, during, and after the performance—becomes the product that is subject to entrepreneurial treatment. So while I'm pretty sure that the Masses of the Renaissance master Josquin des Prez were not created with any entrepreneurial principles in mind, entrepreneurship can absolutely be employed to create a compelling and value-laden *experience* of those works for a modern audience.

Meanwhile, despite the enormous range of needs that exist in the musical marketplace there is one category you'll notice is absent: the needs of the musicians themselves to practice their art. At first glance this might seem like a strange omission: after all, the opera singer needs roles to perform, the string quartet needs gigs, the composer needs commissions, and so on. So why can't the necessity of making a living be included in the entrepreneurial question of "need"?

To answer this, let's remember the point of the entrepreneur's maxim: to define a process by which the entrepreneur can unlock value for the product—or, in a musical context, for musicians to unlock value for their work. If value can be unlocked, the musician's survival naturally follows. Traditional instruction in career development addresses the fundamental need to *survive* by teaching the tools needed to book engagements, promote concerts, fund initiatives, and so forth. These skills constitute what I call the "musician's toolbox," and they are extremely valuable to learn and are essential to professional success. The problem is, if musicians focus exclusively on developing their musician's toolbox solely in service of their *own need* for a sustainable and profitable career, a critical piece of the equation is left out: *what makes you think anybody will want what you have to offer in the first place?* By overlooking this fundamental question, many musicians who have studied marketing, are active in social media, and are polished communicators about their work may feel well-equipped for success in the musical marketplace—and still hit the brick wall of failure once they leave school and attempt to build their careers. Why? Because *unless you can connect your product to a need in the marketplace you cannot unlock value for it.*

Ultimately, entrepreneurship does more than simply facilitate the current notion of career success; it also provides a way you can discover and capitalize on opportunities you may not have ever seen and your professional tools alone will not reveal. It's like developing your musical technique (your musical tools) but never learning how to make music with them. Your muse wants you to use your tools to make *music;* to do the same with our careers, you must turn the issue of need from "This is what I need for my career" to "How can my music help meet the needs of others?"

To summarize the issue of need:

1. Needs are what define markets: when a sufficient number of individuals have a shared need, a market is born.

2. Needs in the musical marketplace are extremely diverse, from the broadly humanistic to the very concrete. Many needs are extramusical, hinging on aspects of the experience unrelated to the art itself.
3. The larger the market, the more diverse the range of potential needs, and the greater the opportunity for product differentiation and specialization.
4. Musician-entrepreneurs do not look for ways the market can support their own need for work; the entrepreneurial approach requires you to ask how your work can be used to meet needs in the marketplace. The answer to this question often resides in needs beyond the experience of the music itself.

When you direct the question of need away from yourself and toward the needs of the market you seek to engage, you are beginning to think like an entrepreneur. You are also able to pull together your product, your market, and the needs that are met to generate the final component of the entrepreneur's maxim: value.

Unlocking Value

At this point you can probably see how the question of value fits into the entrepreneur's maxim: if the market's need has been met through your product, then the market will value that product. You can easily see this in your own daily lives: name any product or service that you want or need on a regular basis, and you will likely have a very specific idea of how you prefer to meet that need and how valuable that solution is to you (and, by extension, how much you're willing to pay for it). In the case of the musical marketplace, the wide range of products and needs makes this question somewhat more complicated. But the core principle remains: *value is created when needs are met.*

Of course, since one product can meet multiple needs, it is extremely difficult to parse out a specific monetary value for each component of such a product. When I go to the Metropolitan Opera, for instance, how is my $200 ticket divided between the value I get from the particular opera I'm seeing, the singers on stage that night, the excellence of the Met orchestra, the novelty of the production, the person(s) I'm sharing all this with, and the thrill of excitement I get every time those starburst chandeliers begin to dim and retract into the ceiling? I can't possibly make that determination, of course. What I do know is that, on (rare) occasions, those factors align such that I'm willing to pay $200 for a ticket to the Met. Some are willing to pay that much (or more) on a regular basis. For others it might be a once-in-a-lifetime indulgence, and still others would never dream of attending the Met for that or any other price. And for each of these individuals, the criteria they employ and the relative weight of each factor used in determining the value of the Met's product will differ.

This is where the long tail once again comes back into play. Remember that the power of the long-tail market is not just that products for which there is a smaller market can be supported by the "hits"; the long tail also unlocks value simply by virtue of its diversity. So while the thing that makes the long tail valuable to the customer is the range of products it provides, the thing that makes it valuable to the entrepreneur is the opportunity for differentiation it enables. This means that even in markets already full of competitors there may still be ways to differentiate your product such that you can tap into unmet needs or underserved sensibilities. And since the musical marketplace is one enormous long tail, chances are there is a spot on that tail for what you have to offer: as with all aesthetic objects of that we consume, the uniqueness of the work itself is a huge part of its value.

You can now see that value is not always easily expressed in monetary terms. After all, a family heirloom might not be worth much monetary value on eBay, but the memories and associations you have with it render it priceless and irreplaceable for *you*. And the value of an experience has many different facets that differ from person to person. This is why it's so important for those of us in the arts to take our focus away from how we've been taught to view the value of our product (that is, as self-evidently and intrinsically high) and instead focus on where our product can thrive in the marketplace. Ironically, putting the needs of the marketplace ahead of your own need to produce music will unlock the very support you seek for yourself: if the market values the thing you offer, that value will translate into the support required for your personal survival.

Now that you understand the dynamics of the entrepreneur's maxim, you can see that it not only helps you unlock the value of your music, it can redefine your very purpose. The mindset of meeting needs means that your wedding band is no longer playing the music in a vacuum, nor are you playing for your own edification—you are now *entertainers,* playing a critical role in the success of an event that is one of the most important days of your customers' lives. More than getting the money you need for your rent, you're now using your music to make a difference, to touch people and bring them joy, to create community and connection they can't experience any other way. And suddenly, rather than being a potential obstacle to reaching a market, your most unique artistic voice becomes your most important *asset*. As the ultimate product differentiator, your own artistic identity becomes the most effective way to meet a specialized need in the marketplace—and, in turn, to create value for your musical product.

To review the question of value:

1. Value is created when needs are met.
2. Value is subjective: it can vary from individual to individual. Understanding the need(s) of your market will help you determine what the value of your product is *for those who need it.*

3. Because diversity and uniqueness are of prime value in the long tail of the musical marketplace, the unique artistic voice of each musical product is of paramount value. Rather than being an obstacle to finding support for your work, it becomes the primary way through which you will unlock value for what you do.

PULLING IT TOGETHER: THE VALUE PROPOSITION

Having worked your way through the entrepreneur's maxim, you will need to find a way to express those principles in terms of a specific product, market, and need. This is the role of the *value proposition*, a critical tool for every entrepreneur. The value proposition will clearly and succinctly describe what your product is, its distinguishing characteristics, who it's for, and how it benefits them. Think of it as a sort of mission statement, except much more specific and, as a result, more useful in guiding decisions ranging from broad strategies to day-to-day operations. The value proposition embodies all the key elements you must keep in mind at every stage of your venture. Said another way, realizing the value proposition is every entrepreneur's ultimate goal.

The form of the value proposition is straightforward:

[XYZ] is a(n) [entity]. Through its [distinguishing features] it delivers [benefits] to [target market].

Let's start with an example of a value proposition outside the arts, to better understand the concepts:

McGuckin Hardware is a Boulder-based home improvement store. Through its knowledgeable salespeople and specialized inventory, it provides expert and personalized customer service to homeowners and high-end contractors in the greater Boulder area.

One key to a strong value proposition is carefully crafting phrases that carry maximum descriptive clarity in as few words as possible. The reason for this is twofold. For one, your finished value proposition should be something easily remembered and frequently shared. It should always be in the forefront of your mind and roll off your tongue—so clear, concise language is essential. In addition, delving deeply into the language of your value proposition helps you clarify and refine your vision for this venture and may even reveal issues you haven't really thought through. So spending the time to find *just the right words* is important. As any writer knows, however, this can be easier said than done, and value propositions are no exception! Two areas that can be especially challenging are describing the distinguishing characteristics of your product and articulating the benefits that are provided to customers. In the example above, what, precisely, are McGuckin's distinguishing characteristics? To answer that question, one must not only know McGuckin but also their competition: what are McGuckin's *distinguishing* characteristics (that is, what makes them different from Home Depot or Lowe's)? It's their knowledgeable salespeople and specialized inventory. Those things are not the *only* descriptors of the store, but they are the core characteristics that *separate it* from its competition; they're what make McGuckin McGuckin.

Customer benefits are obviously intrinsically linked to distinguishing characteristics; think of them as two sides of the same coin. Having identified distinguishing characteristics, how do those features translate into benefit for McGuckin's customers? The knowledgeable staff and specialized inventory means you get amazing customer service from people who know what they're talking about and who can then go into the aisles full of bins and pull out just the part or gadget you need. Since this is in such stark contrast to big box home improvement stores, McGuckin thrives—and just two blocks away from an equally thriving Home Depot. The two businesses are both doing well because they have distinct value propositions: Home Depot's value proposition is built around low price and the *range* of items in their inventory; if you need something standard and know just what you need, you'll probably go to Home Depot to save a few bucks. If you need something more unusual, or you need expert guidance on your project, you go to McGuckin.

So how does the value proposition serve the good folks of McGuckin Hardware? That is, why does it benefit them to know and understand their value proposition? Because a good value proposition can (and should) guide all strategic decisions. It would be a mistake, for instance, for McGuckin to cut its staff in an effort to lower expenses and compete with Home Depot on price. A manager who didn't understand the nature of why customers go to McGuckin might make that mistake; someone who understands the value of distinguishing the business from Home Depot would not. Crafting a value proposition—and then *using it*—ensures that you have a clear understanding of where the value in your enterprise resides, who experiences that value, and why.

In the arts, the challenge of identifying distinguishing characteristics and benefits gets harder—again, due to the abstract nature of the artistic product and the almost infinite number of ways that people experience it. It takes many iterations and a lot of trial and error. But like so many other things, the more you work at it, try it out, and work some more, the better it will get.

Coming a little closer to home, here's an example from the arts:

BDT Stage is a professional dinner theatre company in Boulder, Colorado. Through compelling shows, seasoned performers, excellent food, and an intimate venue, BDT Stage offers first-rate entertainment for families, seniors, musical theatre–lovers, and groups from throughout the northern Front Range of Colorado.

BDT Stage is one of my favorite venues in Boulder. In writing their value proposition, I gave a lot of thought not just to describing *them*, but also doing so as a kind of implicit refutation of the common knocks against dinner theatre: that the quality is substandard, the food is not great; basically, that it's community theater with a rubber chicken. Since there are some other dinner theatres in the region, I decided that the real key to BDT Stage's value proposition was simply the quality of each element of the experience: the shows they program (not just the standards), the cast (regulars whom one gets to know and who are terrific performers), the food (far better than you normally get in a dinner theatre), and a venue in which there are no bad seats. In other words, BDT Stage's value proposition is centered around the idea of differentiation from their competition.

The other issue that the BDT Stage value proposition illustrates is how to articulate who your target audience is. Yes, it's true that it's the BDT Stage experience that its customers value, but if you're going to engage those customers in today's media-saturated world, you'll have to know, with some degree of detail, who exactly makes up that audience, where they reside, what sorts of things they spend their money on, and what are the best ways to reach them. The audience in BDT Stage's value proposition covers a lot of territory (both figuratively and literally), but the value proposition identifies specific groups that can be determined by research and quantified with relative ease. That's the yardstick by which you should measure the audience portion of your value proposition: if you can't identify qualities that can be researched and quantified, then your value proposition is probably too general. That in turn will seriously limit its utility.

What might the value proposition for an individual artist look like? How do we capture someone's unique artistic voice in a few words? I'll admit: it's not easy! But remember that the value proposition isn't just about describing yourself, it's about identifying the characteristics that distinguish your musical product from everyone else's. What makes you *you*. Also remember that your particular impact in the marketplace—that is, the things that unlock value for your work—might center around those "auxiliary" needs mentioned earlier, as opposed to your dulcet tone being so remarkably different from that of the next person in line.

Let's look at a couple of examples from two folks we've already met, Jennie Dorris and Adam Tendler.

Jennie Dorris is a Pittsburgh-based percussionist and author whose infectious personality is both outgoing and empathetic. Her innovative "Musical Storytelling" curriculum combines creative writing with musical performance, bringing healing, hope, and self-discovery to young people, cancer patients, and not-for-profits throughout the greater Pittsburgh region.

Who is Jennie? She's a Pittsburgh-based percussionist and author. Why mention her personality? Because that combination of outgoing energy and empathy is a key component of what makes her "Musical Storytelling" curriculum so compelling. What is the defining characteristic of that curriculum? The combination of creative writing and musical performance. Who is it for? Cancer patients, young people, and not-for-profits in the Pittsburgh region. How do they benefit? They experience healing, hope, and self-discovery.

Now you'll note that Jennie's value proposition doesn't attempt to describe every aspect of who she is, nor does it provide a detailed explanation of her curriculum. What it *does* do is provide a description that is detailed enough for us to understand what she's about, and how her venture delivers value to her customers.

Let's look at Adam Tendler for another example:

> Adam Tendler is a nationally known pianist, composer, and author. Based in New York City, his grassroots career embodies the contemporary DIY movement among classical musicians and focuses on innovative programs that feature modern/contemporary repertoire and appear in a wide range of traditional and nontraditional venues. His performances are both physically exuberant and confessional in nature, creating a fresh and intimate experience for a loyal following that cuts across the genre and cultural spectrum.

In Adam's case, his focus on contemporary repertoire, collaboration, and nontraditional venues provides a fairly detailed picture of the segment of the music market he occupies, while the description of his performances as both innovative and exuberant *and* personal and intimate tells us that a concert with Adam is not just another piano recital.

The way Adam's audience is described is also worth noting because patrons of the arts may not always fall into easily defined demographic categories. For Adam, his audience is anyone who is seeking something novel and unconventional, perhaps a bit edgy. This is a more descriptive way to capture an audience of people who might be fairly diverse demographically but share similar tastes and sensibilities. In a case like this, then, how do we conduct the sort of quantitative audience research I mentioned for BDT Stage? A good way to start is to survey your audience and track classic demographic markers like education, income, home zip code, and so on. Then find out what other sorts of arts venues they frequent and the genres they most like. This data can then start to help paint a portrait of your customers in terms that can help you discern how to contact them, the nature of that interaction, and so forth. As with all the other elements of the value proposition, describing the customers is harder for the arts than for a hardware store—but it's not impossible. Making sure you base your descriptions on data and not assumptions is the first step.

With the entrepreneurial paradigm inverting the traditional way artists view the act of advancing their work, it's understandable why it might be a scary prospect for some. After all, it cedes the illusion of control to an external body (the marketplace) and forces us to address the needs of others instead of remaining in the safe cocoon of our own artistic desires and personal views of "value." By definition, the entrepreneurial process takes us down new and unfamiliar paths, paths that require us to view the advancement of our music and our careers in ways that are completely different from what we've always known and may even challenge our notions about the role our music plays in our society. And that can be some scary stuff.

But remember this: rather than limiting artistic expression to a small and narrowly defined body of "accessible" music, entrepreneurial thinking *opens up* creative action to encompass an infinite array of components. Rather than being antithetical to the "pure" expression of art, entrepreneurship acts as an *extension* of creativity to every aspect of the artistic experience we create for our audiences. Applied well, entrepreneurial thinking empowers both creators and performers/presenters to devise new and compelling ways to reach their markets—and unlock value for their art in the process.

EXERCISE: CREATE YOUR VALUE PROPOSITION

So how do you go about creating your own value proposition? This series of steps will take you through each element. Spend some dedicated time with each of these, and remember that the value proposition is a living thing that can change and evolve over time.

Activity

1. Decide which part of your professional portfolio you're capturing in this value proposition. Remember: you might have multiple value propositions for different parts of your career (teacher, performer, blogger, etc.), so don't try to cram everything you do into a single statement.
2. Determine the best way to describe your product. ("Karl's Koffee is a coffee shop and bakery in the Washington Heights section of Manhattan.")
3. Assemble a list of adjectives that illustrate the characteristics of your venture. Be as specific as possible, and try to focus on the things that distinguish your venture from your competition. Don't try to cull this list down just yet: get as many descriptors as possible for now.
4. *Reality Check 1.* Show this list to a friend or colleague who knows your work well. What have you overlooked? What do they see as the most important distinguishing characteristics of your work?

5. Then go on to identifying your target market. If you're already in business, describe your existing customers as clearly as possible. If you're getting ready to launch a venture (or expand your current one), describe the sorts of customers you hope to attract. Gather as much data as necessary to understand who these people are and how willing and able they will be to pay for your product. (You'll notice that you haven't begun writing yet; you're still just making lists and collecting data.)

6. Now determine the customer needs your product will address. This is the trickiest part of creating your value proposition because there is a very real danger that you will make two assumptions that might be completely invalid. The first is assuming that your target market wants/needs/likes certain things; the second is assuming that your product will satisfy the needs in question. To avoid falling into this trap, collect as much data as possible. Conduct surveys. Look at what works and what doesn't work for your competition. *Talk to people.* Do not take anything for granted. Be willing to shift some aspect of your product (or some aspect of your target market) if your information reveals a disconnect between the product as you initially envisioned it and what you're hearing from potential customers.

7. This step goes hand-in-glove with step 6. You've described the characteristics of your product, and you've articulated the need you hope to address. Now you have to bridge these two things by expressing how your product's characteristics satisfy the need(s) of your customers. Again, make sure you're grounding your language in data you've collected. Avoid assumptions!

8. *Now* you're ready to begin writing. Cull your various lists down to no more than three descriptors for each section of your value proposition. Be as clear, specific, and concise as possible. Start to think about the syntax you want to use, keeping in mind that a value proposition should not contain more than one or two sentences.

9. *Reality Check 2.* Show your draft to the same friends/colleagues you reached out to before. Do they think your value proposition accurately captures the essence of what you do, who it's for, and how they benefit?

10. Revise, polish, repeat. The value proposition is a living thing. It should be concise enough to be easily committed to memory and referred to on a daily basis as you go about operating your venture. It should be descriptive enough that anybody who hears it will understand you and your work. And you must be willing to constantly revisit and revise your value proposition as you gain experience and insights into your distinctive traits and how your venture benefits your customers.

CHAPTER 4
Where the Rubber Meets the Road

Stimulating Demand

So how does the entrepreneur's maxim, and the question of value in particular, translate into *action* on the consumer's part? What is the point of connection between, say, identifying your neighbors' musical needs for a teaching studio . . . and getting your neighbors to sign up and start paying you for music lessons? The answer is the last foundational concept we need to explore in order to decode "the E-word": *demand*.

Professionals in the fields of economics, business, and marketing spend a tremendous amount of time trying to understand the complex dynamics of demand, and for good reason. Demand operates within a complex web of impulses and factors tying together products, consumer sensibilities, price, demographics, macroeconomic conditions, and a host of other issues. Given the complexity of this field, what follows is merely an introduction to get you thinking about how these factors might play out for your entrepreneurial endeavor. As with all other economic and theoretical topics I've explored, there are abundant resources online or at your local library should you desire to dive into this one more deeply.

That said, it's important that you have some basic understanding of the core issues at play with regard to demand because the entrepreneur's maxim by itself does not guarantee a successful launch of your product or venture. That is, identifying a solution to a need in the marketplace does not guarantee that the market will, in turn, respond by purchasing your product. There's another critical step in the process: the point where the value that resides in the satisfying of a need is translated into currency (both literally and figuratively) in the marketplace. That's where demand comes in. Demand is expressed when value for a product is *realized in the marketplace,* via consumption of that product. This chapter explores different types of demand and how demand is stimulated, beginning with the transactional event that drives it: the act of *consumption.*

CONSUMPTION: THE ACTIVATION OF NEED

Before getting into the particulars of demand—the various types and the complex dynamics between a product and its market—we need to look at the moment at which a need for a product translates into a purchase. That's the moment of consumption, and it's the moment of truth for every entrepreneurial endeavor: without it, you can't survive. Consumption is the oxygen required for any business to breathe, grow, and thrive. Think of it as the point of *activation* for the need in question. Let's take a closer look at the factors that drive that moment of activation.

Consumption takes place when a transaction is made; that is, a payment of some asset (usually money) is given in exchange for a given product. The measure of all the consumption for a given product in the marketplace is the demand for that product. Sounds simple enough, right? But what are the factors behind the act of consumption? After all, the transaction in question is not an abstract thing; consumption takes place on the part of *customers,* individuals with a particular need they are seeking to meet. This means that each act of consumption involves a personal decision by each individual consumer. Because of this, it's not as simple a formula as "Identified Need + Cool Solution = *Voilà!* Instant Consumer Consumption!"

This whole enterprise would be easier if that were so, wouldn't it? But, of course, it's not because for each consumer who decides to go ahead and buy your product, there are likely others who have decided *not* to buy it. So what factors are behind those decisions, and how can we understand them better so as to maximize the number of those who say yes? There are countless examples of products that were launched in response to an unmet need . . . yet the market remained unmoved. Clearly, there are other factors behind the consumer's decision to purchase a product. That the product fills some level of need is absolutely necessary, but it is not sufficient in and of itself.

One big piece of the answer to these questions lies in what market researchers call the psychographics of a market: the emotional sensibilities and psychological associations that a given market has vis-à-vis the product in question. Understanding consumer psychographics is at the heart of the art and science of marketing, and it began with the seminal work of Sidney Levy in the 1950s. In his 1959 work "Symbols for Sale," Levy, a behavioral scientist, remarked that "people buy products not only for what they *do,* but also for what they *mean.*" This sentiment helped define the field of modern marketing, in which the symbolic associations consumers make with a given product are at the heart of how that product is packaged, promoted, and delivered.

Levy's work also helped spawn important work on how the symbolic significance of products might help us understand the differences between consumption of utilitarian objects and consumption of products that are primarily aesthetic in nature. In a series of articles published in the 1980s, Elizabeth Hirschman and Morris Holbrook built on Levi's work and developed a theory of what they called "hedonic consumption," a theory that was applied specifically to music in the work of Kathleen Lacher and Richard Mizeski in the late 1980s and early 1990s. The concept of hedonic consumption, defined by Hirschman and Holbrook as "those facets of consumer behavior that relate to the multi-sensory, fantasy and emotive aspects of one's experience," articulated a critical divergence in consumer behavior between consumption of products that are primarily about an aesthetic experience (a perfume, for example) and traditional consumer products defined by their functional utility alone (an electric drill). In traditional models of consumption, the value of a product is determined solely by its utility, whereas the concept of hedonic consumption recognizes that the emotive and sensory aspects of a product can be equally powerful determinants of value on the part of consumers.

This is good news for those of us in the arts because it means that consumption of an artistic product is driven by a different set of sensibilities from the set that drives utilitarian ones. This makes sense to us; we intuitively understand that the artistic product is not a utilitarian one but rather one that speaks to a more subtle and ineffable set of needs and experiences. There's a problem with the utilitarian/hedonic duality, however, and it's this: products only rarely fall squarely into one category or the other. More often, products exist somewhere along a *continuum* between the purely utilitarian and the purely aesthetic. And that means that the decision to consume a given product is likewise driven by a combination of utilitarian and aesthetic considerations. As chapter 3 already began to explore, this applies even to products that are, at their core, aesthetic (i.e., hedonic) in nature.

To understand this better, we can start by viewing the question of utilitarian versus aesthetic consumption not as a duality but as a continuum: with purely utilitarian products, containing "minimal aesthetic dimension" and embodying traditional consumption, on one end and aesthetic products, embodying hedonic consumption, on the other. This continuum is illustrated by the Australian scholar Steve Charters: as we move along the continuum to the right, the degree to which aesthetic considerations drive consumption increases, until we come to products whose aesthetic qualities are now the primary motivating factor in consumption (fig. 4.1).

What's interesting about this continuum is that it shows that many utilitarian products (perhaps even most of them) have some aesthetic component

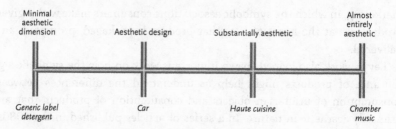

Minimal aesthetic dimension	Aesthetic design	Substantially aesthetic	Almost entirely aesthetic
Generic label detergent	*Car*	*Haute cuisine*	*Chamber music*

Figure 4.1 Charters's range of aesthetic consumption

to them. There's the fusion of function with form that goes into the design of that new toaster you bought for your mom last Christmas or the box design you like for the Kleenex in the guest room. The primary need for the product is utilitarian—your mom's need for a new toaster or your need for tissues in the guest room—but the decision to purchase one particular product over another likely is driven by a combination of utilitarian *and* aesthetic considerations. Said another way, when it comes to stimulating consumption of a utilitarian product, the determinative factor may be a secondary one—the aesthetic qualities of one product over another (provided it still fulfills its primary utilitarian function).

Likewise, the continuum reinforces something already discussed in previous chapters: that even a highly aesthetic experience has utilitarian components to it, such as the transportation logistics associated with your trip to Symphony Hall, the ease of advance ticket purchases for that summer festival in Italy you plan on going to next year, the PayPal page you have set up to receive payments for lessons. Identifying which aspects of your product are aesthetic in nature and which are utilitarian, and (perhaps even more important) understanding how those aspects *interact with each other*, is critical in identifying the nature of consumption of your product. Is that consumption primarily driven by aesthetic tastes or utilitarian needs? Are there secondary drivers (the primarily aesthetic product is driven in part by utilitarian considerations, or vice versa)? And to the extent that consumption of your product is driven by aesthetic considerations, what are the specific psychographics of those considerations? That is, what are the emotional and psychological associations people have with your product? What does it *mean* to them, and what do they *feel* when they experience it? Most important, clarity with regard to how aesthetic and utilitarian considerations drive consumption of your product helps you maximize the extent to which you satisfy the needs of your customers in a way they will respond to. And that's the key to stimulating demand for your product.

In the study of orchestra audiences discussed in chapter 3, the central element of the product the audience was consuming (the Boston Symphony Orchestra concert) was decidedly aesthetic in nature: the initial draw of the product resided in the experience one expected to have by attending a concert by a professional orchestra of world-class caliber. But the study also showed that the aesthetic component *alone* was not sufficient to keep first-time attendees coming back: the primary "driver of revisitation" was parking—a completely utilitarian part of the experience.

We revisit this example because it is absolutely central to the paradigm shift classical musicians must make if they are to adopt an entrepreneurial approach to their careers. We're all raised (and trained) to believe that the aesthetic value of our performances is the sole driver of consumption of our music. Moreover, the notion that other factors that make up a concert experience—like parking, availability of restrooms, or any other of a host of nonartistic things—should overrule the artistic content of our performances is an affront to us and our art. The art alone *should* be sufficient, so the thinking goes; realizing that it isn't always sufficient is a stinging blow!

The problem with this viewpoint is that it flies in the face of what we know about human behavior. Decades of research in behavioral science proves that things are far more complicated than perhaps we'd like to believe. In the case of the arts, most consumers (with the exception of our most diehard fans) are just not that single-minded. For most, a host of diverse factors are under consideration, and not every would-be customer weighs those factors in the same way.

A great illustration of the many factors influencing consumption of artistic products (or the lack thereof) can be found in a 2012 study from the National Endowment for the Arts, "When Going Gets Tough: Barriers and Motivations Affecting Arts Attendance." In this fascinating study, researchers focused on two primary sets of data. They first attempted to determine the leading factors influencing folks who were interested in attending arts events to end up not going. The second asked whether or not there were traits/issues disproportionately common among those who *did* attend arts events. The results were quite striking.

For those attending at least one performance or exhibition a year (nearly 54 percent of U.S. adults), the most commonly cited reason for doing so was socializing with friends or family: 76 percent of attendees reported this among their reasons for attending. Those who attended were also shown to be more interested in adventure, excitement, risk-taking, and creative or original ways of presenting things than interested nonattendees were.

For those who were interested in going to an arts event but did not, the top reason was lack of time. For example, nearly 60 percent of parents with young children cited this as the most important reason for not attending. Another big chunk (37 percent) of interested nonattendees cited problems with finding or getting to the venue as their reasons for not going; an equal percent cited ticket prices.

These numbers illustrate how the decision to consume is complicated, personal, and often unrelated to the art. In fact, "lack of interest in the content" did not even appear among the reasons why some interested consumers elected not to attend an arts event! We can ignore this reality, but if we do, we shouldn't be surprised when we struggle to stimulate demand for our product. The alternative is to look at untangling the various drivers of consumption and devising ways to stimulate them as a creative endeavor in itself, a challenge that needs our unique artistry if it is to be addressed. Not only will this have a greater chance of success, doesn't it also sound like a lot more fun?

So now we have two overriding concepts to keep in mind as we delve more deeply into the question of how consumption stimulates demand:

1. Consumption exists along a continuum between products that are primarily utilitarian in nature and those that are primarily aesthetic. For most products, and especially in the case of the performing arts, consumption is often driven by a combination of aesthetic and utilitarian considerations.
2. Consumers are not automatons; they are individuals whose decisions to consume a product (or not) are shaped by a complex set of emotional and psychological factors—their psychographics. Understanding the particular sensibilities and associations of your audience helps you create the experience that will most powerfully speak to them, stimulating consumption for your product in turn.

Since demand is the *quantification* of consumption of your product, to understand consumption—why your customers purchase your product—is to understand the essence of demand for it as well. Let's go there next.

UNDERSTANDING DEMAND

At this point it might seem like demand and consumption are the same thing. While they are obviously intrinsically linked, there is a subtle distinction. Consumption is the act of purchasing a product; demand is the aggregate of that consumption. *Individuals* express the value they assign to a product through consumption of it; demand embodies the collective consumption of the *market*. To understand this more clearly, recall the discussion of markets in chapter 3. Remember that markets are made up of individuals who share a common need/sensibility. When a product comes along that meets their need(s) and satisfies the various conditions required for consumption of that product, demand is created; the more individuals consume, the greater the demand. Understanding the particulars of the phrase "satisfies the various conditions required for consumption" is the end goal of our discussion. This chapter has begun to explore the matter with the questions of hedonic consumption and consumer psychographics. Let's continue to parse it out with an exploration of two different types of demand and how they can be stimulated in the marketplace.

The sum total consumption of a given product is its "expressed demand." In terms of the entrepreneur's maxim, we might define demand as "the quantitative expression of value for a product in the marketplace." To the extent that some portion of the market is unable to purchase that product (either due to price, access to the product, or simply lacking information about it) there is a "latent" (i.e., unsatisfied) demand for that product. For instance, there are areas of the world without Internet access; once the Internet is made available, at least some citizens of those areas will sign up for it. That's an example of the latent demand for Internet access translating into expressed demand once it's available. Or, to take an example closer to home, perhaps a rapidly growing suburb doesn't yet have a grocery store nearby; as the population of the neighborhood grows, there is increasing latent demand for one. Eventually, conditions will be such that somebody will decide to open a store in the area, causing the latent demand for convenient groceries to translate into expressed demand for that particular store. Businesses are always looking for ways to convert latent demand into expressed demand, first by doing a lot of market observation and research and then through things like special offers, advertising, opening a new store, creating an online portal for purchasing, and all manner of other marketing and promotional tools. All of these are designed to minimize the amount of unexpressed (latent) demand and inspire consumers to consume your product over that of your competitors.

You can now see how tapping into latent demand often presents entrepreneurial opportunities: the new venture that delivers a product to a market with latent demand might very well unlock considerable value. In the grocery store example, the first store to open in the new neighborhood will likely do well. The catch, however, is that if a suburban neighborhood is growing fast, you can bet that one or more of the big grocery chains already have their eyes on the area; it's just a matter of time before they swoop in with a supercenter and wipe out any local mom-and-pop operation that attempts to compete with them. But that doesn't mean there isn't latent demand for something more specialized: an artisanal bakery, specialty butcher shop, or organic market. This example illustrates why it's narrowly defined niche markets that often provide the best opportunities for solo entrepreneurs: large reservoirs of latent demand are likely to be gobbled up by big competitors, but more specialized types of latent demand are found pretty much everywhere. We just need to practice our strategic observation skills to find them.

Another way that latent demand can play out is with regard to price. When Tesla first introduced its fully electric sports car, the Tesla Roadster, the base price of $109,000 limited the market to only affluent consumers. There was significant latent demand throughout the automobile market for a fully electric car that was stylish, was sporty, and had a long-lasting battery, but Tesla's Roadster only converted a small slice of that market into expressed demand. (From 2008 to 2012, Tesla only sold 2,450 cars worldwide!) As the company's brand became more established and Tesla's pricey cars began to sell more, however, lower-priced models were introduced (their S-model sedan had a base price of $59,900 when it was introduced in 2012). At that point, a much larger reservoir of pent-up (latent) demand was unleashed: from 2013 to 2015, nearly 75,000 Tesla S models were sold, followed by more than 50,000 in 2016.

Price and latent demand can work in the other direction, too: let's say the only jewelry store in town is the discount chain Kay's. Depending on the market characteristics of your community, there might be latent demand for a high-quality, custom jeweler whose products are far more expensive. With many items, including the arts, sometimes latent demand exists for a product that is *more* expensive, not less. (Just imagine if there were no luxury car dealerships in Beverly Hills!) These can be the best opportunities of them all: trying to compete on the lowest price can lead to a price war, where the one with the deepest pockets will always win. Instead, as entrepreneurial mentor Frank Moyes often counsels students, the key to success often lies in finding ways to charge more for your product, not less.

The thing to keep in mind about latent demand is that it pertains to *existing* products with *identifiable characteristics*. This poses a dilemma for those of us in the arts, where a whole range of products don't really fall under the heading "existing products with identifiable characteristics." Indeed, huge swaths of the musical products galaxy contain things with characteristics that are often ineffable and extremely difficult (or nearly impossible) to define in concrete terms, particularly if we're talking about newly created content. And even if you're performing known repertoire, there is still (hopefully) a significant element of your own personal artistic voice, or any number of other elements that make the experience new or novel. How do we engage with the concept of demand when these are the sorts of product we're talking about? Is there really latent demand for your next (as yet uncomposed) symphony, your new group's debut, or your upcoming solo album? By their very nature, these products cannot have latent demand: they haven't been created yet, and when they are, they'll be, by definition, new and unique.

This is where we come to another type of demand: *inchoate demand*. Inchoate demand expresses a need that does not exist until the product is created. This is the proverbial "I didn't know I had to have this until I saw it." Since there can't be latent demand for such a product until it exists, inchoate demand remains, in a sense, an abstraction—until an actual product is introduced into the marketplace that addresses the need(s) driving that demand. To better understand this somewhat elusive concept, here's an example we're all familiar with: the smartphone.

Before the smartphone existed there was no market for it. Moreover, there was no latent demand for it because latent demand is pent-up, unfulfilled demand on the part of consumers who know a product and what it does and who *want it* but don't/can't consume it. That state can't exist if the product itself doesn't yet exist! So in the case of the smartphone, how did something that didn't exist give birth to a global megamarket that literally changed the way we live our lives? The answer lies in the dynamics of inchoate demand.

Let's go back to the 1990s, when two important (though at the time unrelated) markets were about to converge. In the one market, the Internet was coming into widespread use with a vengeance: the ability to connect one's personal computer into a web of information spanning the globe was about to revolutionize the way we gathered, disseminated, and applied information. In a remarkably short span of time, the Internet went from something only used in government labs and academia to something every business (and a huge number of individuals) would find indispensable. At the same time, the cell phone was becoming ubiquitous as well. The ability to access the benefits of a telephone without being tied to a landline in your home or office fundamentally changed the nature of our communication. Cell phones would soon be able to do more than just transmit the voice, too: the advent of texting meant we could communicate asynchronously with the written word. Phones started to have cameras. "Personal data assistants" (PDAs) allowed you to keep an updated calendar with you at all times and keep track of your spending. And as more and more commerce and social interaction began to take place online, things were quickly evolving toward a point where customers would want access to information all the time, regardless of whether or not a landline or Internet hookup was available. But how would such access be accomplished? What was the next step?

With the benefit of hindsight, we can see how these two revolutions—the cell phone and the Internet—were destined to intersect. The Internet meant we had more access to more information (and more quickly) than ever before; cell phones meant we could stay connected to our homes or offices without having to be physically present at either one, or even tied into a physical connection at all. The natural progression of these trends was to create a device people could use to access the benefits of the personal computer and the Internet when away from an Internet modem or desktop computer. *What if those things could be accessed by using the portable cellular device that already exists?* And that, ladies and gentlemen, is how the smartphone came about.

Products like the smartphone might appear to spring forth from the visionary minds of their creators, but even the most innovative products are likely to be grounded to some extent in an understanding of existing needs, the dynamics of the marketplace, and where those needs are headed. Needs that are on the cusp of being expressed in the marketplace are called "emerging needs." By recognizing the rising use of cell phones and the increasing use of the Internet for finding and exchanging all manner of information, developers concluded that the market very likely possessed the inchoate (as yet unseen) need to access the vast information of the Internet while away from one's computer. In other words, they identified an emergent need by observing broader trends and sensibilities in the marketplace. This is why developing the practice of strategic observation is so important: we can't expect to connect with any given market if we don't understand the things that make that market tick, the things that market desires. And only once we have that understanding can we devise something that consumers may not realize they want until they experience it.

This story is a little more complicated than my presentation of it here, however. The smartphone concept existed before the iPhone came along and changed the world, and a related tool, the Blackberry (and other PDAs) held on for a long time before eventually falling by the wayside. You see, in the early years of this emerging technology, one piece of the puzzle was still missing, and the resulting gap was keeping the smartphone from taking over the world. The technology existed, but a product that would ignite a new market had not yet been created. There was, in essence, one more inchoate need lurking in the market: an easy-to-use, stylish user interface with multiple features that could be customized for each user. Steve Jobs and the folks at Apple recognized this and set about creating a device that would address this inchoate need. When they had developed their product, the potent inchoate demand for something that was stylish, easy to use, and personal was transformed into pent-up (latent) demand for a particular product: the iPhone. And that latent demand was enormous: so many people wanted iPhones that Apple could hardly make them fast enough. Competitors emerged, and the market then did what markets do: exercise competition among products, winnowing out some while driving others to prosper. The war between Apple and its competitors continues today.

We can capture the relationship between the continuum of needs (from functional/utilitarian to existential/aesthetic) and types of demand (latent versus inchoate) by assigning different types of new and existing products to what I call the needs/demand matrix (fig. 4.2). This matrix illustrates how existential needs can be met through either newly created aesthetic products (new works of art or newly birthed cultural institutions) or existing aesthetic products (existing works of art and established cultural institutions). Similarly, utilitarian needs can either be met through new and innovative products or existing ones. Applying inchoate and latent demand to these categories completes the other axis of the matrix and shows how inchoate demand can operate for products filling both utilitarian and existential needs.

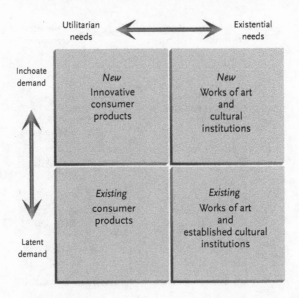

Figure 4.2 The needs/demand matrix

As the iPhone example illustrates, finding ways to translate inchoate demand (as defined by a vague need that has no concrete solution) into latent demand (pent-up demand for a specific product with identifiable characteristics) is where the biggest entrepreneurial opportunities reside. The scholar Paul Gerosky articulated this relationship in his book *The Evolution of New Markets*. Gerosky argues that inchoate demand is at the heart of anything that results in the creation of new markets where none existed previously. Consequently, addressing inchoate demand is also what drives the greatest entrepreneurial successes.

Inchoate demand is also at the center of artistic creativity. After all, how can there be latent demand for a composition that hasn't been created yet or a new chamber group that's just formed? And this, of course, begs the question that is central to this discussion: how is inchoate demand for artistic products in general translated into expressed demand for your particular product in the marketplace?

To help untangle this question, we can take the needs/demand matrix and modify it slightly to reflect consumption versus demand. Remember that consumption is the *activation* of a need, so existential/aesthetic needs will be met through hedonic consumption while utilitarian needs will be met through functional/utilitarian products. The new matrix (fig. 4.3) illustrates how different consumption/demand combinations result from different types of products and needs.

Note that entrepreneurial opportunities exist for the musician-entrepreneur in each quadrant of the consumption/demand matrix. On the

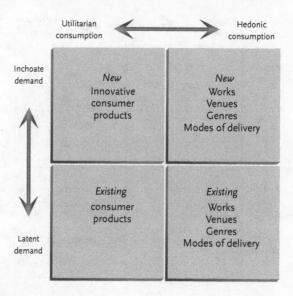

Figure 4.3 The consumption/demand matrix

utilitarian side of the matrix (the quadrants on the upper and lower left) you have things like the equipment, supplies, and tools that we rely on to produce our music. These can be new markets driven by innovative products (inchoate demand that was activated by the invention of the MIDI sequencer, the structural and material changes that caused the modern piano to eclipse the forte-piano, etc.), or they can be the huge number of existing musical products and their respective markets (microphones, digital keyboards, manuscript paper, music stands . . . ad infinitum). Either way, the value of products in the left quadrants of the consumption/demand matrix exists in their utility—their ability to perform a specific, defined function.

On the hedonic side of the matrix things are a little more interesting. Remember that for hedonic consumption the primary value of the product exists in what Hirschman and Holbrook called "the multi-sensory, fantasy and emotive aspects of one's experience." But which of these products belong in the latent category and which are inchoate? For instance, where does something like private teaching fall? What about a chamber music concert that presents standard repertoire in a traditional venue? To answer these questions, remember that latent consumption refers to existing products with specific characteristics. While it's clear that a ticket for known repertoire presented in a traditional way represents hedonic consumption, the nature of that experience is sufficiently familiar to most people that it qualifies as an "existing product with known characteristics." That puts the traditional, mainstream classical concert squarely in the "latent-hedonic" quadrant. A private teaching studio that employs mainstream pedagogy in a traditional manner would likewise share enough known characteristics to reside in the lower right corner of the matrix. Something that's entirely new—a new composition, a new kind of concert presentation using various media in a nontraditional venue—belongs, by definition, in the inchoate realm.

With the infinite variety of the arts, some classifications might seem elusive. Take, for example, the African-themed production of *The Magic Flute* by the South African company Insango Ensemble. While the opera itself is very well known, this particular production is completely new and novel. Where does a product like this fall on the quadrant? The answer lies in the degree of innovation/novelty. In this case, one could argue that the production is sufficiently new and novel that it belongs in the inchoate-hedonic quadrant. A contrasting example would be a traditional staging of *The Nutcracker*. (Is there any other kind?) Audiences around the world have made an annual holiday tradition out of seeing this beloved work, and when children grow up and are parents themselves, the tradition is passed down to the next generation. Moreover, since companies tend to present the same production every year, the audience knows what to expect—and even eagerly anticipates certain favorite moments. Orchestras and ballets are therefore wise to program *The Nutcracker* every year: there aren't a lot of examples of reliable, latent demand in the performing arts; when you find one, stick with it!

Grappling with where certain artistic products fall in the consumption/demand matrix isn't just an intellectual exercise. It's an incredibly important tool to help you understand the nature of, and dynamics behind, consumption of your product. With this understanding you can better connect with your market and stimulate consumption, you can better capitalize on your successes and gain insights into your failures, and you can take a more strategic and informed approach to developing new products and initiatives. For instance, if you see your venture as mainly residing in the latent-hedonic quadrant, then stimulating greater consumption lies in understanding what's behind the "latent" part of the equation. Is your market simply unaware of your product? Is your product too hard to get to, poorly scheduled, or in an unappealing venue? Is it too expensive—or is it not expensive enough to convey its superior quality? Are there other unmet utilitarian needs standing in the way of consumers buying your product?

And what if your research shows that there isn't really any latent (pent-up) demand for your product? Does that mean there are no opportunities for you? Not necessarily: the inchoate side of the consumption/demand matrix is, as of yet in our scenario, unexplored. So in the entrepreneurial spirit of strategic observation and customer empathy, spend some time pondering the needs and sensibilities of your target market that are *not* currently met by existing products. Perhaps there are utilitarian needs that could be met in new or novel ways (inchoate-utilitarian: a fun and festive way to serve refreshments at intermission without the long lines) or perhaps what's called for is a completely new artistic product (inchoate-hedonic: a new, multimedia ensemble). Maybe the most exciting scenario is one that involves stimulating inchoate demand for both the utilitarian *and* hedonic needs of your market (a multimedia ensemble that incorporates food into their performances)!

What the consumption/demand matrix helps us see is that different types of products and markets tap into different sorts of need, and the satisfaction of those needs can play out in myriad ways. What's perhaps unique in the world of the arts is the fact that any given artistic experience likely has elements to it that occupy several, or all, of the quadrants: the artistic product might be a combination of new work and existing works, or perhaps existing/known works presented in new ways, while the presentation of that artistic product involves both standard and novel ways of addressing utilitarian needs like access and venue. And while it's absolutely true that once the audience is seated, the artistic value of the production must be of the highest order, it's equally true that if you can't get an audience to show up in the first place, then the inchoate demand for your artistic product will not be stimulated.

SIX DRIVERS OF DEMAND

So far I've discussed how the aggregate consumption of a product by the individuals of a given market equals the demand for that product. I've shown how consumption is driven by a complex web of psychographics, utilitarian needs, and aesthetic sensibilities. And I've shown that markets can either respond to known needs with known products to satisfy them (latent demand) or to vague, unexpressed needs that don't come into focus until a new product stimulates that market in a new way (inchoate demand). Finally, I've explored how these various drivers of consumption, and different types of demand, can operate in tandem with each other when it comes to artistic products, because consumers are responding to both the art itself and its framing, presentation, and avenues of access.

While identifying utilitarian needs and quantifying the latent demand for them can usually be addressed with solid research and through interaction with your existing and/or potential customers, the realm of inchoate demand is, by definition, far more uncertain. You might be convinced that you've identified some aspect of your market that nobody else has tapped into yet; you might even have some data to support your idea . . . and it can still flop. So are there some common characteristics possessed by products that have successfully stimulated inchoate demand? Are there principles you can employ that will increase your chances of an emerging or inchoate need translating into expressed demand for your particular product? Adrian Slywotzky and Karl Weber have identified six such principles in their book *Demand: Creating What People Love before They Know They Want It*. Let's take a look at these six principles and see how they apply to those of us in the classical music world.

Make It Magnetic

The first key step in unlocking inchoate demand is in creating a product that is what Slywotzky and Weber call "magnetic": it has emotional appeal that generates buzz in your intended market and somehow tickles the sensibilities of your customers. Remember Sydney Levi's words as he launched the field of modern marketing: "People buy products not only for what they *do,* but also for what they *mean.*" Levi's maxim is certainly true in the world of classical music! But again you must be careful to avoid the assumption that what is "magnetic" to *you* will be equally magnetic to your *audience.* That is, you must avoid assigning the meaning *you* associate with your work to your audience. We're insider practitioners, after all; we understand, on a personal level, the power of music to touch our souls and enrich our spirits, and our tastes and preferences are passionately held. So in evaluating the potential magnetism for our products, we have to remember all the things I've talked about so far: look at things from the customer's perspective; use your strategic observation to learn about your target market's behavior and sensibilities; gather data before acting; observe what works and what doesn't, and adjust accordingly. Equally important, remember also that magnetic qualities may need to first exist in the ways the art is marketed, presented, and framed; once you have an audience in their seats, you can then proceed to deliver an experience that will fully realize the magnetism that got them there in the first place—and stimulate them to keep coming back.

Simplify the Hassle Map

Slywotzky and Weber note that many of the greatest product successes are borne out of addressing a "hassle" in the marketplace. The example they cite is that of Netflix, which began when one man discovered that he'd neglected to return his movie rental and was facing a fine far larger than the cost of buying a new copy outright. The hassle of fetching and returning a movie and the steep penalties for messing up that process got Reed Hastings thinking about a different model; eventually, Netflix was born.

Chapter 1 talked about the "bug list," a catalogue of the flaws we identify in products we interact with on a regular basis. Now you're going to create a "hassle map," a sort of experiential "bug list" for a specific product.

Let's take an online purchase as an example. Was the website easy to find? Were the products easy to browse? Were the descriptions, comparisons, and customer reviews helpful? (Were they even there?) Did the payment go smoothly, or did the page get hung up as soon as you pressed "Confirm Purchase"? A comprehensive listing of each element of the consumption experience constitutes the hassle map for that product; often such hassles can be critical factors in a company's failure to keep customers coming back. The hassle map might also be keeping customers away altogether: we've probably all had someone give us a website to check out only to have "Page Not Found" appear on our screen when we enter the address we were given. At that point we can either try to hunt down the entity in question . . . or decide that the hassle just isn't worth it. On the flip side, the foundation of Apple's success in the 1980s and 1990s was the simplicity of its interface: the mouse and the "point and click" paradigm completely wiped away the significant hassle map that was the DOS user interface. The impact was so great that Microsoft had to create the Windows operating system to compete. The revolution in the market for personal computers was driven almost entirely by the product that simplified the hassle map. The hassle map is a powerful thing indeed!

When it comes to live performances of music, there are many things that commonly make up the hassle map. We've already talked about parking and ease of access in congested urban areas. Purchasing tickets may not be as easy as it should be. Some venues are woefully ill-equipped in the restroom department. Seating may be uncomfortable. Perhaps there are no nice restaurants nearby for before or after the show. These are the utilitarian needs I've been discussing all along, and when it comes to classical music concerts, these are hassles we often simply accept because "it's always been this way." But the astute entrepreneur sees "it's always been this way" as a great opportunity to improve the customer experience in some tangible way. That's simplifying the hassle map. The next time you go to a concert or interact with some other musical product, make some mental notes of any aspect of the experience that is less than ideal; when you get home, draw out the hassle map and see how you can simplify it. If you can do that in such a way that your product is also more magnetic (i.e., using your creativity and artistry to solve a utilitarian problem), so much the better.

Build a Complete Backstory

The backstory of a product is often critical to its success, yet it is usually not seen by the consumer. The backstory consists of the research and experimentation that took place during a product's development. It's the previous failures and what was learned from them; and it's the reliable functionality and efficiency of the product that ultimately makes it to the marketplace. The ultimate goal of a strong, complete backstory is for the hassle map to be completely eliminated and the product to exist in its optimal form. The backstory then continues for the life of the product as the sum of all the activities required to create and deliver it to its customers. It's the "behind the scenes" things that may not be visible to customers but are nonetheless critical for a successful consumer experience.

It's easy to imagine what the backstory is with a product like the iPhone: the development of the technology, the design process at Apple that led to the iPhone's unique look and user interface, the partnerships with cell phone providers that put the product in customers' hands. But what might the backstory be for the classical music venture?

The backstory for the classical musician is everything that goes into making your musical product the very best it can be. Certainly practice tops the list, but that's only the tip of the iceberg. Every aspect of your performance should be subject to the building of a complete backstory.

For example, how many times have you been to a concert featuring some piece of technology—a live interface for real-time digital processing of sounds or a video that needs to sync up with the music—and something goes wrong? Not only is the experience seriously marred, it's an enormous turnoff to anyone but the most diehard electronic music groupies. For a general audience, used to experiencing multimedia extravaganzas at pop concerts, in their video games, or at a Broadway show, the breakdown of media in the concert hall smacks of amateur hour: they won't be back.

Or how about stage logistics? How often have we watched a concert come to a complete halt—often for five minutes or more—while chairs and instruments on stage are shuffled around between pieces? If the stagehands are professionals, it might go relatively quickly; more often, set changes resemble a scene from the Keystone Cops! Concert veterans accept this as "just the way it is"; musicians on stage will often insist that it's unavoidable. But the fact is that with careful planning and putting greater emphasis on creating a seamless experience for the audience, set changes can, at the least, be dramatically simpler and less distracting—at best they can be used to actually enhance the overall experience. Technology can be reliable. All manner of elements that jar the audience out of their connection with the performance can be modified (or eliminated) in service to creating a more continually engaging experience. But to do so requires time, trial and error, and additional rehearsal time to make everything run smoothly—and that's the backstory for these elements of your product. It's not something you can shortchange if you want every aspect of your product to be its very best.

Let's take a nonperforming backstory: your private teaching studio. Creating a quiet, inviting space in which to receive students and conduct lessons is an important element to have in place if you want to attract and retain students. You could be an awesome teacher but still be turning off your customers if you overlook this key piece of the backstory.

So much of what I've talked about in this book has to do with how your musical product is framed: the venue, how the concert is designed, how the audience's experience is shaped by every aspect of the experience around the music, the space you use for teaching. This backstory is every bit as important to your venture's success as the time you spend in your practice room. As you can see by looking at many products that ultimately failed in the marketplace, failure to build a solid and complete backstory can be your venture's undoing.

Find the Triggers

Often the biggest obstacle to generating consumption of your product is simply human inertia. We get stuck in our regular habits, or we haven't really taken notice of information that's at our disposal. We've been meaning to go check out that new restaurant, but somehow we always end up going to the places we already know. Maybe we're interested in going to that show next Friday, but then the evening arrives and our friend bailed on us and it's been a long week . . . and so we tell ourselves, "Next time." This inaction is not the exception, it's the rule. So how do we motivate potential consumers to overcome their indifference and act? The answer lies in finding the right "trigger"—that thing that moves consumers to engage with your product rather than remain on the sidelines.

We see triggers all around us every day. They're the weekly specials at the supermarket that entice you to buy that cut of meat you love but is normally just a bit too pricey for your budget. They're the "sales events" that happen at key times during the automakers' model year. They're the special financing offers from appliance stores, furniture retailers, and credit cards.

But triggers can be more than just sales or special financial incentives. Sometimes a trigger can reside in making it easier for customers to purchase your product—once again, you see the importance of simplifying the hassle map (or eliminating it altogether). For instance, in the Netflix story, part of the trigger was the simple fact that you no longer had to leave your house to receive and return DVDs. The Netflix trigger was more than just this business model, however; the company's leaders soon realized they needed to design an envelope that would be sure to (1) deliver the DVD in good condition, and (2) ensure that customers put the DVD back and closed up the return envelope such that it was sure to make its way through the mail back to the warehouse. It took literally hundreds of prototypes before the design was perfected. And *even then*, one problem remained: unless you happened to be close to Netflix's warehouse in California, it could still take the better part of a week for your DVD to arrive, and even longer for your next selection to reach you once you returned the first one. Regional warehouses were required to keep delivery and turnaround times as short as possible. *Only then* was the hassle map reduced sufficiently for Netflix to be a significantly better option than going to the local video store. So in the Netflix story, developing the right trigger involved trial and error and a continual process of problem-solving and customer feedback. (Making their trigger work had a full backstory indeed!)

Slywotzky and Weber give a lot of space to the Netflix example because it demonstrates some very important things about triggers. The first is that even the most savvy of businesses require some trial and error to find what works. You have to be willing to experiment and be willing for those experiments to fail (provided you learn the lessons that failure can teach you). And you have to persevere in your efforts, continuing to get feedback from customers and potential customers about what they want from your product and how things can be improved *for them*.

So how do we focus our "trigger experiments" such that we can more effectively find ones that work for our particular venture? As with so many other things, having good data about your customers and what they want/need/expect from your product is a good start. In addition, the differences between hedonic and utilitarian consumption can provide some insights.

To go back to Charters's consumption continuum, with consumption of primarily utilitarian products at one end and primarily aesthetic ones at the other: if you think about the products that exist at various points along the continuum, you'll notice that completely utilitarian ones (the generic brand laundry detergent) are also the ones that are most readily available: a generic laundry detergent will be on the shelves of your local supermarket, discount retailer, bulk retailer, dollar store, and big-chain pharmacy. The hassle map for purchasing such products is virtually nonexistent. You can even order laundry detergent online and have it shipped to your door! Since products like these are so readily available (and with many different brands that are all more or less the same), the most effective triggers are most likely going to revolve around price. Think about it: you're standing in your supermarket aisle looking at generic laundry detergents, and one is on sale or offers 50 percent more for the same price (or some similar sort of savings incentive). If you're already buying generic laundry detergent, then price is already a major factor (perhaps the determining factor) in your purchasing choice; additional savings will likely be an effective trigger for you.

As we move along the consumption continuum toward aesthetic products, however, personal tastes, and/or the hassle map, start to become more important. This is because the more products are specialized and distinctive, the less price becomes the trigger for purchasing them. That's not to say that price is irrelevant; it's simply less likely to be the thing that *triggers* consumers to overcome their ambivalence about a product and make a purchase. For an example of this, let's take Maserati sports cars. There are fewer than twenty dealerships in the United States that sell Maseratis; guess where they are? In major cities with significant affluent populations, of course. Now imagine that you live three hundred miles away from a Maserati dealership but have always wanted one. What's going to motivate you to take the plunge and buy one: the yearly closeout sale or the closest dealership offering to come to you with a test car for you to try out for the day? At this end of the consumption continuum, it's often not price that is the most compelling trigger: it's reducing the hassle map.

What we can take from these examples is another important paradigm shift for those of us in classical music: since our work resides on the hedonic end of the consumption continuum, the most potent triggers for our audiences might be things other than price. That's not to say that discounts or special offers have no place in our classical music venture. (As already noted, it's dangerous to paint our customers with too homogeneous a brush.) But for those folks who are already lovers of classical music and/or belong to a higher socioeconomic class (as much of our audience does), we need to get more creative about what kinds of triggers we try rather than assume that lower prices will always be the solution for our lack of customers.

What would be some examples of the sorts of non-price-centered triggers we might try in the classical music world? Let's recall the National Endowment for the Arts study introduced earlier. If things like socializing, time, childcare, and access to a venue are keeping people from attending arts events, then perhaps we should explore solutions to those problems. In so doing, we are likely to uncover possible triggers that will entice those consumers to attend our event. Perhaps free (or inexpensive) childcare during a concert will entice parents of young children to finally make it to the symphony. If you're a studio teacher, perhaps offering some free master classes at your local school will help potential students experience your teaching and motivate them to sign up. For your chamber music group, perhaps a special concert, tied to some event or issue of importance in your community, will encourage people to come and hear you when a normal concert would not. Finding the right triggers for your venture (and there will likely be more than one if you're doing it right) is another opportunity for fun and creativity to come into play.

For decades at my alma mater, Franklin and Marshall College, there's been a concert of student ensembles on the night of the Super Bowl. Precisely because it's so counterintuitive (the Super Bowl is, after all, the most-watched television event all year), the event has a festive atmosphere, creates a lot of buzz in the community, and provides a fun alternative for folks who are otherwise abandoned by their Super Bowl–watching spouses and friends. The concert brings in a surprisingly big house, consistently surpassing other concerts during the season. In this case, the trigger for the Super Bowl concert resides in its novelty as a fun alternative for those folks who have no interest in watching the game. It only works once a year, but its return year after year proves its effectiveness. The point is, like everything else in the entrepreneurial realm, the particular solution you come up with will be unique to you, your organization, and your artistic voice. Think about how those things can be expressed as "hooks" for your audience, and use trial and error to learn more about what works for them and how best to engage them. The end goal is about more than mere purchases of your product; done well, triggers for consumers at the hedonic end of the spectrum will result in a community of loyal patrons, folks who not only buy your product but share it with their friends and assist you in building a brand of lasting impact.

De-average Your Customers

You may have noticed that the coauthor of *Demand* is Adrian Slywotzky, who wrote "How Symphonies Grew Strong Audiences by Killing the Myth of the Average Consumer," discussed in chapter 3. The theme of that article returns in his book as one of the key factors in stimulating demand: though we tend to look at our customers as possessing more or less the same characteristics, this is rarely the case. While markets are made up of consumers with a shared set of needs and sensibilities, the particulars of how they are best met, the range of psychographics, and the most effective triggers for the individuals in that market may be quite diverse.

One way the needs and sensibilities of our individual customers can vary is in their hassle maps. For the patron who lives within walking distance of your downtown performance venue, transportation issues are irrelevant; the patron who lives in the suburbs feels quite differently. While a cheap ticket might be meaningless to your season subscriber, it might mean a great deal to a student of limited means. And even for those suburban patrons whose hassle maps all include getting into town, the solutions that work best for each one of them might vary.

The orchestra survey Slywotzky first introduced in "Killing the Myth of the Average Customer" drilled down more deeply into the problem of customer "churn" (that is, new attendees not becoming regulars). They found that the audience for the orchestras surveyed fell into several groups, including "core audience" (those who buy a full subscription every year), "trialists" (first-time attendees checking it out), "special event attendees" (they only attend one or two concerts but do so consistently every year), "snackers" (those who buy smaller subscription packages), and "high potentials" (folks who attend multiple concerts but have never subscribed). In other words, despite the common stereotypes regarding the homogeneity of the classical music audience, it's clear that those audiences are, in fact, quite diverse in terms of the nature of their engagement with their local symphonies. This is important because it means that a "one size fits all" approach to engaging those constituencies is not likely to be effective. Instead, there is the need to gather information about what each group wants and expects from the concert experience, how their hassle map might be simplified, and what triggers will most likely motivate them to return more often and more consistently.

The "myth of the average customer" is not just a problem for performing organizations. It applies to every single market out there. And the larger the market, the more diverse it is likely to be. That's not to say that you can always perfectly customize your product to meet the personal idiosyncrasies of each individual customer. But what you can do is make sure you know your customers as thoroughly as possible, note the trends and subgroups that emerge, and be willing to try different things for different constituencies. At all costs, avoid the trap of painting all your customers with the same brush; that's an excellent way for "one size fits all" to become "one size fits none."

Maintain a Steep Trajectory

Successful companies from across the spectrum of industries have a characteristic in common that will be very familiar to us in the classical music world: an ongoing commitment to improving excellence. In the businesses Slywotzky and Weber cite in their book (like tech and manufacturing), continual improvement is critical to keeping ahead of the competition: without regular updates and upgrades, today's must-have piece of technology becomes yesterday's obsolete news. For the manufacturer, ever greater efficiency is a key factor in maintaining profit margins and being able to continue to beat your competitors on price.

For us in the arts, the need for the "steep trajectory" is somewhat different. Because hedonic consumption depends on stimulating emotions and sensibilities and because much of the value of hedonic products resides in their unique or novel quality, we must be sure that we are continuing to grow and improve—both as musicians *and* in all the ways our art is presented to the world. One of the biggest reasons for the stagnation of the classical symphonic music audience lies in the fact that there's essentially no trajectory at all to the orchestral product: it's been more or less unchanged for over a century! Conversely, if you take a look at the classical music organizations that are thriving, you'll see organizations that are constantly trying new things, raising the bar of not just their musical performances but the way they present their music and engage with their audiences. They are continually revisiting their customers' hassle maps and looking for ways to improve them. They're regularly trying out new triggers and evaluating the effectiveness of the ones already in place. And they're experimenting with new artistic content, too, from new repertoire or additional media to innovative venues and exciting collaborations. Maintaining a steep trajectory for our ventures—whether our individual careers or the organizations we're part of—means constantly asking "What can we do better?"

For a real-world example of the six drivers of demand, let's travel to Miami Beach, Florida, home to the New World Symphony. When New World built its new facility in Miami's South Beach, they brought with it a commitment to building an organization that was in sync with the hip, cosmopolitan vibe of their neighborhood. They wanted to live up to the "new world" part of their name, to create an organization that was an active part of the community and not just an edifice that only certain people visited some of the time. They also wanted to embody a broader mission as a leader in the movement to actively reshape both the perception and the reality of the symphony orchestra concert.

Because they were relocating to a building they would design from scratch, New World was in the enviable position of informing every aspect of that process with their mission and vision. So from the outset they realized that they had to do more than build a performance space. Indeed, even a beautiful concert hall in the hip neighborhood of South Beach would not, by itself, unleash a torrent of latent demand for their product. "Build it and they will come" has no place in the entrepreneurial process: either you must have hard data to prove that latent demand is present (and have a very clear understanding of how exactly your venture will satisfy that demand), or you must try to activate inchoate demand through programming, events, outreach, social media, and other tools designed to attract people who didn't previously *know* they wanted to go the symphony. The only way to accomplish the latter is to have a firm understanding of the broader characteristics, sensibilities, and needs of the community you wish to engage, and to use both physical space and programming to reflect those sensibilities.

New World began with the renowned modernist architect Frank Gehry, who designed a building that is both visually stunning and designed to accommodate many different types of presentations and programming. The main concert hall can be arranged in a variety of ways, from a traditional concert stage to one that is in the round. A stunning array of surfaces around the hall allows for sophisticated visuals to be incorporated into the musical experience. The hall is scaled so that even the back row feels intimately close to the performers. The result is that the audience feels enveloped by the performance—as opposed to being passive observers.

This idea of enveloping the audience with the performing experience extends to the exterior, where a large plaza is outfitted with a state-of-the-art audio system that truly brings the sound of the orchestra outdoors. A giant windowed wall allows the public to casually observe rehearsals, while the public spaces of the building are airy and uplifting. Another section of the hall's exterior wall serves as a projection surface so that patrons can have a high-quality experience of concerts from the plaza. The result is that from the moment one sets foot on the New World plaza, one feels surrounded by music and drawn ever more closely into experiencing it.

The architecture was just the beginning, however. Without innovative programming to embody the ideals of Gehry's design, the building would simply be another edifice: visually impressive, perhaps, but standing aloof from the community surrounding it. While music director Michael Tilson Thomas went about exploring new concert formats in New World Center's performing spaces, the rest of the organization set out to encourage more than simple concert attendance; their goal was to become an integral part of their community, to embody both the existing vibrancy and diversity of South Beach and stimulate the continued growth of Miami's artistic ecosystem.

New World then embarked on a series of special offers and events designed to bring in new audiences and, in essence, dissolve the wall (physical and metaphorical) between the orchestra and the broader public—the audience outside the concert hall. Through careful study of their community, they identified a population of young, fit professionals who had limited opportunities for communal experience outside the bustling South Beach nightlife. In order to engage this demographic, however, they would have to come up with some sort of "hook" that would resonate with their existing habits and sensibilities—the right trigger. They came up with two such initiatives.

The first was to designate certain concerts as "bike nights." Patrons who cycled to the concert would be able to store their bikes in a secure area—and then receive a discount on their admission. Another invited people to gather for a mass yoga session while viewing a projection of the concert on the side of the building and listening to the music through the plaza's state-of-the-art audio system. Both proved to be huge successes. The question is, Why?

First, these initiatives were carefully thought through and informed by observing and understanding the dynamics, needs, and sensibilities of the community the organizers were attempting to reach. In the case of the bike nights, cycling around congested South Beach was something New World's target demographic was already doing. But the key to getting those individuals to bike to the symphony and leave their bikes unattended for several hours, at night, even if locked, was another matter in a city with a high level of bike theft. So providing a secure corral for bike patrons was key. The discounted ticket was simply the icing on the cake. Bike night also directly addressed the very real problem of poor parking and high congestion in South Beach. (There's parking and traffic again!) Once they could ride their bikes to the symphony, the ease, security, and financial incentive of bike night resulted in a significant influx of patrons for those performances—patrons who might not have otherwise come at all.

While the yoga events might seem a bit more "out there" than bike night, they worked precisely because of their novelty—a novelty that was in sync with both the artistic product being offered *and* the sensibilities of the young, fitness-conscious community New World was trying to reach. So while this portion of the city's population wouldn't have previously identified a desire for mass yoga at an outdoor plaza with symphonic music piped in from the concert hall, once they experienced it they knew they wanted more. It was a good fit for them because it resonated with their needs—in this case, their social and cultural needs for a shared, unique experience utterly unlike all the other options in their community. The demand for the event didn't manifest until the product was present, but there was still a clear market whose needs were met by that product. And that's what happens with inchoate needs are stimulated. The success of the yoga events benefited New World in other ways, too: the high visibility of these events brought the concert outside the building and spilled it out onto the streets for all to see (and hear). Some yoga attendees were sufficiently moved by the experience to buy a ticket next time and come inside for the full concert experience; meanwhile, some passersby who saw the mass yoga decided to check it out next time. Needs were met, yes, but demand wasn't stimulated until several other key ingredients were added into the mix.

Let's look at the New World examples in terms of the six elements of demand discussed above.

Make it magnetic. New World Symphony performs in a stunning space designed to uplift and inspire patrons. The plaza, with its state-of-the-art sound system, high-quality video projections, and glass-walled rehearsal space, is a place where the casual passerby can interact with the orchestra on a regular basis—and not just when it is performing a concert. Inside the concert hall, intimate seating and sophisticated sound and video make for a unique experience that feels fresh and relevant to the times. The sum total of these and other qualities makes New World a magnetic product for its community; because people can experience something meaningful to them, and in a variety of ways, the New World product is a magnetic one. Rather than needing to "push" customers into the concert hall through traditional marketing, the community is *"pulled" toward it* because of the magnetic nature of the experience they encounter.

Fix the hassle map. Studying the hassle map of their target market revealed two things to the folks at New World. The first was the familiar hassle of traffic and parking, particularly acute in the congested urban zone of Miami's South Beach. Bike night was their solution, encouraging folks to bike to the symphony and avoid the hassles of driving and parking. The second was a more inchoate issue: making it easy to integrate concertgoing into the outdoorsy, fitness-oriented lifestyle of the young professionals New World wished to attract. The yoga allowed patrons to experience the symphony in a casual setting, combining it with something they were going to do anyway: their yoga practice. This combination of ease of access and integration into an established part of the audience's lifestyle made this initiative the perfect match for hundreds of patrons.

Build a complete backstory. The yoga events would not have worked were it not for the extremely high quality of the sound and video available at New World's outdoor plaza. When I visited there a few years back, I could hear music playing as I came down the street toward the New World building. As I got closer, the sound was so good that I was convinced there must be an outdoor concert going on. But when I rounded the corner and surveyed the plaza, there were no musicians to be seen. It was a recording, piped through a web of speakers ingeniously placed throughout the plaza and camouflaged as contemporary-styled lamp posts! The average yoga attendee might not pay attention to the extraordinary quality of the sound, but you can bet that if the sound were as shoddy as most piped-in music outdoors, the events would never have taken off. When I asked my hosts about it, I discovered that New World had contracted with a leading sound designer and a team of technicians to re-create the fidelity of the concert outdoors on the plaza. This, combined with the building's seven-thousand-square-foot projection wall, makes the plaza an outstanding place to experience a New World Symphony concert. These "Wallcast" concerts are not just a novel but poor substitute for the concert inside, they're a unique and quality experience in their own right, made possible by meticulous attention to the quality of the sound and video—an excellent example of a complete backstory that makes all the difference.

Find the triggers. It's important to note that for bike night, the reduced ticket by itself was not enough to make the initiative a success. After all, these folks were presumably already biking around South Beach; how likely was it that the only reason those folks weren't riding to the symphony was the price of the tickets? The real issue—the trigger—was security for their bikes while they were inside (especially if the concert was at night). It's entirely possible that New World might have tried a bike night with only the ticket discount, publicized it, tried to drum up excitement on social media, and then when it flopped concluded that the whole bike thing wasn't going to work. Instead, they paid attention to the needs of bikers and identified the real issue at play: security.

In the case of the yoga events, the trigger was simply a novel and fun event, one that brought together a community of like-minded individuals (yoga practitioners) for an evening of great music, physical/spiritual nourishment, and shared experience.

De-average your customers. While it's plausible that there might be some overlap between yoga attendees and bicyclists, the two initiatives were designed to provide different avenues for different patrons to come to the symphony. Rather than make assumptions about what "their [homogenous] audience" wanted, New World recognized that different segments of their community would respond to different things—and engaged in a diverse range of initiatives to hook them.

Maintain a steep trajectory. The events I've described continue to evolve. The yoga events are now monthly gatherings that take place in the mornings and feature different prominent instructors. Because these events are now using concert recordings, some of the yoga attendees are undoubtedly returning to purchase a ticket for a live concert. And if they aren't, they have a relationship with the organization that builds community visibility and goodwill, essential elements to an orchestra aiming to be an integral part of its community.

Meanwhile, a host of new events can be found via New World's active social media portals, including late-night club events and cocktail receptions (definitely in sync with South Beach's active night life and club scene). A membership program provides free or discounted admission to these events, while nonmembers can still gain access for a reasonable price. The diversity of these events shows that the folks at New World are continuing to advance their community engagement on multiple fronts simultaneously, experimenting to see what works and refining the initiatives that resonate with patrons.

Armed with our understanding of what drives consumption—and with it, demand—we can see how the entrepreneurial process can take our products from the idea stage to being launched in the marketplace. Understanding the drivers of demand also underscores the critical importance of observing the dynamics and sensibilities of our audiences, replacing assumptions about what they want and expect with as much data as possible. We can see the importance of experimentation and the willingness to try something that fails—a process entrepreneurs embrace but musicians often find daunting. And, perhaps most important, we see how the integrity of our art remains of paramount importance: while "being entrepreneurial" may begin with such "non-artsy" concepts as understanding the needs of the market and how to stimulate demand for our products, in the end it still boils down to creative problem-solving. How do I make my product magnetic? How do I develop compelling triggers? What new things can I try to keep my art fresh, vibrant, and relevant in my community? These are all creative challenges. And who better to envision creative, nonconventional, buzz-creating solutions than an artist?

EXERCISE: MAKE A HASSLE MAP

To develop your ability to create a hassle map, start with a product or service with which you are very familiar. Where are the "pain points" in the process of purchasing and experiencing that product? Then, literally map out these issues to visually show where they show up in the process, and then begin thinking about how the hassle map for that product could be improved. Try this exercise for a product you find easy to use and one that has a large hassle map: paying attention to how companies do this well can be as illuminating as studying the ones that don't. Finally, talk to your customers (or potential customers) and find out where the hassle points are in your own venture: listen carefully to what you hear, even if it's hard to accept!

EXERCISE: EXPLORE THE SIX DRIVERS OF DEMAND

Take a product/service you admire and work through each of Slywotzky and Weber's six drivers of demand: how is this product magnetic, how was the hassle map simplified, etc. Then try the exercise again with a product you know of that has failed or is currently struggling in the marketplace. Finally, look at the arts organizations in your community—both the ones that are thriving and those that are struggling. What insights do the six drivers of demand give you about why these companies are flourishing (or not)?

EXERCISE: PLAY WITH THE CONSUMPTION/DEMAND MATRIX

List the various musical activities you engage in, identify the products associated with them, and then see where those products fall in the consumption/demand matrix. What elements of your product are hedonic in nature, and which are utilitarian? Can you identify sources of latent (unmet) demand for existing products? What inchoate needs/sensibilities might you exploit to unleash demand for something new and novel related to your musical activities?

CHAPTER 5

A Dream with a Plan

Five Questions and an Imperative

The funny thing about fortune cookies is how often they contain a message that actually resonates with some aspect of our lives. Shortly after I started teaching entrepreneurship at the University of Colorado I got one that perfectly expressed the reason why aspiring music professionals need to acquire entrepreneurial tools. It said: "A dream is just a dream. A goal is a dream with a plan."

As musicians, most of us do not lack for dreams about what our career might look like. Whether we dream about fame or performing at the highest level in a particular genre or building a teaching studio of talented students, we can usually identify pretty quickly the "ideal career" for ourselves. And while having goals and aspirations is a good (and necessary) thing, if we don't have a clear sense of how to proceed toward those goals we're only setting ourselves up for frustration and disappointment. In this we once again see the value of entrepreneurship, which is designed to help us develop a process by which we can realize our goals. If the tiny cookie fortune had had more space, it could just as easily have said "*Entrepreneurship* is a dream with a plan."

Previous chapters have discussed what constitutes an entrepreneurial mindset, the traits of entrepreneurial action, how to identify and articulate your value by exploring the entrepreneur's maxim, and the dynamics behind the act of consumption. It's now time to draw together all these concepts into a simple and coherent process for developing and implementing an entrepreneurial idea. I call this process "five questions and an imperative."

Why questions? Doesn't describing a process usually consist of a series of steps (do this, then do this, then do this)? Well, as already discussed, entrepreneurship is not about generating a predetermined outcome. It's not like a recipe in which combining a set of ingredients in the proper amounts and sequence will generate the desired result. For entrepreneurship, the only measure of success is whether or not you've unlocked value for your product in a given marketplace. How that plays out is entirely defined by you, the entrepreneur. So rather than characterizing the entrepreneurial process as a set of prescriptive steps, I frame the process as a series of questions that every aspiring entrepreneur must answer; those answers, in turn, inform the next step in the process. (Besides, entrepreneurs are always asking questions anyway, so it seems appropriate for the entrepreneurial process to embody that form!) Answers to these questions might not always come easily, but that's also the point of asking them: working through tough questions is almost always a prerequisite for success in any endeavor, and especially in entrepreneurship. Answering these questions will also engage your strategic observation, opportunity recognition, customer focus, flexibility/adaptability, risk assessment, resourcefulness, and storytelling skills in service to your idea—or, as often as not, a new and better idea that emerges from the process. As you address each question in the entrepreneurial process, therefore, be sure to keep one of your eyes on ways your idea might be improved, modified, or even replaced by something that is more feasible, does a better job of meeting the needs of your customers, or is a better or more inspiring use of your skills. If there was ever a field in which knowledge is best acquired by asking and answering questions, it's entrepreneurship.

THE FIVE QUESTIONS

Question 1: What Do I Have to Offer?

We begin the entrepreneurial process by taking stock of our own gifts, skills, and passions (and those of our team or group if we're working with others). After all, before we can begin planning our entrepreneurial endeavors, we have to know what we care about, what we bring to the table, and what gaps exist in our knowledge or experience that we might need to address.

A good way to take inventory of your skills is to combine two exercises my colleague David Cutler uses in his book *The Savvy Musician*. The first is to ask yourself what you're passionate about. What things really get you excited? (These can be musical things or, often just as important, nonmusical things.) What kind of impact do you want to make in the world? What's the one thing you want to accomplish before you die? (How's that for a stimulating question!) Beginning with these questions helps put everything that comes after in perspective, and reminds us why we're engaging in this process to begin with: if we're not about trying to realize our dreams, there's not much point.

If you have a specific dream, make note of that for sure. But also note broader things like a love for teaching, or working with young children, or public service, or certain pressing issues in society. Cast the net more widely than just your musical/professional dreams because these other passions can often provide entry points for our music or can combine to create unique opportunities for our talents to find value.

Cutler's second exercise involves assembling a skills inventory in four categories. I've modified the fourth category ("distinctive skills" replaces Cutler's "unique skills") and added a fifth:

> Primary musical skill(s)
> Secondary musical skills
> Nonmusical skills
> Distinctive skills
> Areas for growth/improvement

When giving this assignment to students, I've found that most do not have any problems with their primary and secondary musical skills. "I'm mainly a violinist, but I'm also pretty strong on the piano and have done some conducting." Pretty straightforward, right?

Nonmusical skills can sometimes trip us up, though. I've actually had students assert that they didn't have any skills outside music! But of course, once you spend some time thinking about it, you'll absolutely find skills you possess and perhaps take for granted. Maybe you're a whiz in the kitchen, a great public speaker, or an empathetic listener. Maybe there's a sport or other hobby you excel at, or you're proficient in languages. Perhaps you've had some experience with Photoshop or had a summer job one year in which you learned spreadsheets backward and forward. It doesn't matter what these nonmusical skills are, and the more you can identify the better. Remember: at this stage in the entrepreneurial process, you don't yet know for certain what your venture is ultimately going to look like. Sometimes the very process of identifying the range and depth of your skills can inform your vision for the future. If nothing else, it will help you determine what sorts of things you can do yourself and what things you might need outside help for.

Cutler's category "unique skills" is perhaps the hardest to define. Because it's so often misused, it's worth recalling that the word "unique" means "*singularly* distinctive." And while we are all unique individuals, few of us possess any specific skills that are *truly* "unique" (i.e., the *only* person in the world with that skill). I've therefore tweaked this category just a bit, renaming it "distinctive skills": what skills help define your individuality and set you apart from others in your field? While the answer to this question might be some obscure skill or knowledge that few others have, more likely the things that make you distinctive consist of some *combination* of things. For instance, a good friend of mine is an outstanding conductor, a visionary theatre director, and a gourmet baker of bread—and all of those things have played a role in his creative life (even the bread-baking!). I have degrees in both geology and music, a combination that may not be truly "unique," but it's something that distinguishes me from most other composers and is something I've used to my own entrepreneurial (and artistic) advantage. Perhaps you are equally proficient on more than one instrument—again, something that may not be unique but is of great value in places like community music schools or the musical theater pit. These examples illustrate how the category "distinctive skills" is in some ways the most important, because, as a later question will show, distinguishing yourself from your competition is a critical part of entrepreneurial success.

Before leaving this step, check yourself by running your skills inventory past some people who know you well: they'll likely remind you of some things you've missed or perhaps point out something you didn't even realize you possessed!

Question 2: What Problem/Need Exists in the Marketplace That I Can Address with My Skills, Resources, and Passions?

This book has already talked a lot about the question of "need," and that's because defining the problem or need is in some ways the most important step in the entrepreneurial process—and one of the most challenging for musicians to articulate. Remember that needs are at the center of the entrepreneur's maxim: it's in the meeting of needs that value is unlocked. You'll also recall that needs exist on a continuum between purely utilitarian and hedonic (aesthetic/existential) and that some products (especially ones related to the arts) may embody multiple needs simultaneously and at different points along the utilitarian-hedonic continuum. And while it's true that identifying a need and then determining the fulfillment of it can often run together as virtually simultaneous acts, I've separated them into two discrete steps in the entrepreneurial process. It's critically important that you fully understand in every way the need you are addressing before you decide on the best way to address it.

Keeping these things in mind, we can identify three parameters of a need that we must work through in order to properly address this second step in the entrepreneurial process. These are:

> WHAT problem are you solving?
> WHO has this problem/need?
> WHY does this problem/need exist?

Though I've been using the phrases "meeting a need" and "solving a problem" to mean essentially the same thing, I use "solving a problem" for this stage of the entrepreneurial process with great intention. Putting the first question in the shape of a problem forces us to go beyond the all-too-simple answer "people's need for music." This is because, unless your chosen market has no access to music *whatsoever*, consumers are likely to be already filling their need for music in some other form. So asserting that your clarinet playing will meet people's need for music doesn't really get you anywhere; you have to ask: *Why do people need YOUR music? What is it that makes what YOU do so special?*

Answering these questions is admittedly hard, especially for classical musicians, who are not generally trained to develop a unique, distinctive voice (at least, not one that is identifiable by audiences outside the profession). But getting too caught up in this question is something of a red herring: while your playing, by itself, might not stand out as radically different from everyone else's, you can still find ways to meet the needs of your audience through the use of your unique, distinctive personality and the other gifts, skills, and passions you bring to the table. Here we come back to the idea that audiences' needs extend far beyond the existential need for shared, aesthetically oriented experiences. Their needs are both broader than that and more subtle.

Needs are more broad in the sense I've discussed before: every aspect of an experience can influence whether or not someone finds it valuable, including a whole range of utilitarian needs such as parking, adequate restrooms, the comfort of the seating, and many others. It might be in addressing these needs that you can stimulate demand—and value—for your musical venture.

The need for shared, aesthetically oriented experiences is not met by just *any* experience, either. If it were, then attendance at classical music concerts would not be in decline, and a ticket to a Chicago Symphony concert would command the same price as one to see Taylor Swift. In the Brooklyn Rider example, the key audience need that is being met is to have a compelling, holistic experience, one in which the audience feels like it has gone on a journey *with* the performers rather than passively observing a performance. For a group like Brooklyn Rider, *connection* is the primary driving need being addressed.

So you have to go deeper into the question of what, exactly, is the need you're addressing through your particular product, and posing that question as a problem helps you get to a more useful answer. Maybe the problem you're solving is that there are no music teachers in a community—find out why and then ponder solutions. Perhaps there is no orchestra in your city because there is no proper facility for one to perform in—so you come up with a creative way to address that without having to raise millions for a concert hall. Or maybe the need is more subtle, further down on the existential end of the spectrum of needs. Perhaps, like Brooklyn Rider, you recognize that the classical music experience needs to continue to grow and evolve with our times, that audiences today are looking for live concert experiences in which they are more actively engaged. Perhaps your own experience has given you insights into some specific things that can help audiences feel less passive in the concert experience, help them feel like they're joining you in a journey. Now you're in the territory of solving a problem (the disconnected nature of most classical music concerts), because only now are you beginning to think of your musical activity as filling a need for someone *else*.

If you're feeling right about now that you don't have any insights into how you might create a unique musical product, go back to the method of strategic observation discussed in chapter 1. If you're interested in a new concert format, spend some time going to concerts and observing what works and what doesn't. Talk to members of the audience—and not just the regulars: seek out people who are attending for the first time or who look a little uncomfortable or out of place. Find out what *they're* feeling about the experience. Take note of accomplished individuals in your field and spend some time learning what elements constitute a potent and compelling stage presence. Talk to enthusiastic audience members to find out what they love about the experience, and try to catch a person leaving at intermission to find out why she or he has packed it in.

If you're wanting to be a teacher, observe how teaching operates in your community, and ask yourself what you might offer that's distinct and personal. Identify the traits of successful teachers (as well as less successful teachers), and be intentional about interacting with those who employ different styles from the ones you're used to. Then draw your own conclusions about which practices are the best reflection of your gifts and will best serve the students you seek.

Let's say you're thinking of starting a music camp; visit as many as possible and study both what tends to work and where problems tend to emerge. Talk to potential campers about what they want to get out of their experience (both the kids and their parents). And take note of how you might apply your own gifts, skills, and passions to make a better, more effective, or more fun music camp for all.

In other words, whatever your particular field, instrument, or area of focus, study success stories to understand why they've succeeded. And ask yourself what those who fall short of greatness lack. Use your powers of inquiry, observation, and reflection to gain a fuller understanding of the complex dynamic between the musical product and those who consume it. You'll begin to develop a deeper and more comprehensive understanding of the needs of your customers and the problems you can solve for them, and you'll likely uncover completely new needs and problems you hadn't considered before. (Perhaps, rather than another music camp for kids, what's really needed is a music camp for *adults*.)

Identifying the *What* of a need, challenging though that is, is not sufficient, however. In order to address a need successfully, we also have to know *Who* has it and *Why*. Once again, you can see how needs at the utilitarian end of the spectrum are easier to articulate. For instance, if you've identified that a lack of parking is a problem, then it's pretty easy to see that it's drivers who have that problem and that they have it, well, because they're driving to the concert and there's no place to park. But as soon as you move down toward the existential end of the needs spectrum, things get murkier. As noted earlier, we can assert that "everyone" has the need for a compelling live music experience, but that doesn't really get us very far: does *any particular* art form reach "everyone"? So again, we have to dig deeper, and again, our powers of strategic observation help us do so. Identify a range of events in your community—not just classical music concerts—and observe who goes to them. If you're fortunate enough to have the opportunity to see a nonstandard classical music group, go to every show you can and make careful observations of the audience demographic. Who's there—and who's not? Talk with them: why did they come? Would they do it again?

What's most important about this process is that you avoid making assumptions about what people need, who those people are, and why they have that need. Nowhere is an assumption more dangerous than in determining the dynamics of the need you are addressing. More often than not, the people we assume want something may not, and the reason an existing problem hasn't been addressed might be more complex than is apparent at first glance. For example, I'm often surprised by the age and socioeconomic diversity of new music concerts: the common assumption that the older classical music crowd doesn't like new music is repeatedly debunked. Yet that assumption still prevails in much of the classical music world. Another common assumption is that young people don't come to the symphony because tickets are too expensive—yet those same young folks will happily save up for months to buy a ticket to a pop show that costs five times as much. Clearly, there's something driving their decision other than the price of the ticket. Making assumptions about the needs and sensibilities of your target market is a very easy trap to fall into, and you must be forever vigilant in avoiding it.

If assumptions are the entrepreneur's curse, then data and strategic observation are the entrepreneur's salvation. Use every resource at your disposal, from online research to conversations with potential customers, to make sure your characterization of the need—what it is, who has it, and why it exists—is grounded in reality.

Carefully working through the three parameters of "need" can take considerable time, research, and contemplation. But it's critical that you don't shortcut this step in the process. Take the time required, be careful to avoid assumptions, and verify your conclusions with data whenever possible. Run your ideas past trusted colleagues and potential customers. Make sure you fully understand the dynamics of the need you're addressing before moving on. Failure to do so will seriously hamper—if not downright doom—your efforts moving forward. Clarity with this step, on the other hand, will be the foundation of everything that follows. Make sure the foundation is a solid one.

Question 3: What Is a Solution to That Problem/Need That Utilizes My Distinct Artistic Voice?

Having identified a problem/need, the next step is, obviously, to come up with a solution. Recall that entrepreneurial action can take one of two forms: "direct" entrepreneurship (identifying an unmet need and developing a new product/service to meet that need—the smartphone example) and "applied" entrepreneurship (an existing product is delivered in an entrepreneurial way—the teacher who employs the entrepreneurial process to launch and build her studio). "Direct" entrepreneurship usually involves some sort of innovation—something that redefines the market, either through something completely new or the novel use of something already in existence. At the very least, it will address customer needs through a product with emergent properties that combines existing concepts or functions in new or novel ways. "Applied" entrepreneurship generally does not require a paradigm-shifting innovation; it operates in an existing market and meets needs through traditional methods. In either case, the five questions of the entrepreneurial process are the same—only the answers will be different.

Chapter 4 introduced the consumption/demand matrix to illustrate the relationship between needs and the demand for products that meet them. To help us sort out what type of entrepreneurship our venture will encompass, let's visit the last of the entrepreneurial matrices, the needs/action matrix, which shows the relationship between needs and their fulfillment through either direct or applied entrepreneurship (fig. 5.1).

The needs/action matrix demonstrates how an arts-based venture can conceivably operate in any one of the four quadrants, or perhaps more than one simultaneously. Existential needs can be met by the creation and/or presentation of completely new paradigms of art (Brooklyn Rider, eighth blackbird, Alarm Will Sound, and many others) or by established channels (a traditional symphony orchestra, chamber group, or opera company that performs existing repertoire or performs new works in a traditional way). On the left side of the matrix, known utilitarian needs can be met by delivering their established fulfillments to a market that currently does not have access to them (applied action that fulfills latent demand) or by devising a new type of fulfillment (direct action that stimulates inchoate demand).

Let's go to Broadway to look at some examples for the four quadrants of the needs/action matrix. At the lower right we have a standard musical, *Fiddler on*

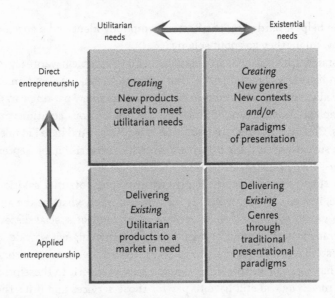

Figure 5.1 The needs/action matrix

the Roof. In the upper right is the groundbreaking hit *Hamilton*, with its innovative mix of genres and unique take on its subject. At the lower left is the standard-issue printed program *Playbill*, which provides information on the production and cast.

What about the upper left quadrant? In all the examples given so far, we haven't talked much about that part of the needs/action matrix: meeting utilitarian needs in new and innovative ways. This quadrant is of special interest to us in the arts because it might very well be a key piece to creating an identity and presence in our community/market that is distinctive, memorable, and compelling. What we're talking about here is a utilitarian need—one whose fulfillment probably doesn't *require* an artistic or creative approach—and meeting that need in a new, creative way, a way that also helps define to your audience who you are. The creative element—and perhaps even an artistic element—exists in the solution, one that creates emergent properties through new and novel combinations of familiar elements. For the Broadway example, the upper left quadrant might be something like a new app that provides online access to all the content of *Playbill*—and then goes beyond that to create an online community made up of lovers of Broadway shows.

Remember the study a group of orchestras undertook to better understand their audiences, particularly why first-time attendees often did not return? You'll recall that the leading reason was parking and that it was particularly acute for the Boston Symphony; lack of parking and just the logistics of driving in the city center created a significant disincentive for repeat visits. So with the help of hard data, the Boston Symphony identified a specific problem. How might they go about solving it?

For starters, it's reasonable to assume that if the problem were easy to solve, it would have already been solved. But when we're talking about an already-developed downtown (no room to simply slap up a new parking garage) and the complex infrastructure of an entire city, the obvious solutions are non-starters. Clearly a more creative solution is required. (And here I'm taking the real-life survey and turning it into a hypothetical exercise in entrepreneurial problem-solving.)

Let's start with the factors at play with various potential solutions. For instance, if access by automobile is the problem, then what are the alternate ways to get to Symphony Hall? Perhaps some kind of special discount for public transportation could be created, or a partnership with a ride-sharing service, so that symphony patrons could get to their destination without personally having to drive there. There might be some merit to these proposals, though *somebody* will still have to pay for those services and if it's the symphony, that may not be such a great solution: over the course of the season, the bus fares or ride-sharing charges for hundreds of patrons (or even several thousand) would get expensive fast! Something like valet service might help with the parking issue, but newbie patrons might not be willing to pay an additional fee for that luxury.

These solutions, and many others like them, might be worth researching further and perhaps gathering some more data to gauge viability. Depending on what you find, you might decide that you've found something that will make a significant dent in the problem.

But that's just scratching the surface. Might there be a way to not just "solve the problem" but actually make a positive contribution to the organization's artistic mission? Is there a way to tackle this problem in a creative way, something that would give voice to the Boston Symphony's artistry while also solving a logistical problem that needs to be addressed? These are questions for our entrepreneurial muse to address, in the hope of finding ways to create an experience for customers that is *holistically artistic*. The art we present is at the center of that experience, but it could now be contextualized such that the entire experience is compelling, fun, artistically engaging, and in support of the music we perform.

So here's an idea: let's say the Boston Symphony launches an "Art Bus" that travels around the city to pick up folks, bringing food trucks, a mobile bar, and a flatbed with musicians performing in tow (weather permitting). Perhaps the price is the equivalent of an evening of parking downtown. Décor, drink choices, and volunteer docents would all be designed to set the stage for the music being presented that evening. Partnerships with local restaurants and bars would result in publicity for them—and low-cost food and drink for the Bus. There's virtually no end to the variety and fun that could be had with each unique, custom-designed Art Bus excursion. Such a solution not only would address the mundane need for more convenient ways to get downtown but also would become a "thing" in and of itself, creating buzz and fun and making a creative and artistic contribution to the overall experience.

The Art Bus also illustrates the second half of question 3—"that utilizes my distinct artistic voice." It's these words that cut right to the heart of the question so many musicians struggle with: *Where does my creative identity fit within the entrepreneurial process?* One of the most potent places our creativity drives entrepreneurial activity is right here, at the problem-solving stage. It's in solving problems that we activate the creative tools, such as "conceptual combination" (discussed in chapter 2). It's in the problem-solving stage that brainstorming with "three good friends and a couple six-packs of beer" comes into play. It's also at this stage that the entrepreneurial quality of "authenticity" is critical because the more your solution reflects your unique personality, your unique voice, the more powerfully it will resonate with your audience and distinguish your product from everyone else's. And in the world of the arts, distinctiveness and personality are essential. It's an important reminder that the purpose of entrepreneurship in an artistic context is to create value for your creative voice, to empower your muse to find *artistically fulfilling* ways to support your professional life. Moreover, your distinctive characteristics are essential to distinguishing yourself from everyone else in the field. It might be that the Art Bus isn't the right solution for Boston; on further study, there might be any number of reasons why it's not the best idea. (One that springs to mind is the simple fact that a lot of the Boston Symphony's season takes place during the winter months, when the weather would likely put a significant damper on the festivities.) The point is, looking at the problem-solving stage as an inherently creative endeavor will yield far more interesting and compelling solutions to the challenge at hand, all the while activating your artistic voice beyond just your music making.

A fun example of this is the Pittsburgh New Music Ensemble, one of the nation's oldest ensembles devoted exclusively to new music. (Full disclosure: I was executive director of this ensemble from 2003 to 2007 and am still the company's president.) When the ensemble moved to a summer season in 2002 and began its first concerts without their founder, David Stock, they wanted to reboot their brand such that it honored Stock's legacy but also launched a new chapter in the company's life. As part of this initiative, a new logo featuring the colors black and lime green was designed; to reinforce the new brand, the colors were incorporated not just into marketing materials but also into the staging of the concerts themselves. The presence of lime green soon became a "thing": performers incorporated it into their concert dress, folks started to look for ways in which lime green would show up in the ensemble's new theatrical stagings of music. After a season or two, patrons began wearing lime green to concerts—and soon began to be known as "Limers." The color was becoming an essential part of the organization's brand.

In 2004, the company identified a problem that needed to be addressed: its unique "theatre of music" approach to presenting concerts (which I'll discuss more in chapter 6) was hard to describe to people who had never experienced it. Once they came, though, they were usually hooked (an example of inchoate demand if ever there was one). So how could the ensemble solve the rather straightforward need to get more first-time attendees in the door? With no money for a traditional marketing campaign (not to mention money to create media that could accurately convey the experience to begin with), the group decided to look at it as a creative problem. Something quite new, something bold and perhaps even a little crazy, needed to be devised. The buzz created from it would be its own marketing. If it failed, there was nothing lost; if it succeeded, not only would attendance be boosted, but the ensemble's brand— its identity in the eyes of its patrons and the community at large—would be enhanced as well. In pondering a solution, the group relied on a key piece of information about their audience: the profound enthusiasm and loyalty of their existing patrons. So they focused in on that as an asset that could possibly be leveraged. What was the best way to do that? The solution was the "First Limer" program. Anyone who was attending for the first time got in for free (in exchange for contact information, of course), while any *existing* patron who brought a First Limer got in for half price; if they brought two, they got in for free as well. (Though I implemented the First Limer program with abandon, I can't claim credit for its creation. Credit resides with our artistic team, something itself worth noting: the solution to a "business" problem was, in essence, an artistic one—and took on a life of its own driven by artistic impulses, not "business" ones.)

The program was a huge success: attendance nearly doubled the first season it was implemented and has continued to grow. Of equal importance, however, is the way that the First Limer program contributed to the group's organizational identity. Being a Limer was becoming a point of pride. Patrons competed with each other to see who could bring the most First Limers. Others tried to see if they could manage to bring two new people to every show and thus see the entire season for free. Whatever ticket revenue was lost by such tactics was more than made up by returning First Limers, who would then have to start paying for their tickets. Soon donors and important volunteers were called "Key Limers," and the extraordinary group of artists making up the ensemble became "The Lime Green Dream Team." Fundraising goals were presented by adding limes to a giant fishbowl. Postconcert receptions incorporated various lime-themed snacks and drinks. The playful incorporation of all things lime evolved into a central part of the organization's identity— as well as that of its audience. Through this initiative, and the many rituals that sprang from it, the ensemble began to build a sense of *community* for its audience. And community is the key ingredient to building and sustaining a thriving cohort of patrons for your art.

The First Limers story is a great illustration of how we can exercise our creativity to solve otherwise mundane problems. There was no shortage of guides and consultants out there who would have been happy to advise the Pittsburgh New Music Ensemble on how to build their audience, and all of it would have been very standard arts admin fare. That is, those tactics would not have been any different from what every other arts organization in town was doing. But the Lime Green tactic proved to be so effective (and, I believe, was more effective than a traditional approach would ever have been) precisely *because* it was different from the standard tactics. Moreover, it was an *authentic reflection* of the artistic voice of the organization: fun, a little quirky, and absolutely unique. And the continued incorporation of the theme is an ongoing creative endeavor for everyone involved in the company. It's an extension of their own artistry. This is the entrepreneurial muse at its best: engaging a problem *through* one's artistic voice. In this approach, the use of mailers, social media, brochures, and all the rest becomes a supporting mechanism for something bigger—making them far more potent and effective. Said another way, more brochures and mailers and whatnot, by themselves, did not have much of an impact in attracting new patrons; using those tools to communicate a novel idea driven by an artistic impulse most certainly did.

And so, as we contemplate solutions to the problem/need identified in question 2, we can see how the intersection of creative expression and problem-solving serves both entrepreneurial and artistic ends. And the more our creativity is given free rein, the more power it has to engage the people we're trying to reach—and create value for the art we're presenting. If you're unsure of how to start the process of creative problem-solving, take the information you've acquired in question 2 and stir it into the pot of your own interests, passions, and sensibilities: you might be surprised at the delicious, unique stew that will result!

Understanding the nature of your solution (does it meet a utilitarian need or an existential one?) and how it interfaces with your market (through direct or applied entrepreneurship?) brings important clarity to the question of how to proceed with your venture. Next up: feasibility and implementation.

Question 4: Is My Solution Financially and Logistically Feasible and Sustainable?

Here is the point where the entrepreneurial process turns from strategic observation, creative problem-solving, and engaging our distinctive qualities to more practical questions. How will I make money? What are my costs? Do the numbers add up? Can I sustain this endeavor over the long run?

The answers to these questions make up what's called your "business model." Simply put, your business model describes how you'll make money (income), the resources required to operate (physical, financial, etc.), defining your market (who are your customers, how many of them are there, and how you will reach them and interact with them), what your primary activities will be, and whether or not you require any external partners or relationships to operate your venture. Addressing each of these components of your business model will help you determine whether or not the venture is feasible. Are the costs too high to be recouped? Can you reach enough customers to make the venture worthwhile, and if so, how will you reach them? How much will your customers be willing to pay, and can you generate enough revenue at that price point to make a profit? (Seeking to start a not-for-profit venture? Take note: even not-for-profit ventures must have a business model with math that adds up! Even if your motivation isn't to get rich, you still need a business model that is viable and sustainable over the long run.)

These components are elegantly portrayed in the Business Model Canvas, an open-source tool for organizing your business model and seeing how the various parts relate to each other. You can see how the Canvas works and is laid out in appendix 3.

Of course, the Business Model Canvas is only as good as the information you put into it, so, once again, we come to the need for careful research and avoiding unsubstantiated assumptions. Much of this research, such as estimating costs for materials or rental space, can be done relatively easily via the Internet. General market analysis, including things like demographic information and geographical distribution, is also just a few clicks away. But, as already discussed, subtler issues like determining the precise needs of your customers, setting a price for your product, and determining how much of it they will consume over a given period of time requires more granular data than we can easily pull off the Internet. It requires honest feedback from real people. This data complements and enhances your own observations and experiences to give you a much fuller and more accurate picture of how realistic your business model is.

Of course, just as our Canvas is only as good as the information we put into it, the data we use is only good if we are thorough and unbiased in gathering it. Here are a few traps entrepreneurs can fall into when they're gathering and analyzing data on their target market.

Data Gathering Flaws

Flaw 1: Sample Size

When starting up a venture, it can be difficult to engage prospective customers to find out what they want, need, and are willing to pay. Consequently, novice entrepreneurs may only talk to a handful of easily identified prospects. The problem, of course, is that such a small sample may produce wildly divergent results (which won't be useful) or, by chance, misleadingly consistent ones. There isn't any hard-and-fast rule here (unless your venture is aimed at a sufficiently large market to warrant a formal statistical analysis of your results), but what I would suggest is to think about the capacity of your venture: if you're looking to open a studio that will have forty students, you'd probably want to talk to at *least* fifteen prospects. If that number doesn't reveal any clear trends, then find another ten. The point is that just talking to half a dozen folks (especially if they already know you) likely will not give you an accurate view of even a small, local market.

Flaw 2: The Sample Misrepresents the Market

Targeting the right individuals for your research is perhaps even more important than the size of your sample. For instance, if your teaching studio targets adolescents and you want to find out how much to charge, you want to be sure you talk to the *parents*: after all, they are the ones who will be paying for the lessons, not your students. The targeting of your survey should be directed toward the individual(s) who will actually be making the purchase.

Flaw 3: Asking the Wrong Questions

A common pitfall in gathering customer feedback is that we either ask the wrong question or ask it in the wrong way. For instance, rather than saying "Would you pay $10 for this product?" you should ask something like "Do you feel that $10 for this product is Extremely high / Quite high / Somewhat high / About right / Somewhat low / Quite low / Extremely low?" If your business model requires repeated purchase of your product (as in a monthly fee for lessons), the issue isn't just about whether or not your target customers will pay $50 for a lesson; it's equally important to ask "Would you pay $200/month for four lessons on a monthly basis?" The online survey company Survey Monkey has an excellent guide to wording questions such that you get the most useful data possible.

Flaw 4: Tipping Your Hand—Asking the Right Questions in the Wrong Way

Related to the questions we ask is the problem of interview bias. If you're conducting your survey in person (which can provide a valuable opportunity for immediate follow-up or additional feedback), the way you conduct the dialogue can bias the response. Are you leading the respondent in a certain direction with your body language? Are you registering disappointment in your reactions to the respondent's comments? If you're conducting the survey yourself, you must be very careful to put on your poker face and do everything you can to ensure you're getting an honest and unbiased response. If you can get objective, third-party individuals to conduct your interviews, even better. Collecting bad data can be just as damaging (or even moreso) than collecting no data at all.

Data Analysis Flaws

Flaw 1: Confirmation Bias

A very easy trap to fall into when it comes to gathering and analyzing data is to subconsciously give greater weight and importance to the data that confirms what you already believe or hope to find. We see examples of this all the time in our social media: we tend to search for, notice, and recall the posts, articles, or memes we already agree with, while we tend not to seek out or notice the ones that don't. Over time, this reinforces our notion that our opinions and beliefs are the correct ones, to the exclusion of opposing opinions and beliefs. The same thing can happen as you try to analyze the viability of your product in the marketplace: if you are passionately convinced that folks are going to go wild for your venture, you are likely to place greater value on feedback that confirms that rather than feedback that does not.

Flaw 2: The "Semmelweis Effect"

Related to the problem of confirmation bias is what's known as the "Semmelweis effect," in honor of Ignaz Semmelweis, the Hungarian physician who noted that handwashing helped reduce the instances of disease in his community. Because this correlation predated Pasteur's work on germs, Semmelweis's colleagues in the medical field rejected his data: they simply couldn't see how washing their hands could possibly make a difference to patients. The "Semmelweis effect" (sometimes called the "Semmelweis reflex") is therefore the refusal to accept data that confounds conventional wisdom or contradicts established norms. This is a big problem in the world of classical music, where assumptions about who makes up our audience and what they want are rampant and deeply entrenched. So while numbers may not "lie," how we collect and interpret them can cause us to reach the wrong conclusions.

Forecasting and Financial Projections

Related to the challenge of collecting sound data on what the people in your market want, how much of your product they will consume, and how much they'll pay for it is the task of making reasonable forecasts of income—both in terms of the sources of that income and the amount of it. There's no doubt that as you start out, some guesswork is required: after all, nobody can predict the future. The trick is to make that guesswork as informed with hard data as possible.

As with the phenomenon of confirmation bias, we must be careful not to let our optimism get the better of us. Let's say, for instance, that you've identified the potential market for your product as consisting of one thousand people in your community; let's also say that this number is based on good data and constitutes a reasonable estimate of your target market size. What comes next is critical: how many of those one thousand people are actually going to consume your product? As chapter 4 revealed, many factors are involved with converting a need in the marketplace to a demand for your product. So even if you make what you think is a conservative estimate for that conversion—say, 2 percent—you could still be way off.

Another common mistake is business models that rely on unrealistic projections of growth to make their ventures viable—and if those projections fail to materialize, things disintegrate quickly. I often see students predict growth of 10, 20, or even 30 percent a year. High growth numbers like these are probably not very realistic. If your venture is being introduced to a large market that you are confident will embrace it, you might achieve high growth numbers in your first few years, but that kind of growth is not likely to continue over the long haul. So if your business model requires high growth just to be viable, proceed with caution.

So, once again, you must be sure you're not just pulling numbers out of the air, even if you think they're conservative: make sure your estimates are supported by as much data as possible, and the more personalized that data is (i.e., from individual people as opposed to extrapolating data from broad statistics) the more useful it will be. This, in turn, will help make your estimates and forecasts more reasonable as well. Then, err on the side of *underestimating* market size rather than *overestimating* it.

Understanding Your Margins

The next important component in determining the viability of your business model concerns *margins*—the size of the gap between what it costs to make your product and what you can charge for it. Low-margin business models, where the gap between the cost of each individual product-unit and the sale price is a small one, require two things to thrive. The first is maximizing efficiencies during production so as to make the per-unit cost as low as possible. The second is high volume, particularly when increased volume doesn't add considerable costs. (Once you've built a factory and hired workers, producing ten thousand widgets doesn't cost appreciably more than producing one thousand—a principle known as "economies of scale.") As a result of these two qualities—volume and efficiency—successful low-margin businesses tend to be ones that deal in mass-produced products for markets of considerable size.

High-margin businesses, on the other hand, generally rely on quality and customer service to thrive: the cost of producing the product is high and volume tends to be small, meaning that, when you do make a sale, you need to clear considerably more profit in order for your business to be sustainable. My brother David is a jeweler. He sells high-quality merchandise, much of it made-to-order, and his prices reflect this. Because volume—the number of sales he makes—is far lower than it is for a mass-produced product or service, he needs to make sure the profit he clears from his sales is considerable. His is a high-margin business, sustained by delivering high-quality products and personalized service—something that customers who are looking for such things are happy to pay for.

Under ideal circumstances, musical products are high-margin ones. When you calculate the time and expense of our training, our instruments, and our hours of unpaid practice, the cost of delivering our product (whether it be a performance, a lesson, or a composition) is considerable. The only way to recoup those costs is to charge a premium; of course, the problem is that the market may not be willing to pay that premium.

On the other hand, the rule that high-margin businesses thrive when products are of high quality and are delivered with excellent customer service is good news for musicians. We thrive on presenting a quality product! And while focusing on customer service—the customer experience—is often overlooked by musicians, I hope you're beginning to see how the broader context in which we deliver our musical products (combined with our own creativity) offers myriad opportunities for unique and compelling customer connections. When these opportunities are fulfilled in a marketplace that values them, we unlock the key to successful high-margin business models.

Logistical Feasibility

Another key part of feasibility is less about numbers and more about logistics. This is addressed in the "key activities" portion of the Business Model Canvas, and it's an incredibly important component that we must carefully work through. Take this example from a few years ago, when I had a student studying different models for opening a private teaching studio. She latched onto the idea that there were surely young students who needed teachers to come to them rather than students coming to their teacher's studio. She defined her market and its need in very astute terms: so-called "soccer moms" who would be willing to pay a premium for the convenience of one less event to drive their kids to. This is not a novel idea, but it was not common in her community; she sensed a potential untapped market. Her market research indicated that there was, indeed, a fair number of potential customers in the area to support her venture, but it also revealed something else: that market was sufficiently dispersed geographically that she would be spending a *lot* of time in her car. And in this single logistical issue the entire business model fell apart: in order to cover the wear and tear on her car *and* address the value of her time spent getting to and from a given lesson, her rates would balloon past what the market would pay—no matter how desperate the parent might be to avoid driving the kid to yet another lesson or game. If she kept her rates stable and simply booked more lessons, the problem only got worse: more wear on a car that had already seen better days, more money spent on gas, and more time spent sitting in traffic—when she could be practicing, gigging, or just having a healthy work/life balance.

This example illustrates how assessing the viability of our venture is more than mere number crunching. You have to work your way through every aspect of the venture in logistical terms: who will do each task, what is required of them to do it, how long it will take, and are there additional costs associated with that action? Is there an opportunity cost to these actions? When you factor in additional time, such as driving, is your hourly wage still acceptable? In other words, you can't look at the cost/income numbers in a vacuum. You have to put them into a broader logistical context in order to accurately assess whether or not they'll stand up to real-world conditions.

Risk Assessment

As discussed in chapter 2, risk entails both business factors (legal liabilities, the potential for changes in the marketplace to render your venture obsolete or impractical) and personal factors (how much of your resources—personal, financial, emotional, etc.—this venture will require of you). Use the information you've gathered in your Canvas to inform your SWOT analysis—and remember to stay as coldly objective as possible, avoiding the tendency to see the results you want to see instead of what the information is actually telling us. Outside sets of eyes are particularly helpful at this stage, especially if those eyes are skeptical and are not swayed by friendship's desire to be supportive. Find a mentor or a businessperson outside your discipline, and ask that person to give you her or his honest assessment of your model. What's missing?

What could be done better? What assumptions can they expose? While brutally honest feedback can be hard to hear sometimes, it's worth enduring—and listening to—if you want your venture to succeed.

Sustainability

Having assessed whether or not our business model is feasible, question 4 also asks if our venture is *sustainable*. Just because a venture is viable today doesn't necessarily mean it's sustainable over time. The question of sustainability has several components, including (1) How easy will it be for you to maintain the features that make your product valuable to the market? (2) How vulnerable to changing circumstances is your business model? (3) Will success force you in unforeseen (and unwanted) directions? (4) Can you personally sustain what's required of you to keep the venture thriving? Let's take a little bit of time with each of these questions.

Sustainable Competitive Advantage

In discussing questions 2 and 3 of the entrepreneurial process, I talked about the dynamics of identifying unmet needs and devising solutions that employ our skills and passions. Implicit in those questions is what's called "competitive advantage"—the feature(s) that make your product different from, or better than, the competition. Without this differentiation, your product is no different from what already exists—and, therefore, will have a much harder time finding value in the marketplace. Competitive advantage can take many different forms. Sometimes it can be as simple as moving into a geographic area where competition is minimal or nonexistent. Or it can be as complicated as keeping control of top-secret proprietary information essential to your product (the recipe for Coca-Cola). It can be a more efficient production method (allowing you to make your product more cheaply) or a better/different customer service model (competing on service rather than price). In the world of music, it might be a distinct repertoire or a unique way of presenting it, or your particular knowledge and experience, which render what you have to share special and valuable to others. No matter what form it takes, however, you must address the question of whether or not you can *maintain* that competitive advantage over time. Certain kinds of competitive advantage (like that secret recipe for Coke) can be sustained indefinitely. Something else, like underselling your competition, might not be sustainable at all: what's to keep them from turning around and undercutting you? If your venture relies on material for which you own the copyrights, what will happen when that material enters the public domain? Perhaps your venture operates in a specific geographic area; you are the ruler of your market—until somebody else decides to move in on your turf. So a critical part of determining the feasibility of your venture is how reliably you can maintain your competitive advantage over time. Nobody can predict the future, of course, but just as in the SWOT analysis, identifying how vulnerable your competitive advantage is will help you better evaluate the viability of your venture over the long haul. If it's easy for competition to come along and erase your distinctiveness, then you may need to revisit your product design. At the very least, you'll have identified something in your market to keep close tabs on so that you can adapt/evolve if competition starts eroding your competitive advantage.

Resilience during Change

Another aspect of sustainability has to do with how resilient your venture is in the face of changes. Such changes can be internal (you've relied on your business partner to run key areas of the venture, but now he or she has decided to focus on other things) or external (a competitor moves into your market, or some other threat from your SWOT analysis materializes). When such wrenches get thrown into the works, how much damage might they do to the viability of your business model? Will they be your undoing, or might they just be catalysts for adapting your venture in such a way that it continues to move forward? Do you have any sort of cash or credit reserve to help you through a lean patch, or are you sufficiently close to the edge that one downturn will do you in? In essence, what are your key vulnerabilities? Revisit the weaknesses and threats of your SWOT analysis: how significant are they? Are the weaknesses you've identified easily addressed, or will they be an ongoing problem? How likely to occur are the threats you've identified? And if they do occur, how destructive will they be to your ability to continue your venture successfully? It's one thing to determine that your business model is viable when things go according to plan; it's something quite different to look at how easily things will fall apart when they don't. Answering these questions will help you see how well you can ride out the storms that every venture eventually encounters.

The Double-Edged Sword of Success

Sometimes the biggest problem a venture can face is "too much" success. Ventures that grow incredibly quickly, for instance, might have difficulty managing that growth and making the necessary changes to keep things running smoothly. Perhaps some key component you need is not easily available in larger quantities, causing delays in delivering your product and resulting in unhappy customers. Sometimes success can create a false sense of invincibility that causes entrepreneurs to stop listening to their customers or observing the marketplace. Success is a great thing, but it can also pose significant—sometimes even fatal—challenges.

A common problem accompanying a successful venture is personnel: increased business requires more help, but the increase is not yet *enough* to support the costs of additional employees. Having a handle on your margins and the costs of the kinds of employees you will need will help you evaluate how big the hiring dilemma might be (as well as how you might address it if it arises). If you operate a high-margin business, is there some room to tighten up those margins in the short term in order to hire additional staff? If you're a low-margin business, will the new employee immediately allow you to increase your volume sufficiently to pay for her or him? Will you require highly specialized personnel (who will likely command a higher price) or can you get by with low-wage, unskilled labor?

Your supply chain can also be stressed if your business starts to grow. For instance, your prime supplier of cane for your reed business can only provide limited amounts every month, and you're now getting more orders than that supplier can fill. Are there other sources you can have on call in case they're needed? Is the quality as good?

The bottom line is that, while we don't need to spend a lot of time planning for success that may or may not come, understanding how your business model will be impacted by growth will help you evaluate the sustainability of the venture over time.

Personal Sustainability

The last piece of the sustainability question is a personal one. For almost all entrepreneurs, the early stages of a venture will likely be very time consuming: getting anything off the ground nearly always requires a lot of energy and commitment. For musician entrepreneurs, though, the question of how long we can sustain that energy is critical: if the venture requires so much of us that we no longer have sufficient time to maintain our musical activities, then it will not be sustainable for very long. Or perhaps there are other personal issues looming: you know you'd like to start raising a family, and that will require you to cut back the number of hours you spend each week on your venture. Figuring out the right work/life balance is of course not unique to the field of music, but for musician-entrepreneurs the challenge has the added component of the time required to maintain their craft through practicing, studying, and so on. As you are evaluating the viability of your business model, you must not forget to factor in time for your music—that is, after all, the point of all this. A venture that will initially require 150 percent of your capacity to get it off the ground is one thing; a venture that taxes your capacity that much in order to *continue* to run will not be sustainable for the long haul.

The opportunity cost also factors into the question of personal sustainability. For instance, let's assume that your teaching studio venture takes off and you're soon inundated with students. That might be fine in terms of paying your rent, but now you can no longer accept pit orchestra gigs—when those gigs are ultimately what you'd prefer to do! You're now in a bind, one where success in one area of your career exacts a cost in another: each additional block of lessons you accept means fewer playing gigs you can accept. The business model for your teaching studio might be extremely solid, but it's not sustainable for you over the long run because of the high opportunity cost.

In all these scenarios, the business model might be feasible in the short term but not sustainable in the long term. This means that you'll have to either modify your business model (now or down the road) or pivot to something else entirely (remember flexibility/adaptability!). In other words, the question of sustainability is both a business and a personal one—and the choices presented might be difficult ones, especially if your venture is doing well. That's why trying to identify them in advance is so useful. Questions of sustainability might be the ultimate trump card in the game of determining whether or not your venture is worth pursuing.

Working through each component in the Business Model Canvas, therefore—and supported with as much data and research as possible—will help ensure that you've covered all your bases, that each component of your business model is viable. The Canvas will also help reveal weaknesses or flaws in your model, giving you the opportunity to revise (or even completely reimagine) your idea.

Question 5: How Will I Implement My Solution?

"I've got this idea for a new venture, so I'm starting to work on a business plan . . ."

"Whoa, there! Hold on just a minute!"

This dialogue, or one similar to it, is common for anyone who works with would-be entrepreneurs. It's understandable: a business plan is probably the only entrepreneurial tool that most people have heard of. And it seems reasonable that if you've got an entrepreneurial idea and have spent some time thinking about it, a business plan is the first concrete step in working out the details and determining whether or not your idea is viable in the marketplace. Problem is that's not the purpose of a business plan; those who dive into making one too soon are skating on some very thin ice.

In some ways, a discussion of business plans doesn't belong in a book about entrepreneurship. A business plan enters the picture late in the game, and isn't even particularly "entrepreneurial" at that. A business plan is simply a blueprint for implementation. Only when you've done your homework and thoroughly worked through the first four questions in the entrepreneurial process are you ready to write a business plan. In relation to the Business Model Canvas introduced in question 4, the business plan lays out the steps needed to take the venture that lives in your head, your spreadsheets, and on your Canvas and *manifest it* in the marketplace. By the time you get to your business plan, your homework should be done. Your entrepreneurial thinking and problem-solving are completed. There should not be any additional research required. The business plan is purely about implementation. It's your master to-do list.

Business plans can take on various forms, depending on the nature of your venture and whether it's solely an internal document or will be used to present your idea to potential investors, donors, or partners. There are entire books on writing a business plan, so there's no point in reinventing that particular wheel here. But for the sake of completeness and to inform your thinking on this last of the entrepreneurial questions, let's take a quick look at the basic elements most business plans have in common.

Mission

The mission is a simple statement of your venture's purpose. A great way to articulate your mission is simply to use your value proposition, since it embodies all the elements of a mission statement: who you are, what you do, who it's for, and why they value it.

Example: "Green Valley Music School is a community music school in Atlanta, Georgia. Its outstanding faculty provides high-quality, affordable music lessons and performances, in a safe and nurturing environment, to low-income and at-risk youth." In other words, if someone asks "What is the Green Valley School of Music?" the mission statement—your value proposition—provides the answer.

Vision

A venture's vision is similar to its mission, but it's more about where you see your mission taking you. Your vision is an articulation of what success for your venture looks like. It's a "big picture" expression of what you hope will ultimately result from your efforts.

Example: "Green Valley Music School will become the leading community music school in Georgia, with branches in economically challenged neighborhoods throughout the greater Atlanta area. Later phases will bring satellite campuses to locations throughout the state such as Macon, Valdosta, Savannah, and Albany."

Keep in mind that your vision need not be one of growth and expansion; not every venture need take over the world. Perhaps your vision is to maintain a "lifestyle venture" that provides ongoing and stable financial support for your teaching or performing . . . and that's enough. Again, entrepreneurial outcomes are *yours* to determine, and while the mission describes what *is*, the vision describes what you want to *accomplish* and, ultimately, where you want to *end up*.

Objectives and Strategies

Some business plan templates place objectives and strategies in separate categories, but I've joined them together to underscore their intrinsic connection. The vision expresses your long-term, ultimate goal(s); objectives are a series of specific milestones—the progressive steps—that will get you there; strategies detail how you will achieve your objectives. You'll notice a pattern here, too: the business plan takes you from the "big picture" to progressively more specific points of action. The benefit of this is twofold. First, it forces you to support each goal with a specific activity to achieve it. Second, it gives you a means by which you can measure your progress. Without these two things, you're just bouncing around between task A and task . . . *K* without any strategic direction or coherence.

In order for your objectives to be useful and effective, you need to keep several things in mind. The first is that your objectives must be measurable—otherwise, how will you know you've achieved them? For instance, in the hypothetical example of the Green Valley Music School, "Get funding for initial phase" is not a very helpful objective. How much money do you need, and how will that money be allocated? Furthermore, such a vague objective makes determining a strategy that much harder. ("Get money for initial phase? Umm . . . how much? From where??") Better to go back to your Business Model Canvas, look at the items you've identified under "key resources," and come up with a specific list of items you need. That concrete list will, in turn, help reveal strategies for acquiring each item. Here is where you recall the entrepreneurial trait of resourcefulness, for it is at this stage that you begin by taking stock of what you have at your disposal and determining what you can do *right now* to get your venture off the ground.

Objective: Acquire three pianos. Strategy: Hmm . . . where could I find these? Maybe some schools are replacing their old instruments? Maybe there are some cheap ones on craigslist? I bet my childhood piano teacher has some ideas! I should talk to Aunt Millie, too—maybe she still has those two pianos in her rec room . . ." And so forth. The specificity of your objective (acquire three pianos) in turn helps dictate the strategy ("How can I go about getting three pianos, cheap?") and provides a concrete metric for success ("I could only rustle up two pianos . . . what's next, then?").

The second thing about objectives is that they exist in multiple, interconnected timeframes. There are long-term objectives (three to five years out), mid-term objectives (eighteen to twenty-four months out), and near-term objectives (six to twelve months). You might want to go one step further and identify immediate objectives: perhaps the first day of each month is given over to assessing the previous month and establishing specific objectives for the coming one. What's critical, though, is that your objectives build on each other: immediate ones should aim to achieve your near-term objectives; near-term objectives move you toward accomplishing your mid-term objectives, and so forth. The farther out your objectives, the more general they will be, too. After all, even the most savvy and experienced entrepreneur can't predict the future. It's like those maps of a hurricane's projected path: the next four hours are predicted with a high degree of certainty, but the farther out the projection goes the wider the area of potential impact becomes. Think of your objectives the same way.

And speaking of predicting the future, it's important that you continually evaluate your objectives and modify them when necessary. A business plan—and especially this section of it—should be a living, flexible document. You should not look at it as set in stone, particularly if this is your first entrepreneurial venture. It's inevitable that some of your projections will be off, for instance (some you thought were conservative when you made them may prove to be overly optimistic and vice versa). Perhaps the timing of things is different from what you anticipated (your first year fundraising goal is met in six months). Or the response of your market isn't quite what you anticipated (initial registrations yield twice as many guitar students as expected but half as many pianists). Perhaps, even after all your careful research, you overlooked a detail that changes some aspect of your business model. Or maybe something unforeseen and completely out of your control has thrown a wrench into things. If the business plan is to be of any use at all, then you must be willing to revisit it in the light of such changes and adjust accordingly. Otherwise, the document will be useless and obsolete with remarkable speed.

The "objectives" section of your document may turn out to be the most detailed and extensive. Here is where you carefully map out what you need to accomplish and in what order, making sure that each objective has a mechanism for measuring its success. But this begs the question: how do we go about determining objectives and the best strategies for achieving them? As you'll recall from our discussion of Caspar Badrutt and his bobsled track, the entrepreneurism resided in defining the nature of the problem and devising a solution; "the rest [the implementation, the business plan] was just good business." The problem for us in the arts, of course, is that we might not know how to go about practicing "good business." You can learn to think entrepreneurially, to observe strategically, and to address unmet needs. But ultimately, you will have to address the presence (or absence) of business skills—that is, how complete your "toolkit of skills" is. You need to either acquire those tools yourself or team up with someone who already has them.

Now I can hear you saying, "So does this mean that in addition to mastering my music and learning to think/act like an entrepreneur, I *also* have to get an MBA, a law degree, become a marketing expert, and sit for the CPA exam?" No—though I won't lie: the more of those skills you can acquire on your own, the fewer of them you'll have to hire out to somebody else.

Fortunately, many useful resources are out there to help you determine effective strategies and business practices for your venture, whether it be a for-profit business, a sole proprietorship, or a not-for-profit organization. In addition to these DIY resources (online or in print), consider creating a "board of directors" for your entrepreneurial life. This is a group of three to five people who have agreed to mentor you, encourage you, and hold you accountable to your mission and goals. These individuals can be family, friends, colleagues, or business mentors from the local arts council or chamber of commerce. But they should be people you trust who will give you honest feedback (even when it hurts) and who have knowledge and experience in the areas you lack. Someone with legal and accounting experience is highly recommended; expertise in marketing and social media is extremely helpful. And for emotional support, a fellow artist-entrepreneur who can share with you his or her own lessons and experience can be extremely valuable. And remember the number-one rule of networking: if you don't know somebody in a particular field or with a particular set of skills, you probably know somebody who knows somebody who does. Even if your entrepreneurial venture is a venture of one—you—it doesn't mean that you have to tackle this unfamiliar territory by yourself. In today's digital world you have access to an incredible amount of information and resources, as well as generous individuals who enjoy sharing their expertise with aspiring entrepreneurs. Avail yourself of these.

The Target Market and the Marketing Plan

You'll recall that your target market is the body of consumers you currently reach or hope to reach. In this section of the business plan, you'll pull together data from the customer-related portions of your Canvas—"customer segments," "relationships," and "channels"—to define the characteristics of your target market and outline a strategy for reaching them.

As you'll recall from chapter 3, markets are made up of individuals with shared needs and sensibilities. Now we'll see why it's so important to define your market as specifically as possible, and to have a clear understanding of its characteristics: without this knowledge, your efforts to connect with your market are seriously hampered.

A market's characteristics can be defined in two ways. The first is demographically: where the people are located, their socioeconomic status, age, gender, race, educational level, marital status, and so forth. The Internet is a great boon to entrepreneurs seeking information about a given group of people: the data is everywhere. (In fact, sifting through all that data is probably the biggest challenge. A research librarian at your local university or community library can be enormously helpful to you in getting to the data you need.)

Remember, too, the "psychographics" of your market—the sensibilities of the individuals making up the market. What do they tend to like? What factors influence their buying decisions? What other sorts of hobbies and activities do they tend to engage in? What styles or attitudes tend to resonate with them? Psychographics can be harder to identify, but this is where talking to potential customers during question 4 of the entrepreneurial process comes back into play: in addition to determining what problems they share and how they feel about your proposed solution, use that interaction to gather a broader data set of information on their lifestyle, preferences, and attitudes.

The more information you can gather about your target market, the more effective your marketing plan will be. This is because a marketing plan must be tailored to the market you are trying to connect with: its sensibilities, preferences, and behaviors. This information is critical to determining the nature of the customer relationships you seek to establish and will dictate the channels you employ to facilitate those relationships.

The idea that your marketing should both reflect your product and be tuned to the sensibilities of your target market might seem obvious, but many entrepreneurs overlook this point. They blindly employ the standard promotional methods (print ads, social media, posters, mailings, etc.), assuming that all channels are equally effective and appropriate for any venture. They are not. Moreover, the content of your marketing materials (whatever they might end up being) must also be in keeping with the identity of your brand and the sensibilities of your target market. For instance, if your house concert series aims to attract cultured individuals seeking an intimate musical experience, then a mass mailing and posters tacked up around town are not likely to be very effective channels for your marketing. Something more personal, something that embodies the nature of the experience you're offering, needs to be devised. Remember the "target" in "target market": your marketing should be tailored—targeted—to the particular consumers you most want to reach. Despite the common notion to the contrary, marketing is not just a fancy word for "advertising." Advertising is just one marketing tool among many. Which tools you use are determined by the nature of your product and the demographics and psychographics of your target market. The ultimate goal of marketing goes far beyond getting "butts in seats" (or customers in the door);

the ultimate goal of marketing is to help create and facilitate a *relationship* with your customers.

While the field of marketing is enormously complex and sophisticated, you need not have the resources of a company like Procter & Gamble or Coca-Cola to create an effective marketing plan. Common sense, informed by observations of, and conversations with, potential customers, can take you a long way. And as with the development of objectives and strategies, abundant resources exist online and in print to help you with basic marketing strategies. Consider adding someone with marketing expertise to your "board of directors" as well. Marketing can be fun and creative, especially when it's informed by these basic principles and its implementation is guided by an expert. Done well, even the simplest marketing strategy can be an extension of your artistic and organizational identity (recall the "First Limers" of Pittsburgh). When this happens, the delivery of that strategy is often self-evident.

Budget and Finance

This section takes the income streams and expenses identified in your Canvas and adds the element of time: what income and expense figures can you project for your first year? Your second year? What might things look like in three to five years? In addition to these financial projections, this section of your business plan should identify how much startup capital you need (if any) and where you will get it.

Financial projections have one potential pitfall, but it's a big one: there is no place where "garbage in, garbage out" is more true. Your spreadsheet software will happily tally your income and expenses and churn out an ever-increasing sequence of profits from one year to the next. But the totals will only be as reliable as the numbers you put into each calculation. It's important that you do as much research as possible into both the expenses required by your venture and the capacity of your target market to grow in the future. Financial projections are a "guestimate" on the best of days; be sure, then, to plug in the most grounded numbers you can. Once again, data is your friend. Here are some questions to be sure you answer as you gather information for your budget and financial projections:

INCOME
1. If you have competitors, find out how much they charge: this can provide a valuable context as you figure out what to charge for your own product.
2. When you talk to potential customers, start out by asking them how much they'd be willing to pay for your product. Then follow up and try to gauge the maximum amount they'd be willing to pay; in other words, at what price point will you price yourself out of the market?

3. Depending on the structure of your venture, another follow-up as you speak with customers should seek to get at the relationship between the price they pay and the mode and timing of payment. For instance, if you're starting a concert series, find out whether or not customers like the idea of buying a subscription to the entire season up front in exchange for a discounted ticket price. Some organizations rely heavily on subscriptions, but it doesn't appeal to all audiences (and appears to be going somewhat out of style, for a number of reasons). Another example would be paying for lessons week by week or monthly (or quarterly or by the semester). There are lots of payment models, each with its own set of advantages and disadvantages. Find out which ones work best for you *and* your customers.

4. Be sure you have a clear understanding of whether or not payments for your product will be ongoing (income from teaching Jon the guitar will continue as long as Jon is a student), intermittent (Julie is a "regular" at your concert series, but some years she comes to all six concerts and others she only makes one or two), or one-time (considering its $250,000 price tag, Antonio isn't likely to buy more than one Bösendorfer piano for his living room).

EXPENSES

Gathering data on the expense side of the ledger is a little easier, because when it comes to something you'll need to buy, rent, or outsource, you can simply get online and do some cost comparisons. The key is making sure you're not leaving something significant out of the equation. Here are some things to keep in mind:

1. Make sure that every element from the key activities and key resources segments of your Canvas have been addressed in your budget.

2. Make full use of key partners to reduce or eliminate monetary costs through mutually beneficial relationships.

3. Remember the quality "resourcefulness" discussed in chapter 2: be as creative as you can in coming up with ways to acquire as many resources as possible without paying for them outright. Use the "three Bs" of the "lean startup": *borrow, barter,* and *beg.* Adding a dollar cost to your budget should be the last resort, not the first.

In calculating the costs of doing business, it's important for you to have worked things through on both the granular level (the cost for a single unit of your product) and the global level (total estimated costs of materials, labor, time, and overhead versus total estimated income).

Once again, be sure to avoid the temptation to let your optimism carry you away when it comes to financial projections. Unless your research supports it, projecting continued hefty growth for your venture, year after year, is simply not a good idea. It's far better, and more useful, to see how *low* your sales can go and still keep your venture afloat. Shoot for the moon, sure, but have a very clear understanding of how short of the moon you can fall before you crash back to earth.

Once you've created the leanest budget possible, you'll have a much more realistic picture of what kind of initial investment your venture requires. If it is still more than you feel you can reasonably acquire, then you may need to scale back the scope of your venture to the point where the numbers work for you *now*. Later, when things get off the ground and you begin to have some operational success, you'll be in a much better position to borrow money, attract donors or investors, or finance your expansion from within.

When it comes to calculating your bottom line, the bottom line is this: be as informed and conservative as possible with your inputs. Wishful thinking has no place in your financial statements. And as your experience gives you real-life numbers, be willing to look at what those numbers are telling you—and adjust your projections accordingly.

Administration

This section is quite simple: who will do what? Even if you are a venture unto yourself, you may not have to see to every aspect of the venture personally. Regardless the size of your team, use the components of your Canvas to determine your venture's main areas of operation. Certain areas (such as marketing and finances) are common to pretty much all ventures. Depending on the particulars of your venture, however, there may be other operational areas. If you're a touring chamber group, then booking engagements and making travel arrangements is a key operational area. If you're a community music school with branches in church basements across the city, then managing your partnerships is critical. Once you've identified the main areas of operation your venture requires, revisit your skills inventory (and that of your team's, when appropriate) and determine who is best suited to each area. If there is nobody with the requisite skills to oversee certain tasks, well, then you will need to figure out how else to get them done. Perhaps some DIY research is in order. Maybe there is a barter to be made where you and the needed vendor can trade services. This is a place where your "board of directors" might be helpful. Hiring someone to take care of a functional area might be unavoidable—especially as you grow—but like anything else that requires cash to buy, it should be the last option.

Determining operational areas and how they will be staffed is important for several reasons. Perhaps most obviously, it helps ensure that nothing gets overlooked or falls through the cracks. A great business plan, with carefully considered objectives and sound financials, can still fall flat on its face if there is a lack of clarity about whose responsibility it is to execute critical tasks.

Keeping things from falling through the cracks is only the first benefit of mapping out an administrative plan, however. For one, if your venture is just you, defining operational areas can help you determine whether or not it's even possible for you to tackle everything by yourself. This is one of the biggest challenges for the musician-entrepreneur: how do you find enough hours in the day to tend to your venture *and* maintain your musical chops? There's no question this challenge is real under the best of circumstances. But if you don't have your tasks organized, prioritized, and plugged into a larger strategic plan of attack, it's nigh unto impossible. With operational areas defined, you can manage your time much more effectively: *Mornings from 9:00 to noon are for practice; social media is from noon to 1:00 daily; bills and budget is Monday evening after rehearsal,* and so forth.

If there are several members of your team, dividing up the main operational areas both ensures equality of workload in the group and puts each individual in charge of the area he or she is best suited for. Some people despise making travel arrangements; others love it. Some have a great sense of what works on social media; others just don't have the knack. If you can put people in charge of tasks they enjoy (or at least can do competently), they will be more likely to enjoy their responsibilities and maintain a positive attitude in the midst of challenges or conflict. Doing this also creates clear lines of communication and avoids people working at cross purposes or contradicting each other. (Imagine if two members of the group were both negotiating the rate for an upcoming gig!) Finally, this arrangement gives everyone a sense of ownership in, and responsibility for, the ultimate success of the venture.

The implementation stage of the entrepreneurial process is indeed the most daunting for musicians unfamiliar with the nuts and bolts of running a venture. It's an understandable feeling, one that might not ever completely go away even with years of experience and acquired knowledge under your belt. But it's important to keep the end goal in mind: engaging in the entrepreneurial process is meant to enable the practice of your art, to equip you to pursue your professional and creative goals—and on your terms. That's where the payoff is. And in time, your venture may grow to the point where you can farm out the daily tasks you find distracting or tedious or simply the things you've never gotten very good at. This is another place where your "board of directors" can be invaluable: they're there not just there to guide and advise but also to encourage and motivate you when the goal feels like it's a long way off. Of course, it's a challenge to balance the needs of your venture with your need to maintain your craft (not to mention a healthy work/life balance). But that's life: no matter what your course, these challenges will exist. Viewing your performance and practice time as *an essential component* of your musical venture will help you view this challenge in a comprehensive way: rather than maintaining a "music versus business" mindset, you view all of your venture's various components as equally important to empowering your dreams and creating value for your work.

THE IMPERATIVE
Deliver Everything with an Unwavering Commitment to Excellence

The imperative that caps off this discussion of the entrepreneurial process is a familiar one to musicians. We spend our lives striving for excellence in whatever form our music making takes. But there are two reasons why it's important to articulate this in the context of entrepreneurship. The first is that many musicians are so intimately acquainted with how they attain excellence in their musical lives that they almost take it for granted; transferring that to other areas of their professional lives is quite often a significant challenge. (If you doubt that, ask yourself how many times you've heard an outstanding performer deliver rambling, fumbled, sotto voce remarks when asked to address the audience regarding the music she or he is about to perform.)

The second reason why the excellence imperative is important in this discussion is that it explicitly counters the common assumption that entrepreneurship is a substitute for talent or ability in one's music. Many's the time I've heard students (and faculty) utter statements along the lines of "Well, if your performing career doesn't take off you can always fall back on entrepreneurship." It's the equivalent of that insulting (and spurious) assertion "Those who can't do, teach." A less harsh but equally specious misconception is that entrepreneurship is for those who place making money ahead of making art. But as I've been saying all along, these are false dichotomies: entrepreneurship embodies a process to empower and support your creativity, and it is at its most effective when the artistic integrity of your product—its excellence—remains the primary motivating force. A shoddy artistic product that is delivered entrepreneurially is still a shoddy artistic product—and won't cut it in a highly competitive market that is seeking a product of high artistic value.

So for the musician-entrepreneur, excellence must extend beyond the art. Every aspect of your venture must be held to the same high standard as your music-making. Since your goal is for your customers to find value in a product you've spent a lifetime developing—a precious, highly developed, sophisticated product—you insult your customers if any component of that product is less than your very best. (Remember the demand trigger "Maintain a steep trajectory"!) That goes for the music itself and every other aspect of how it is packaged and delivered. Remember: you're selling an *experience,* one in which music is central, but all the other associated elements are the unique and personal things that make your product *yours.* From the initial point of contact (your website, your social media presence) to the purchasing experience (tickets through a web portal; quarterly checks for lessons via PayPal?), from the availability of parking to the ease of locating the venue, from the qualities of the venue itself to the look and content of the programs. For each of the ways you communicate with your audience before, during, and after the show, you must examine *every* aspect of your customers' experience and bring a philosophy of excellence and creativity to each. Giving any piece of that elaborate puzzle less than your full commitment to excellence sells yourself, and your customers, short, and can be the difference between your venture's success or failure.

Achieving entrepreneurial excellence is not fundamentally different from pursuing growth and improvement in any other endeavor. It's a process that requires continual attention, patience, and evaluation. This process can be boiled down to three core elements: homework, feedback, and continuous improvement. Let's briefly review each of these.

Homework

A recurring theme throughout this book is the importance of doing your "homework." Your musical studies require both a foundation of basic knowledge and the ongoing acquisition of new knowledge, techniques, and approaches to your music making. Your entrepreneurial homework is no different: you cannot use your lack of facility with DIY website software as an excuse for a messy, unprofessional website. You either need to spend some time learning the software better or find someone to help you. Most likely, potential customers will interact with you first via your website, social media, and marketing materials or indirectly through other business channels (your relationship with vendors, selling merchandise, etc.). In each of these cases, those potential customers are judging you based on the available information they have. *Does this person appear to be professional? Are they someone I want to associate myself with? Would I want to do business with them? Would I trust them to teach my kids?* Bottom line: before you launch any aspect of your venture, make sure you can do so at a professional level. So do your homework first, identify areas where you need additional knowledge or skills, and make sure you know where to find the resources you need. Everything need not be perfect, but it must be up to a high standard. To calibrate that standard, proceed to the next element of excellence.

Feedback

Just as we rely on our teachers, colleagues, and mentors for feedback on our musical endeavors, feedback on the other elements of our entrepreneurial ventures is essential. It may be even *more* essential than it is for our music, since we may not have the same depth of knowledge and experience to inform our self-evaluations that we have in our musical practices. This is another appropriate role for your "board of directors," particularly those with expertise in the field in question. Get constructive feedback from colleagues, prospective customers, and existing supporters. Listen to them, ask them for suggestions on how things can be improved, and follow up. Feedback is important beyond its obvious use for your venture, too. It reduces the sometimes debilitating sense of isolation that solo musician-entrepreneurs often face. Remember: even if you are a venture of one, you are not alone in your entrepreneurial pursuits.

Continuous Improvement

Also called "continual improvement," the process by which organizations seek progressively better quality was developed by W. Edwards Deming, an engineer and statistician whose post–World War II work in Japan got him interested in how companies maintain their success over time. He began to develop a series of principles around the notion of "continuous improvement," a process by which feedback (both internal and external) is used to determine how an organization can deliver its products/services more efficiently and effectively. Rather than focusing on profits, Deming's approach showed that paying attention to the quality of the production and delivery of the product results in better profits over the long haul. This is a powerful concept for artist-entrepreneurs, since once again it shows how focusing on the quality of your product is key to the creation of value for it.

The continuous improvement process is a circular one, beginning with planning and moving to execution and then evaluation. Evaluation in turn results in planning improvements, and the cycle begins again (fig. 5.2).

Continuous improvement is the driving mechanism behind the entrepreneurial Imperative for excellence: knowledge and feedback fuel successive generations of increased quality and effectiveness. And while Deming developed his principles around large corporations, they are perfectly in sync with the entrepreneurial practices of strategic observation, opportunity assessment, customer focus, and flexibility/adaptability that I've been discussing all along. It's also an *affirming* process in which feedback and lessons learned drive success and progress, not failure and setbacks. It is the glue that holds together the five questions and the imperative.

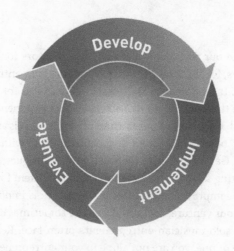

Figure 5.2 The continuous improvement cycle

EXERCISE: EXPLORE THE FIVE QUESTIONS

A good way to begin exploring the five questions of the entrepreneurial process is to answer them for an existing venture you're familiar with. For instance, talk with your teacher about how his or her studio operates and address each question from that perspective. Try this for several different types of venture, such as your local community music school, a for-profit business in your neighborhood, and your nearest performing arts organization.

Once you've gotten familiar with the five questions through exploring how existing ventures work, then you can try it with an idea of your own you've been mulling over. Or, if you've already got something going, it can be an interesting exercise to go back through the five questions for your existing venture: what things did you overlook when you first launched? Do you see your venture any differently now that you've looked at it through the lens of the five questions?

Be sure you're clear, from the outset, about whether you're engaging in "direct" or "applied" entrepreneurship. Where does your venture fall on the needs/action matrix? Is there perhaps a more promising idea in a quadrant other than the one where your current idea lies?

EXERCISE: CREATE A BOARD OF DIRECTORS

As this book's various discussions have shown, entrepreneurs rarely operate in a vacuum consisting only of themselves and their ideas. The feedback of friends, colleagues, and potential customers is a critical resource for all entrepreneurs; don't let your shyness or discomfort over being in unfamiliar territory keep you from seeking out that feedback. Learn to push through those personal barriers and get the advice and wisdom you need from folks who are experts in a given area. The benefits are enormous.

To assist with this, create a "board of directors" for your venture—even if your venture is simply you as an individual performer. This group is not a board of directors in the legal sense—though if your venture ends up becoming a not-for-profit organization, you'll need one. But at this stage we're just talking about a group of three to five individuals who care about the work you are doing and are committed to helping you succeed. They will provide advice and knowledge from their area of expertise, serve as a sounding board for new ideas, hold you accountable to your goals, and provide emotional and moral support as you move forward. Depending on your own areas of knowledge and the nature of your venture, you might look for folks who have experience in things like marketing, social media, financial management, and legal issues. People who are simply well-connected in your community can also be extremely valuable. But most important, assemble a group of people who believe in you and are pledged to be honest and forthright—even if their counsel is difficult for you to hear. Allies like that can be the difference between success and failure; seek them out and engage them from the outset.

EXERCISE: EXPLORE THE BUSINESS MODEL CANVAS

The Business Model Canvas is a powerful tool, but it will take some familiarization before you can unlock its full potential. In appendix 3 you'll find some detailed steps for exploring the Business Model Canvas and learning how it can help you design and implement your entrepreneurial venture. You'll start with some existing examples and then be given some assignments to help you play with the various components of the Canvas and how they relate to one another. Once you've completed these exercises, you're ready to begin using the Canvas to develop your own ideas, game out various different scenarios, and hone your business model into one that has the best chances of success.

CHAPTER 6

Can Entrepreneurship "Save" Classical Music?

If you conduct a quick Google search on the term "classical music crisis," you discover a myriad range of opinions on the subject, best summarized by the number of articles claiming that classical music is "dying" (or dead altogether) and an equal number of articles adamantly maintaining that classical music is *not* dying, much less *dead*. Nevertheless, the assertion that classical music is in "crisis" has become ubiquitous in recent years, with two polarized camps defining the debate: either the whole thing needs to be blown up and reinvented to prevent our complete extinction, or classical music has always been a tough sell and the key to survival is sticking to our artistic guns and educating future generations to the joys this music brings. For the many musicians and administrators who fall somewhere in the middle, a lack of clarity on how to move forward results in most classical music programming maintaining the status quo, with groups of all sizes simply worrying about how to make the next payroll.

So which is it? Is classical music in its death throes, or is it just going through a rough patch? On the one hand, there's no denying that attendance at what the National Endowment for the Arts calls "benchmark events" (performances of symphonic and chamber music, opera, ballet, and modern dance) has declined sharply over the last two decades. It's also hard to ignore the number of bankruptcies, labor disputes, and depleted endowments that some of America's most cherished classical music organizations have undergone, including the Philadelphia Orchestra, Atlanta Symphony, Detroit Symphony, Minnesota Orchestra, San Francisco Symphony, Pittsburgh Symphony, and many others. Not to mention the shuttering of regional orchestras like those of Syracuse and Albuquerque and the closures of major voices like the Brooklyn

Philharmonic and the New York City Opera (the latter since reopened, but only as a shadow of its former self).

On the other hand, orchestras all over the country have developed innovative and compelling ways to build their audiences. And, of course, classical music is not limited to the symphony orchestra; more and more chamber groups of varying sizes and types, not to mention solo performers, are doing truly groundbreaking work, creating entirely new sorts of concert experiences for their audiences and eschewing the traditional use of agents and competitions to pave the way for their successes.

So where does that leave us? Does classical music even need to be "saved"? In my view, the fact that classical music faces some significant challenges is undeniable. The question of whether or not those challenges represent an existential threat to the very genre is open to debate—and represents a distraction from addressing them with effective solutions. So the first step here is to understand the nature of the problems themselves. Then we can look at how entrepreneurial thinking might help address them.

THE CHALLENGES FACING CLASSICAL MUSIC PERFORMANCE

So what's driving the challenges facing today's classical performers and organizations? I believe there are four major forces that the classical music world must address:

1. Changing demographics—in both the concert hall and society at large
2. The need for new business models
3. Failure to adapt to the digital revolution
4. Our "preservationist" mindset

In most cases of a career or organization struggling to survive, you can find the roots of that struggle in one or more of these four issues at play. And in the case of each organization or performer who is thriving, we can see engagement with these issues in new and innovative ways. Let's explore each of these factors in greater detail.

Changing Demographics

As noted, attendance at performing arts events of all stripes has steadily declined since the 1990s, with classical music concerts declining more or less in tandem with other genres. This data is perhaps the most damning evidence that the field of classical music performance is experiencing a systemic and prolonged decline. Debate over the reasons for this decline is fractious and intense. Many assert that the decline in K–12 music education is to blame, even though there's considerable data showing that cities and states with robust music education programs are still seeing declining attendance at classical music concerts. Others blame high ticket prices, a point that has merit in some markets but should still be placed in context: the most expensive orchestra ticket pales in comparison to what it takes to secure a ticket to the current Broadway megahit or your favorite pop diva. Still others see the problem as simply one of marketing, despite the utter failure of countless expensive and spiffy marketing campaigns to make any significant or sustained impact on attendance.

While any one of these issues might be relevant to a particular organization or market, they completely overlook something far more fundamental to the question of why more people aren't coming to classical music concerts, and that is a failure to meaningfully reflect and connect with the sensibilities of our audiences and communities. And a big part of that failure resides in the fact that the demographics of both our audiences and our communities are changing while our programming and modes of presenting it are not.

The classical music audience in the United States is overwhelmingly white, educated, and from the middle or upper socioeconomic classes. While the demographic breakdown of audiences by race, education, and class has remained essentially the same for decades, what's changing is a decided aging of this audience. Despite the often-asserted truism that classical music audiences have always been made up of senior citizens, the data does not bear this out: until 2008, the largest percentages of classical music patrons were distributed more or less equally across the age categories 45–55, 55–65, and 65–75. Patrons in the 75-plus category were roughly equal to those in the 35–45 bracket. Since then, however, the breakdown has skewed decidedly older, with the largest increase occurring in the 75-plus bracket. It might be tempting to see this as simply a reflection of the United States' aging population overall, except for the other change taking place over the last decade: the sharpest decline is in the 35–45 bracket, meaning that while the existing audience is aging (as it will do), it's not being replenished by newer, younger patrons. So the argument that classical audiences have "always been like this" is a dangerous one; the demographics inside our concert halls *are* changing, and not for the better in terms of growth.

This is hardly news to anybody inside the classical music business, but what's getting overlooked are the demographics of the communities *outside* our concert halls. The United States is becoming progressively more ethnically and racially diverse, with the two largest areas of growth occurring among those of Hispanic origin and those of mixed race. While Hispanics constituted 12.6 percent of the population in 2000, the Congressional Research Service predicts that nearly one in three citizens will be of Hispanic origin by the year

2050. Overall, the ratio of white to nonwhite citizens is steadily decreasing, with current trends inexorably pointing to a time when the United States will be a "majority minority" nation.

Meanwhile, classical music performances continue to present work overwhelmingly composed by white European males for audiences overwhelmingly consisting of white individuals of European background. Attempts to change this dynamic tend to be either superficial or downright condescending. If we want to change the demographics of our audiences to more accurately reflect the demographics of our society, it will take more than the occasional performance of a work by a composer of color, sandwiched between more of the same European canon. A much more comprehensive approach, involving every aspect of our programming, is in order.

The data from the National Endowment for the Arts report *When Going Gets Tough* bears this out. Among minority attendees, the leading reason respondents cited for attending an event was to support organizations or activities associated with their specific communities. Forty-two percent of interested nonattendees who were Mexican American and 32 percent of interested nonattendees who were non-Hispanic African American cited not having anyone to go with as the top barrier to participating in an arts event. This proportion is starkly higher than for nonattendees from other racial and ethnic groups, who cited having someone to go with only 17 percent of the time. Mexican Americans were also far more likely to cite difficulty getting to the venue as a barrier (47 percent), compared to other interested nonattendees (35 percent). This data clearly shows that reaching nonwhite audiences goes far beyond the artistic content being presented; issues around social interaction, community identity, and access are far more significant barriers to attending arts events. Yet the majority of mainstream cultural organizations—especially classical music ones—are virtually ignoring these issues. As our demographics continue to shift away from majority-white to majority-minority, these barriers will have increasingly more significant impacts on attendance and, more fundamentally, the relevance and sustainability of classical music entities.

The Need for New Business Models

Classical music has relied on a patronage model for as long as it's been around. Ever since secular music (instrumental, vocal, and theatrical) began to garner the attention of "serious" composers in the Renaissance, patrons from the royal and aristocratic classes were needed to support it. Before that, it was the Church that supported composers as they created music for its various functions. And though concert music began to evolve into a progressively more public affair in the nineteenth century, composers, performers, and organizations continued to rely on some form of patronage to survive. The rise of classical music in the United States in the late nineteenth and early twentieth centuries was likewise driven by patronage, with royal aristocratic patrons being replaced by civic-minded barons of industry and finance. By the mid-twentieth century, the model we have today was pretty much in place: most classical music performance is presented by, or through, not-for-profit organizations which are, in turn, supported by private foundations, public support (in the form of money and infrastructure), corporate giving, individual philanthropy, and earned income through the sale of tickets and merchandise.

Over the last quarter century, this business model has taken numerous hits, such that it is no longer nearly as reliable as it was in the past. Public funding for the arts has dropped precipitously: adjusted for inflation, the budget of the National Endowment for the Arts has dropped more than 40 percent since 1992, a reflection of the "culture wars" that we in the performing arts have largely failed to win. Corporate giving has dropped even more (it's decreased by 50 percent) as corporations are shifting their charitable giving away from the old-school idea of supporting things that make communities better for their employees and are instead looking for the "biggest bang for the buck" in terms of marketing impact and visibility. Many companies have shut down their corporate foundations entirely while others have moved what used to be called "community relations" over to the marketing department.

Giving from private foundations, which has always played a significant role in supporting arts organizations (particularly small ones), has changed as well. Arts funding from foundations has decreased at an inflation-adjusted rate of 18 percent since 2000 as priorities have shifted toward the health and education sectors and community projects judged to have the broadest impact on the most people. The arts are now often viewed by foundations as not having sufficient impact outside their own narrow constituencies; there is also a growing bias against continuing to support small organizations that depend too much on annual operating grants. Consequently, funders are taking a harder line in dispensing their giving, demanding greater accountability regarding outcomes and community impact. Philanthropists in all sectors are looking for ways to stretch their dollars further and increase their impact, which usually translates into supporting specific projects with measurable metrics of success. Even the most generous arts funders are adopting a more businesslike approach, wanting a measurable return on their investment. The more or less "no strings" annual operating grant is becoming a thing of the past, despite many organizations' depending on them for their survival.

On top of all this, competition for grants is greater than ever: the net decrease in foundation gifts since 2000 has taken place alongside a significant increase in the number of not-for-profits applying for them. The pie has gotten smaller while the demand for slices has increased. The days where artists and arts organizations were supported simply because their work was "good for society" are largely behind us.

But the changing face of philanthropy is not the only problem facing traditional classical music business models. As you'll recall from the discussion of feasibility in chapter 4, understanding the margins of your business is critical to assessing its long-term sustainability. Entrepreneurs understand that low-margin businesses, like discount retailers or grocery stores, have to maximize volume, beat their competitors on price, and keep a steady stream of consumer triggers flowing in order for their business to remain viable. High-margin businesses thrive on high-quality products and loyal customers willing to pay a premium for something unique and special.

So is classical music a high-margin or a low-margin business? It depends on which business model we're talking about. Given that our product is of high quality and we are always seeking "loyal customers willing to pay a premium for something unique and special," classical music *ought* to be a high-margin business. Unfortunately, it's often not. From the standpoint of the individual musician or chamber music group performing more or less the same repertoire in more or less the same way, the competition is so high that only the most elite musicians and groups can charge a premium rate. This is classic "supply and demand" doing its thing in the marketplace.

But for large companies (big symphony orchestras and opera houses), the problem is worse. Because these companies have large fixed costs—that is, costs that remain the same regardless of how many customers purchase their product—they end up operating more like their low-margin cousins. Owning and operating a big concert hall and maintaining full-time payroll for a full orchestra, administrative staff, and stage crews represents a mountain of fixed costs, costs that are so high that even selling out every show doesn't prevent a deficit. That's a low-margin business indeed! With philanthropy changing and public funding shriveling up, it's reasonable to wonder whether the "big company" model of the major symphony orchestras and opera companies will be sustainable for many organizations beyond a select few in the very biggest markets. The gap between those high fixed costs and the revenue coming in will simply be too great without something fundamentally changing.

In contrast, it's a lot easier to find success stories—and hope for the future of classical music—when looking at chamber groups and individuals rather than the entrenched, low-margin, behemoth symphony orchestra. By virtue of their size, entities like chamber orchestras, small ensembles, and individual performers have much lower fixed costs, paired with a much higher capacity to be nimble and flexible. Experimentation with new repertoire, new ways of presenting it, diverse venues, and even new business models is a lot easier when you're not chained to an expensive concert hall that demands costly maintenance, utilities, and bond payments no matter how many people occupy the seats. Moreover, an organization made up of a small number of individuals can more easily forge a brand identity that reflects the unique personality of its members and is distinct from the competition.

This is all good news for musicians in the individual and chamber sectors of the classical music marketplace, provided they capitalize on the flexibility their smaller size affords them. For large organizations, the weaknesses of their current business model are a lot harder to solve (and I don't presume to have any easy answers here). But simply doubling down on the old approaches is not going to serve our big cultural institutions for much longer; some new models will need to be found.

As I'll discuss more in the next section, the Internet and social media are frequently heralded as the best source for potential new business models. Unfortunately, the promise of our digital age has yet to be realized to any great extent in the world of classical concert music. For instance, crowdfunding is often pointed to as a revolutionary way for composers and presenters to garner support for their work directly from their audiences. But the truth is that crowdfunding is simply an updated (though admittedly more efficient) way to accomplish what musical creators have been doing for centuries: using the network of their personal and professional relationships to assemble the resources they need to present their work. There is not a fundamentally *new* business model represented there.

Digital streaming, on the other hand, certainly represents a fundamentally new model for recorded music: what used to be a source of income has now become a marketing expense. But again, this seismic shift in the business model for recorded music has not truly changed the situation for classical musicians on the ground: unlike the pop world, the market for recorded classical music was *never* a big money-maker for either recording labels or the musicians themselves. One could argue that the new business models for recorded music are even worse for classical musicians than the old ones: now, the expense for recording is almost entirely borne by the composers and/or performers themselves, with the burden of distribution and promotion likewise transferred away from labels and onto the musicians. Meanwhile, streaming services like Spotify, Pandora, and all the rest reduce what little revenue might be made even further: the power—and the bulk of the profit—remains with the gatekeepers of content. Those gatekeepers used to be the record labels; now they're the streaming services. So while today's ability to make your own quality recording and promote your product gives individual musicians and groups more *artistic* freedom to produce the work they want, things haven't really changed from a *business* standpoint much at all.

Where are the new models, then? Where are the truly new models for funding concert music? Where are the truly new models for monetizing our work on the web? The results are few and spotty—but encouraging. For instance, Claire Chase's International Contemporary Ensemble ("ICE") earns the vast majority of its income from a myriad of innovative educational programs, for which there is more abundant funding than for traditional concert operations.

(Le) Poisson Rouge is, from a business standpoint, a nightclub (and a profitable one); the success of the business side of the venture has, in turn, supported the birth of other, not-for-profit performance mechanisms that take music out of the club and back into the community. The online portal Bandcamp provides streaming and publishing to independent artists and gives them a much bigger chunk of the proceeds than traditional publishers or streaming services.

Unfortunately, groups like these are exceptions that prove the rule: by and large, classical musicians and presenters have not discovered a way to fundamentally upend the traditional triad of public support, private philanthropy, and earned income that is the way the vast majority of classical music organizations survive. That triad continues to be the foundation of virtually every arts organization out there (not just in classical music), and there is an enormous industry devoted to maintaining it. The sheer inertia of that makes the widespread replacement of that model with new ones extremely difficult.

So how can entrepreneurship address the birth of new business models for the arts? One way to start is to remember that entrepreneurship is uniquely equipped to help uncover the right business model for a *particular situation*: "ICE," Bandcamp, and (Le) Poisson Rouge are all entrepreneurial ventures, but they operate with very different models. So while entrepreneurship may not reveal a uniform replacement for the traditional not-for-profit triad of support, it absolutely *can* help the individual performer or organization develop the best business model for their particular venture. With the tools of entrepreneurship in hand, musicians and organizations need not assume that they will be a not-for-profit venture, or that their business model will be, a priori, one using the traditional support triad. They can work through all of the steps in the entrepreneurial process and determine, through research and creativity, the model best suited to their goals. The more ventures employ this process, the more the best and most robust business models will begin to propagate across the landscape of classical music. This is one of entrepreneurship's unique strengths: through trial and error and reiteration, innovative products and business models grow from the ground up. Most will not take off and change the world. But a few will. Somewhere among the classical music entrepreneurs who are developing and experimenting with and refining their individual ventures today are the business models that will transform the industry tomorrow.

Failure to Adapt to the Digital Revolution

The digital revolution that began in the 1980s represents one of the most significant societal upheavals in recorded history. Virtually every aspect of our lives has been changed, from the ease with which we can access and share information to the ways digital commerce has transformed the way we buy and sell products of all types. Concurrent with these changes (and in part because of them) the nature of our interactions with media and information has fundamentally changed as well: more than ever, we are inundated with content of all kinds, from every direction, 24/7. Whether it's through social media or product placements at the movies, advertising has infiltrated virtually every avenue of social interaction; our social media has become so multi-faceted that there are apps to manage our apps!

To think that something as integral to society as music would be immune to such changes would be foolish, and, indeed, the digital age has impacted the way we create, access, experience, sell, and buy musical content of all kinds. What was true about the music business fifty years ago has been almost entirely turned upside down, and the business models of the past have been rendered impotent. The problem is that new business models that allow artists and artistic organizations to thrive in this new digital world have been slow to emerge. Take recordings: it used to be that live performances were used as a way to promote record sales; now, with rampant piracy and streaming models creating precious little income for artists, the role of recordings has completely changed into primarily that of marketing tool for your live performances. Music publishing is another business that's been completely upended, with mixed results: composers can now publish their own scores and pocket all the profits, but they've lost the marketing support and credibility that came with having a publisher backing them and distributing their work.

Related to the question of concert attendance are new statistics around electronic access to music, either via television and radio, a handheld device, CDs and DVDs, or the Internet. The NEA reports that 71 percent of people accessed arts content of one kind or another through electronic means. (This is in contrast to 31 percent of the population who attended some kind of musical performance, all genres.) As you might expect, the use of electronic means to consume art is highest among the youngest age groups and declines steadily in each subsequent age bracket. So it's safe to assume that the use of technology as a primary avenue for consuming music will only continue to increase.

For musicians and musical organizations, the ease with which the Internet connects people to, literally, the entire world means that a genre that is based on patient, reflective listening and that gets more fulfilling the more you know and understand its content appears to be more and more out of sync with the culture at large.

For the most part, classical musicians and institutions have ignored these trends. Those who have experimented with things like encouraging social media interaction during concerts have often alienated existing patrons or received scathing criticism. Attempts at incorporating other media (like lighting or video) are often executed poorly, further alienating audiences from the idea that classical music can (and should) exist outside its own pristine, hermetically sealed container.

Meanwhile, the world around us is becoming smaller and smaller at the hands of social media and the Internet, and technology is becoming more and more integrated into the fabric of our daily lives. This development is only going to become more inexorable with time, so we must stop looking at technology as something antithetical to our artistic goals and start looking at it as a vast realm of possibility.

Classical music is certainly present in many corners of the Internet. Virtually all organizations and performers have websites (some more robust than others); apps like YouTube provide the opportunity to share visual as well as audio representations of one's work; and crowdfunding platforms like Kickstarter, IndieGoGo, and Patreon are transforming the way artists fund their projects and groups. Unfortunately, as alluded to above, none of these has fundamentally changed the two core challenges classical musicians and organizations are constantly facing: the size of their audience and the money they need to sustain themselves. In other words, the classical music industry has not yet figured out how to utilize the Internet in any sort of paradigm-shifting way in terms of either finding a new business model or more effectively reaching new audiences.

This failure to fully take advantage of the digital revolution extends to the artistic realm as well. The rich array of emerging technologies means that the creative and scientific experimentation that is happening across the media spectrum is ready and able to help us in the classical music world, and not just to develop new ways to present and disseminate our music and interact with our audiences but also develop entirely new genres of music and musical experience. Composers like Mason Bates are exploring the full integration of technology into one's orchestral compositions (as well as drawing from nonclassical musical genres like hip-hop and EDM); choral composer Eric Whitacre has created worldwide virtual choirs to sing his works—garnering him enormous media coverage while also stimulating an international market for his music. And a number of chamber music groups and soloists are regularly employing various sorts of technology in their performances. But these are exceptions that underscore just how divorced from technology most classical music practice is. Technology affords us the opportunity to fundamentally transform the music we create, how we deliver music to our audience, and how we make money from it. But for the most part, this vast universe of possibilities remains largely unexplored. We have all the tools we need for bold experimentation and artistic boundary-pushing, but in order for such things to take place, the classical music world has to get past the last of the four forces holding us back.

Our Preservationist Mindset

A lot of lip service is paid in the classical music world to the concept of "reaching out" to communities and tailoring offerings to the tastes of our local audiences; yet classical music programming is more homogeneous than ever. A survey of seasons from orchestras and chamber music societies across the country will show the same repertoire being presented in essentially the same way regardless of the location, demographics, and sensibilities of the community. Moreover, this repertoire and presentational style has been essentially unchanged for well over a century, with organizations relying on the forbidding walls of the concert hall to keep the rapidly changing world around us at bay. This is not a sustainable model. So how did we get to this place?

In the late eighteenth century, as classical music began to move out of private salons and into the public realm, the instrumental concert was very much an expression of contemporary culture. Commentary from that period was highly critical of concerts that did not contain an abundance of new works, and pieces that were a mere five or ten years old were derided as old news: concertgoers demanded new works by the leading composers of the day. Precisely why and how this began to change is the subject of another book; suffice it to say that over the course of the nineteenth century a canon of revered works from the past began to develop. By the early twentieth century that canon was largely established, and the primary role of musicians and institutions began to change into one of preservation.

To make the problem worse, the twentieth century saw the emergence of a divide between "art music" and "popular music." Classical music was decidedly on the "art" side of this high/low divide, further solidifying the musical canon as immutable and beyond reproach and the role of classical musicians and institutions as the guardians of it. By the late twentieth century the classical music world was completely dominated by a fixed body of repertoire—and a fixed approach to presenting it. Those who were committed to creating and performing new works, once the central lifeblood of classical music, were marginalized to the fringes of academia and a handful of new music ensembles in major urban centers.

In the past twenty years, this has begun to slowly change. Music directors such as Robert Spano, Michael Tilson Thomas, Marin Alsop, and others are regularly commissioning and performing new works, while the number of chamber ensembles devoted partly or entirely to new repertoire has increased significantly as well. But the vast preponderance of programming continues to feature the traditional canon, and the larger the institution, the more likely this is. And though there is no apparent correlation between institutions engaging in more adventuresome programming and increased financial struggles, that fear keeps the majority of classical musicians and groups sticking with the same old offerings year after year. The fact is the classical music organizations, large and small, that are doing the best in today's marketplace tend to be the ones that are offering a more diverse range of musical offerings or that have forged an entirely unique identity built around new work presented in new ways. Alarm Will Sound, Brooklyn Rider, the Knights Orchestra, Pittsburgh New Music Ensemble, Third Coast Percussion, and a host of other chamber groups, individual performers, and regional orchestras are willing to engage in programs that actively defy (and in some cases reinvent) the traditional classical concert (both in terms of the repertoire and how it's presented). Of course, there will be exceptions—groups like the Tokyo String Quartet or the Chicago Symphony which present the canon, and precious little else, at an exceptionally polished level that is second to none. But for the emerging professional looking for his or her place in the world or the struggling institution searching for ways to revitalize its presence, the well-trodden ways of the past are not likely to lead to success.

FACING OUR CHALLENGES THROUGH ENTREPRENEURSHIP

As mentioned earlier, the debate about the current state of classical music (and its future) is framed by alarmists at one end ("classical music will go extinct unless we change it") and denialists at the other ("classical music is doing better than ever; this is just a rough patch"). The alarmists tend to focus only on the bad news (the orchestra failure du jour, the utter uniformity of most classical programming) while overlooking the many interesting and innovative things going on across the country. The denialists, in turn, have not internalized long-range demographic and financial trends, which the data reveals conclusively; instead, they tend to blame current struggles on a weak economy, cuts in K–12 arts education, and what they see as an overly demanding musician's union.

A third response, and probably the most vocal and best represented on blogs and op-ed pages, is the assertion that efforts at audience engagement, cultural relevance, and community outreach over the last few decades have largely failed. Programming to the tastes of the audience, so the argument goes, has resulted in seasons of the hoariest of standards to please the core audience and orchestral backup for pop acts to please the mainstream population. The result is a complete lack of anything original or challenging in either category, rendering the orchestra an inert and ineffectual institution. The reason orchestras are struggling (so goes the op-ed) is that they've sold out their mission at the urging of funders and "experts" (who see classical music as an elitist endeavor that is disconnected with its community) and in so doing have fundamentally compromised the experience. In the words of critic Philip Kennicott, "the effort to popularize classical music undermines what makes orchestras great."

There's definitely some merit to this assessment. As I've mentioned, classical music programming, especially among orchestras, is more homogeneous and conservative than ever; "pops" programming is occupying a larger and larger slice of the season's concerts (and supporting larger and larger portions of the budget, too). Somehow the "specialness" of going to a darkened hall, insulated from the constant assault of outside stimulation, in order to engage in a live performance of some of Western culture's finest creations has been lost. In entrepreneurial terms, only a very narrow slice of the market sees sufficient value in that experience to regularly attend and support it with their philanthropy. And that slice is simply too small to sustain these large institutions. Consequently, despite all the money poured into "outreach" and "engagement" activities, attendance continues to flounder and finances continue to tighten. Perhaps it makes sense to discard the myriad and ineffectual attempts to build new audiences that have been tried over the last quarter century and instead try to recapture the core value of the experience itself. Unfortunately, the critics and bloggers advancing this argument have few, if any, substantive ideas on how to actually bring about a recapture of that value.

So what's missing? The answer lies partly in the lack of a critical evaluation of *why* attempts to revitalize the orchestra have generally failed (sometimes spectacularly) and partly in the lack of any guiding principles for designing programming and initiatives that will succeed. Entrepreneurship can help on both counts. Let's revisit some of the concepts explored in this book and see what they can reveal.

Opportunity Recognition

Classical musicians, and especially administrators, have an unfortunate tendency to isolate what they do from the community around them. This results in a host of potential opportunities being completely overlooked by composers, performers, and administrators alike. A great example of this was the 2016 centennial of the National Park Service. Despite many summer classical music festivals taking place in or near national parks, despite a host of existing repertoire that could speak to the treasure of our parks, and despite a tremendous amount of national and local media coverage leading up to and during the centennial, the classical music world was almost entirely unengaged with this milestone. Even Wolf Trap, *our national park for the performing arts,* failed to present any meaningful programming marking the occasion. One pitch to a major symphony that I'm aware of, in which performance of a new American work with direct ties to our national parks was proposed in tandem with educational and outreach activities, was reportedly dismissed by a befuddled administrator who declared, "I just don't see how we'd market this."

Something like the national parks centennial should have been jumped on by classical musicians of all stripes and types. The National Endowment for the Arts even had a dedicated grant program, "Imagine Your Parks," that awarded nearly $800,000 for projects related to the centennial. Of the thirty-three awards, only six involved music—and three of those supported performances of the same piece, "Des canyons aux etoiles," by the late French composer Olivier Messiaen. While this piece is a beautiful work that certainly deserved inclusion in any sort of national parks celebration, it illustrates the worst sort of mindset in classical music programming. Rather than investing the time and effort into creating something new and compelling, something reflective of this quintessentially American celebration, and rather than linking that event to education and outreach activities that would actually help strengthen the bond between orchestras and communities, fully *half* of the meager projects funded by Imagine Your Parks involved a work written by a Frenchman more than forty years earlier. And *none* of the six projects involving music linked performances with other community events designed to explicitly connect the public's experience of the national parks with the musical experience taking place in the concert hall.

The almost nonexistent engagement of the classical music community with something like the parks centennial is a sad commentary on how poorly musicians exercise their opportunity recognition. There was tremendous activity nationwide, cutting across the sectors of education, visual arts, and recreation, but the classical music world was largely absent. What an incredible opportunity to let pass by! If classical music is to regain a more central position in the cultural life of our country, we have to find ways to link our music with what's happening in the world around us, to use outreach and engagement not as clumsy marketing tools but as vehicles for demonstrating the relevance of classical music to our modern lives. We have to find ways to integrate music into the broader canvas of our community and stimulate discourse that is not aloof from our daily lives but a part of it. To accomplish this, we in the classical music world have got to become a lot more observant of the opportunities that surround us, as well as becoming a lot more creative and strategic in the ways we capitalize on them.

Customer Focus

As discussed throughout this book, classical musicians often struggle with the idea of creating programming that is responsive to the needs and sensibilities of their customers—their audience. The fear is that such an approach means "dumbing down" our content, programming only what we know will "sell."

But as this book's discussion of demand clearly demonstrates, simply giving the market more of what it already has is not the path to growth (unless, of course, you can make a clear case for latent demand existing in your market, something that is mighty rare in the world of classical music performance). Remember also that the greatest entrepreneurial successes take place in the realm of inchoate demand, and that the first step in releasing that demand is understanding the dynamics of the customers you hope to inspire and stimulate with your product. I've shown that it's often the utilitarian needs of your audience that most impact their decision to consume your product (or not). And I've explained that hedonic consumption is about the emotional currency of the experience in question, meaning that the concert experience is about much more than just the music being performed.

Taken together, these lessons teach us that customer focus is not about compromising the integrity of our musical products at all. Rather, it's about understanding the needs of our audiences (both utilitarian and aesthetic) and building a holistic artistic experience designed to stimulate and engage those sensibilities. It's about identifying which elements of the concert experience are really the ones drawing our audience in, and gearing our marketing and outreach toward conveying those elements. Customer focus is the central, guiding force behind all entrepreneurial endeavors, and as you'll recall from our look at Brooklyn Rider, customer focus in the form of empathy can be a central, guiding force in everything we do as artists, too.

Flexibility and Adaptability

The stories of Yngve Berqvist and Jennie Dorris in chapter 1 showed how entrepreneurs maintain an open and creative mindset as circumstances unfold and pay close attention to what works and what doesn't. They're willing to learn from their successes and failures and adjust accordingly. Once again, we can see how this ability does not come easily to most folks in the classical music world. Since the foundation of our musical training is a canon of long-established works and performance practice, the mindset of our art being essentially fixed and immutable is pretty much hardwired into us from the outset. Learning to shed that mindset takes conscious, intentional effort, but it's essential for the entrepreneurial success of our careers and the organizations we're a part of. To do this, we have to be willing to reassess the things we think are sacred; when we find ourselves reflexively reacting to something with the statement "That's just not done," we must stop and ask ourselves "Why not?" (After all, as the saying goes, "Sacred cows make gourmet hamburger!") And when we try something that doesn't work, we have to be willing to proceed with version 2.0, based on data and analysis of why version 1.0 fell short, rather than just walking away from the idea and dropping it altogether.

One thing that's interesting about the development of a flexible and adaptable mindset is that good musicians already have one when it comes to their music making. The best musicians are the ones who are constantly looking for ways to improve, and seeking new insights into the music they play. When they try something that doesn't work, they see what they can learn from that and then try something different. But as soon as we get out of the familiar zone of our musical practice, that adaptable mindset often falls by the wayside. Instead, we need to look at our entrepreneurial endeavors in the same way we look at our practice: if something works, see if you can make it work even better; when something fails, figure out why and fix it.

One thing that stands in the way of an ongoing process of flexible, adaptable refinement is the way our classical music organizations, as well as our individual projects, are generally funded. For large institutions, virtually all ongoing operational funding goes toward those high fixed costs I mentioned above; any sort of program or initiative intended to experiment with something new has to be underwritten by a special grant or gift. The same tends to go for smaller groups and even individuals: grants that support experimentation are usually one-time affairs, resulting in one-off initiatives; once the project is completed, there's no opportunity to take the lessons learned and then create a version 2.0 (and then a 3.0, a 4.0, and so on). The result is that traditional programming becomes more entrenched than ever, and even those organizations that want to try new things lack the resources to support the *ongoing*, reiterative process that is key to the development and implementation of entrepreneurial and artistic innovation. Unless we happen to get lucky and find success on our first try, we tend to get stuck in a cycle where lots of things get tried once but few things get refined and tried again. So we have to find a way for flexibility and adaptability to be our central mindset in everything we do and not just orientations tied to an isolated project that we drop when the grant for it is used up. We have to employ the additional entrepreneurial traits of resourcefulness and tenacity as well, in order to leverage our existing resources toward supporting the changes and refinements we need to make to keep growing. The more we can practice this mindset, and the more nimble our reactions, the better chance we have for success with our endeavors.

Lessons From Hedonic Consumption

Sydney Levy told us that people buy things not just for what they do, but for what they mean. And nowhere is Levy's insight more true than on the hedonic end of the consumption spectrum, where aesthetic products reside. What abundant data and case studies demonstrate, however, is that in the case of the performing arts, the "meaning" of the product—and the point of value for the consumer—is a multifaceted thing that encompasses the entirety of the experience. For classical music, that means everything from getting to the venue, purchasing the ticket, interactions with staff and other patrons, creature comforts like chairs and restrooms, how (or if) we connect with the performers, and yes, every aspect of the performance itself: the repertoire, how it's selected and with what it's paired, and how the stage is set up, lit, and changed when needed. The lessons of hedonic consumption clearly teach us that presenting a piece of *repertoire* will only motivate the most devoted of aficionados; presenting a holistic artistic *experience*, designed in every aspect to convey a specific body of *meaning*, can motivate many more.

For an example of this, let's go back to Pittsburgh and the "Theatre of Music" developed for the Pittsburgh New Music Ensemble by its artistic director, Kevin Noe. While the Theatre of Music utilizes a variety of media and theatrical elements (such as lighting, video, etc.), it is a much more unified and holistic approach than other "multimedia" concerts. Rather than a mere sequence of works that employ other elements, Noe aims to construct the entirety of a concert as a *single* artistic entity. Theatrical tools like lighting, stage movement, costumes, spoken word, video, and so forth are not ends in themselves; they are only employed in service of focusing the audience's attention, revealing meaning and relationships between and within the pieces and, ultimately, creating the same kind of dramatic coherence and continuity one finds in a film or play. No element of the experience is taken for granted, and nothing is added to the music that doesn't serve a dramatic purpose. The result is that repertoire that might be considered too esoteric or challenging for a general audience is embraced, contemplated, and appreciated because these works play a role in creating *meaning* for the audience.

In contrast to the Pittsburgh New Music Ensemble's approach, the vast majority of additional elements, like lighting or projections, that are added to classical music concerts fail because they do not, in fact, enhance the experience, nor do they aid in revealing meaning or creating continuity. They are done as add-ons in an attempt to make the traditional concert feel more contemporary and reflective of our multisensory world. But just adding a new element to the concert does not, by itself, accomplish anything; in fact, it might make the experience worse. It's like deciding to make your sandwich more appealing by adding every single condiment in your refrigerator: you haven't created a tasty new sandwich, you've just piled on a bunch of conflicting flavors with no regard for how they taste in the aggregate.

While the Theatre of Music is the center of the Pittsburgh New Music Ensemble experience, the performance is framed by audience interactions designed to reinforce the sense of community among the ensemble's patrons and provide an avenue for processing that experience afterward. A party atmosphere exists in the lobby, with upbeat staff and volunteers greeting patrons as they come in. The stage is configured to eliminate any physical barriers between the first rows of seats and the stage itself. The show is kicked off by personal comments from the artistic director. And afterward, patrons gather for a BYOB reception, with food provided by members of the ensemble and wine brought by the patrons themselves. Artists and patrons share the food and wine together, and discussions about that night's show often go on longer than the show itself!

As the First Limer initiative made clear, the ensemble's audience has not only grown in numbers since the Theatre of Music was developed in the early 2000s but has also cohered into a community that returns each week for an *experience*. The repertoire is often not known in advance, nor do the vast majority of patrons care whether or not they recognize the composer or know the piece. They come because they know they will have a meaningful experience, one that is compelling, unique, and memorable.

Of course, creating such experiences takes enormous artistic thought and a willingness to take creative risks. On a practical level, it takes additional resources in terms of rehearsal time, equipment, and sometimes things like props, costumes, or modest sets. It requires a willingness to throw out the conventions that have kept classical programming in a straitjacket for far too long ("we can't have too much of x or y," "without a big soloist people won't come," and that perennial favorite, "we have to have an intermission"). Most of all, it requires us to disenthrall ourselves from the cult of the "masterpiece"—the idea that the primary motivating factor for our audiences is the particular repertoire being presented. That's not to say that we shouldn't present masterworks or that nobody cares what we perform; what it *does* mean, however, is that the repertoire by itself is not compelling enough to enough people to justify making that the only thing we think about. We have to create an aesthetic product that embraces the entirety of the concert and that facilitates the most focused and personally compelling experience of the music that is possible. That's how we create *meaning* for our audiences, and as the principles of hedonic consumption demonstrate, the meaning this aesthetic produces is what consumers value and seek.

Deliver with Unwavering Commitment to Excellence

As we look at how principles of entrepreneurship apply to the challenges of reinvigorating the classical music concert, it's worth revisiting the imperative that capped off the five questions of the entrepreneurial process. For often even the best intentioned efforts to try something new fall flat for the simple reason that they're not executed well.

Shortly after I moved to Colorado, I was excited to hear about an upcoming concert at the Colorado Music Festival: a performance of Lorin Maazel's orchestral redux of Wagner's *Ring*, complete with commissioned images depicting the action projected over the stage. Being a Wagner nut, I was nearly giddy with anticipation. When the time came for the performance, however, it was a disaster. First off, the images, while certainly inspired by key plot points in the *Ring*, did not necessarily appear in sync with the appropriate corresponding music. This was not a combined musical/visual reliving of Wagner's epic; it was really no more than a slide show, and a repetitive one at that: certain images reappeared throughout, apparently at random and completely unrelated to what was happening musically. And if all this weren't bad enough, about one-third of the way into the performance the screen froze, and the audience was treated to a projection of the computer desktop and the operator's actions as he attempted to troubleshoot the issue and get the program up and running again.

Afterward I made sure I eavesdropped on the comments of the audience, and not a single one was forgiving. The unanimous consensus was that even if the technical meltdown hadn't happened, the visuals were, at best, of no value to the experience and, at worst, were an unwelcome distraction.

It didn't need to be this way. A carefully choreographed and synced series of visuals could have added something compelling to the performance, helping to knit together a piece that, as "pure music," is somewhat disjointed and abrupt. And while sometimes technology is just going to do what it's going to do, I've never seen such a meltdown at a pop concert or a Broadway show. We're simply far too cavalier about our use of technology in the concert hall, and it sabotages our efforts to create something meaningful for our audience.

Another example is in the simple act of speaking before a piece or at the beginning of the concert. I've only seen a handful of conductors or performers who can deliver a set of remarks that are concise, thought-provoking, and fluently delivered so as to perfectly tee up the performance about to take place. To do it well, it's another one of those things that takes extra thought, time, and practice—and because we devote those things only to our musical execution, most remarks from the stage are weak and poorly delivered, *disengaging* listeners from the experience ("Will he just shut up and get on with the piece??") rather than drawing them in.

One positive example that has always stuck with me was the pre-performance talk at the premiere of Kevin Puts's *The Manchurian Candidate* at the Minnesota Opera. I generally don't go to preconcert talks because they tend to not be very interesting or well delivered. But I was by myself that day and dinner had ended early, so I decided to go in and see what was going on. Our host sat at the piano and delivered a thirty-minute monologue of music, plot summary, and musical commentary that was one of the most gripping and entertaining lecture-demonstrations I've ever seen. His command of the music was absolute; his delivery was dramatic, animated, and sincere. And because this is apparently something done for every production, the regulars at the Minnesota Opera knew to come: the room was packed, with folks standing once they ran out of chairs. I don't blame them: this guy was a knock-out! And yes, it enhanced my experience that night. For one, it demonstrated to me that the folks at Minnesota Opera *cared* about my understanding of the opera they were about to present. And because it was delivered so incredibly well, every bit as professionally as the performance itself, I retained the content and recalled it at the appropriate moments in the performance. It was a great example of how excellence in framing the performance can enhance the performance itself.

Musicians and institutions need to develop a view of their responsibilities to their audience that is much closer to all-encompassing, leaving no aspect of the time they're with their audiences for granted. The more you dissect the concert event and evaluate each component separately, the more you begin to see how even the smallest details can taint the experience—and the more you'll start to see creative ways to address those details in a way that is consistent with the overall impact you hope to make. In order to create something that has the maximum impact for the largest audience possible, every detail of your event—*every single one*—must be executed with the same commitment to excellence you bring to your music making. Anything short of that undermines your efforts and is an affront to the very people whose support you need.

Lessons from Stimulating Demand

In the quest to revitalize classical music concerts, every one of the six drivers of stimulating demand needs to be considered. Here are some examples to illustrate how they can work.

Magnetic. Remember that the "magnetism" of the product consists of the emotional and experiential aspects of the product that make us want to consume it—the very thing I've been discussing all along. A particularly good example of a magnetic classical music product is one that resides outside the concert hall, however. It's New York City's "multimedia art cabaret" (Le) Poisson Rouge. Founded by two graduates of the Manhattan School of Music, this cabaret seeks to "revive the symbiotic relationship between art and revelry." The venue presents a huge range of music and other arts, from straight-up classical music (both old and new), avant-garde and experimental music, indie rock, and jazz to film, drama, dance, and even burlesque. The key to the cabaret's magnetism, however, is an attraction beyond the eclectic mix of its offerings. The venue itself is carefully designed so that both the performance experience and the bar experience are delivered at the highest level. A beautiful, soundproof bar provides excellent libations, while the performance space was designed by master acousticians and provides an intimate and personal proximity to performers. And since patrons of the cabaret come simply because they know that whatever is on that night will be good, all manner of patrons who might not normally take in (or even know about) a particular genre get to experience it for the first time.

Reduce the hassle map. This next example isn't from music, but it's a great example of reducing the hassle map in the performing arts. The Colorado Shakespeare Festival presents a summer season of plays at its home in Boulder, and organizers were concerned with low attendance during the weeknight shows. They sought feedback from their audience regarding this and found that the 8:00 start time simply made far too late an evening when the play might stretch to three hours and work beckoned the next morning. Since many of the plays are presented in an outdoor amphitheater, however, the lighting designers objected to an earlier start time because it would mean there was still daylight during the first act, posing a problem for them. In the end, however, the needs of the audience held sway, and the weeknight start time was moved to 6:30. Attendance skyrocketed. And yes, the lighting is not as prominent during the early parts of the play, but there was an unantici-pated upside: the slow transition into a summer night is itself a magical expe-rience, and the shift from ambient sunlight to theatrical lights had the effect of drawing the audience into the experience as the evening progressed. I've talked with many patrons (and experienced this myself), and the overwhelm-ing consensus is that this journey from day into night actually *enhances* the experience of the play. What started as a way to simplify the audience's hassle map turned out to have artistic benefit as well.

Complete the backstory. As in the case of the New World Symphony's tech-nical mastery of sound and video in their plaza, getting things right before showtime is an essential part of stimulating demand for your product. Once again, we need to take something we already do—practicing every nuance of our musical performance—and apply it to every other aspect of our products. This is new territory for musicians: building time into rehearsal to choreo-graph a set change or blocking out where a music stand must be placed in order to receive the proper lighting might seem unnecessary for those who haven't ever thought about such things before, but it's critical. In implementing the Theatre of Music at the Pittsburgh New Music Ensemble, it took several sea-sons to work out the most efficient way to address all the many nonmusical elements of the performance and make sure that the performers understood the artistic intent of the show and its emotional arc. There are now two full, two-hour rehearsals devoted to blocking, walk-throughs, and tech for each show. That's a lot of time when each show is put up in just four and a half days! But it's also absolutely essential to making sure that the elements supporting the music are as rock-solid and strong as the music itself.

Time and time again I've seen (or been involved with) shows where the performers resist taking any time to work out these details. And what results is malfunctioning tech, performers looking awkward and uncomfortable, unnecessary shuffling around of chairs and stands before a piece begins, and so forth—all of which comes off as folks simply not having their act together. The emotionally intimate space created by careful staging and an intentional form for the entire concert is an incredibly fragile thing. That focus is easily disrupted and hard to regain. If our goal is to create a professional-level experience, one that our audiences will want to return to again and again, it's simply unacceptable to skip over the hard work required to make the entire show a smooth, flawless, and integrated experience. And in an era when every other type of performance medium—theater, Broadway shows, pop concerts, film, video games, and so on—delivers an integrated experience that flows seamlessly from one element to the next, a similar approach to concert music is required to stimulate demand from today's audiences and the audiences of tomorrow. But we can't do it on the fly, cut corners, or expect that these elements will just fall into place by themselves. It takes a lot of homework, extra time, and deep commitment. But when it works, it's very much worth it.

Triggers. Remember that a trigger is something that motivates consumption by someone who otherwise was sitting on the sidelines. Let's stick with Pittsburgh New Music Ensemble for a second and revisit their First Limers initiative. While the primary focus of First Limers is the free ticket for anyone attending for the first time, that's not really where this trigger gets its power. In fact, audience surveys show that most First Limers didn't know about the ensemble until . . . wait for it . . . *their friend told them about it.* You'll recall that folks who bring a First Limer get in for half price, and if they bring two they get in for free. So, really, the First Limer program is about offering an incentive for existing patrons to bring their friends: the trigger is aimed at leveraging the existing audience, and the trigger for the newbies is that their friends are inviting them. (After all, if they'd never heard of the group before then they wouldn't know about the free ticket either.)

The lesson here is that as we think about what kinds of triggers would help boost consumption of our products, we have to base our ideas on an understanding of the sensibilities and dynamics of our existing customers. So often (and not just in the arts) entrepreneurs will come up with fun or inventive ideas and implement them with abandon because they just seem so right *to them.* This approach is far too hit-or-miss, however. (More often it's a miss.) With the First Limers, however, the ensemble's leaders spent a lot of time observing and understanding their audience and figuring out the most effective way to leverage patrons' enthusiasm to bring in newcomers. The organization could have spent thousands of dollars on conventional marketing and still not likely generated much new interest, because the Theatre of Music experience was simply too unique and novel to be properly captured in a spiffy brochure or postcard. Word of mouth, friend-to-friend, was the only way, and the First Limer program was the trigger.

De-average your customers. The endeavor of de-averaging customers for classical music is an interesting one because on the one hand we're getting a lot better at it and, on the other hand, we continue to fail miserably. Here's what I mean: most classical music institutions (the larger ones anyway) have gotten pretty good at offering a wide variety of options and triggers for different constituencies in their audience. Students and seniors can get discount tickets. Subscriptions offer much more flexibility than before. Things like shorter "rush hour concerts" that start at 6:00 and include a happy hour are becoming more common. All of this is good, and in some communities these sorts of initiatives have had a significant and positive impact. But where de-averaging loses its way is when it comes to the nature of our programming overall: an orchestra season in Portland, Maine, is remarkably similar to one in Portland, Oregon. This is because those in charge of programming (and not just in the orchestra) continue to operate under a set of unchallenged assumptions about what their audiences want. The assumption that seniors won't tolerate contemporary repertoire, for instance, doesn't square with the fact that pretty much every new music ensemble concert I've ever attended has more or less the same age spread as the symphony. Another chestnut is that going to visit an elementary school once a year will convert those kids into symphony patrons later on, or that the only thing that will attract younger audiences are concerts of music from movies or video games. There's nothing wrong with visiting schools or movie and video game nights, but the assumptions behind them are often misplaced—which is why, despite many such initiatives, attendance is still a problem. We have to stop making blanket characterizations of our audiences, and especially of the *target* audiences we seek, and recognize that the elements that make a product magnetic to them are more diverse than we think (and probably different from what we think).

Maintain a steep trajectory. The pace of change in our world is definitely a double-edged sword. Things are regularly upgraded and improved; new products are constantly being introduced. And we can get our hands on them more easily and quickly than ever before. On the other hand, sometimes the drive to continually upgrade doesn't result in an improved product. (Each new iteration of iTunes, for example, seems to be worse than the last.) And the hectic intensity of a media-saturated society, with its constant flux and stimulus, can be exhausting. Against that background, the contemplative and insulated experience of a classical music concert can feel like a welcome (and much needed) oasis.

Unlike our tech cousins, though, maintaining a steep trajectory in the performing arts doesn't mean continually developing entirely new products. On the contrary, it means continually getting *better* at delivering artistic products—old and new—to our audience, at strengthening our strengths and reducing our weaknesses. And there's not an enterprise out there that can't be better. In the classical music world, though, that preservationist mindset creeps into even those institutions and groups devoted to the new and progressive and their assumptions about venue or seating or duration or a host of other things. It's the mindset that if the musical performance is top-notch then everything else doesn't really matter. But if "just good enough" is not permissible for our music making, why should it be okay for the rest of our presentation? Moreover, if one dynamic of our times is that consumers are constantly on the hunt for the new and novel, then it would behoove us to see how we can tap into that dynamic as well. Again, this doesn't mean throwing out the good in what we do; it *does* mean getting a lot more creative about the repertoire we perform and where, when, and how we present it. And it means constantly evaluating what works, what doesn't, and how to improve it. In the tech world, maintaining a trajectory of continual improvement is an existential imperative: fail to maintain it, and you die. In the classical music world, there is usually almost no trajectory of improvement at all, much less a steep one. Yes, performers continually strive to improve their musicianship, but on a programming and organizational level, things remain incredibly stagnant; when new things are tried, they're often done halfheartedly, are not thought out, or are poorly executed. Then, when they fail, they are dropped until the next idea that seems good comes along. To maintain a trajectory of ongoing improvement, however, things have to be better planned, executed with greater commitment, and, perhaps most important, evaluated after the fact so that the next iteration—version 2.0—will be better than the last. So for classical music, maintaining a steep trajectory is essential both to generating a vibrant and fresh energy for our audiences *and* to the long-term growth and success of our institutions.

Don't Make Assumptions, and Think Things Through

One important thread that runs through this entire discussion is the danger of making assumptions about our audiences and the vital importance of subjecting our ideas to careful, critical thought and direction based in reliable data (when we can get it). Time and time again, aspiring entrepreneurs jump to conclusions about what their customers want, what they should do to inspire new customers to come on board, or why something failed to catch on. It's easy to get caught up with an idea, too, particularly if it came in the guise of a flash of inspiration.

I've been guilty of this, too. I remember one year in Pittsburgh our chamber of commerce was going to try a special, free bus that would go up and down the main street a block from our venue for the duration of the summer. I thought this might be a great way to promote our concerts, so I worked out a low-cost deal with the chamber to put a different ad inside the bus every week for the duration of our season. In contemplating what the ads should consist of, I had one of those inspired flashes, a catchy way to contrast the Pittsburgh New Music Ensemble with the stereotype of a "classical music concert." I could hardly wait to share my brilliance with other members of the team!

Each week's new ad would riff on this idea and hopefully catch on as a "thing": "Because Bach didn't have Google," "Because Chopin didn't own earbuds," and so forth. I was positively giddy with excitement over my brilliance, so you can imagine how deflated I was when I showed it to members of the team and got this response:

"Huh."

I explained my thinking behind it and the response remained "Well, yeah. I guess . . ."

As a last-ditch effort, I took my idea to my husband for a little spousal support. He looked at it for a moment and said, "I don't get it."

"What do you mean you don't get it?" I demanded. "Come *on*. Can't you see how cool and clever that is?"

Then he looked me straight in the face. "Honey . . . No."

I was undeterred. I ran the ads anyway, on the bus and in our more expensive print ads (fig. 6.1). I ran each week's meme in the preshow ads reel projected over the stage and dropped them into marketing materials and program inserts whenever I got the chance. I was convinced that it was just clever and pithy enough to catch on, and that once it did, we could riff on it indefinitely.

Figure 6.1 The slogan that should not have been . . .

Then I asked attendees of our concerts what they thought, fully expecting to be vindicated by our fans.

I had one person, *one*, who saw it the way I did. "Oh my God that's brilliant!" she exclaimed. Triumphantly, I reported this back to my husband. "You see? *Lisa* gets it! Ha!"

"Lisa's nuts," he replied.

"Well, yeah, she is." I had to accept it: I might have thought I'd come up with something brilliant, but I was wrong. Something that made complete sense to me didn't resonate with anyone else. If I'd listened to the initial feedback I'd received I wouldn't have wasted the time and money we put into the ad campaign. But I was so sure I was right.

Another example of running with an idea before working it fully through was the Colorado Symphony Orchestra's 2014 "Classically Cannabis" initiative, which followed the legalization of recreational marijuana in the state. The newly legal cannabis industry was interested in aggressively marketing their product to a variety of constituencies, so they approached the Colorado Symphony about giving them some support. What resulted was the "High Note" concert series, which was to be a set of performances by the orchestra at the famous Red Rocks Amphitheatre at which patrons would be encouraged to come to the outdoor venue and, well, smoke their weed.

The initiative made quite a splash in the community and beyond; you may even have caught some of the national news stories. Leaders of the symphony touted the program as an example of their new commitment to "being entrepreneurial." They also stated their intention that the High Note concerts be a draw for younger audiences—a trigger, in other words.

Then things got messy. For one, organizers neglected to check with the city of Denver, which operates Red Rocks and has an ordinance against consumption of marijuana on city property. Moreover, the ballot initiative passed by voters clearly stated that legalization was for private consumption only. The Red Rocks Amphitheatre was both city property and very public: no weed would be allowed there.

Since it was now apparent that any sort of public concert was a nonstarter, the orchestra decided to create a pair of private, invitation-only chamber music events in a local gallery. Tickets started at $75. The events went off without a hitch, but they were a far cry from the original intent, which was, you'll recall, to reach out to younger audiences. But what young person would pay $75 to do something in an art gallery they could do for free at home? (As it turned out, the High Note concerts went on, underwritten by the cannabis industry, but they were no different from any other concert—including the size and demographics of the audience.)

There are some important lessons to be learned from this fiasco. First off, do your homework before you pull the trigger. (There's the importance of completing your backstory again.) But even if the Red Rocks idea hadn't run afoul of the city ordinance, it's still unlikely the concerts would have had the desired result. In order for them to attract an audience that wouldn't otherwise come to the symphony—in other words, for the ability to smoke marijuana at the concert to be an effective trigger—the lack of smoking would have had to be the reason they *weren't* coming before. That's unlikely. Despite leaders' touting of the concerts as an endeavor by the symphony to act entrepreneurially, they in fact overlooked several key principles of entrepreneurship: they were not solving a latent need in their market, nor did they have any data or even anecdotal information to support a bet that inchoate demand would be stimulated. They did not adequately work through the feasibility of their venture, a failing that then forced them into a new model that was completely out of touch with the original intended market. But because it was so novel, and because there was money on the table to make it happen, they forged ahead. In the end, rather than evaluating and seeing if there was a way to adapt their idea for a more effective version 2.0, the idea was dropped entirely. Unfortunately, from start to finish, the initiative was a far cry from effective entrepreneurship.

So as we assess the state of classical music today, we might still disagree on whether or not things are so dire that it needs to be "saved." But it's undeniable that we face some significant challenges: demographic trends point to a decline in our primary audiences; the digital age has taken over our lives and social interactions, while the nineteenth-century concert model we cling to is becoming more and more of an anachronism. While this chapter has focused a lot on orchestras, the same lessons apply to our chamber groups and solo careers: if we don't find new and creative ways to connect the music we love with audiences that value it, our opportunities will become scarcer and scarcer.

I don't personally believe that classical music will be extinct in fifty years, as some have asserted. But I also don't think it will look the same way it does today. It's understandable that such a thought is unsettling for some of us, even threatening. But in times of great change there are also great opportunities. Employing principles of entrepreneurship can help us identify those opportunities, capitalize on them, and create new avenues of support for the music we cherish.

Magic Beans and Golden Eggs

A few years back I learned that my father, an otherwise rational and practical man, regularly purchased tickets for the Powerball.

"Really, Dad? That surprises me."

He shrugged. "I like to daydream about what I'd do if I won."

One of the things I like about humans is that we are essentially an optimistic species. Even in times of great discouragement, most of us still maintain a little flicker of hope that, one day, our dreams will come true. Even if we've given up such thoughts as a practical matter, we still find ways to indulge that part of ourselves—by purchasing lottery tickets, for instance.

I had a student come into my office one day, sit down with a sigh, and declare, "I'm graduating next month, and I have no idea what I'm going to do after that. So I figured I'd better come see you."

It had been a long day, so it took some effort to resist the snarky comeback that popped into my head: *You realize I'm not the career vending machine, right?*

For many young musicians, leaving school and entering the professional world is the point where their essential optimism runs up against their youthful impatience. They're still holding onto the naïve belief that, as long as they've dotted all their *i*'s and crossed all their *t*'s, their careers will unfold in an orderly and straightforward way. So they're ready for things to happen; and if they're not sure what they want, they assume that a visit to the career guy will give them the answer they need.

Of course, it hardly ever works that way. Studies show that most folks will have as many as five distinct careers during their working life—not five different jobs, five different *careers*. For musicians, it can be even more circuitous, since we often maintain multiple careers simultaneously: performer and teacher, with a side order of day job to plug the financial gap; composer and administrator, with a side order of performance; day job, with a side order of performing. Each of us follows her or his own unique path with its own unique combination of activities. And not only are the particulars of that path unclear to us while we're traveling it, we often don't even have a clear idea of where we think we're going (much less where we're *actually* going).

Chapter 1 talked about how fear of the "E-word" can lead to resistance to, or suspicion of, the precepts of entrepreneurship. Another byproduct of fear is the burning desire to find The Answer in the hope that it will provide a clear path forward and allay our anxiety. So along comes entrepreneurship, and with it an implicit hope and expectation that it will provide that Answer, that it'll give us what we need to realize our dreams: A + B + C = Success!

As this book has shown throughout, it hardly ever works out that way. So as we wrap up our time together, I urge you to remember the following.

FAILURE IS YOUR FRIEND

Despite the long-established allergy musicians have to the notion of "failure," for musician-entrepreneurs, failure is the natural result of the process of continual growth, exploration, and refinement. Remember Yngve Berqvist? If he hadn't endured the humiliating failure of his ice sculpture festival he would never have had the insight that led to the Ice Hotel. Fear of failure is a natural thing for almost everybody, but remember that the only way we continue to grow—as musicians, as entrepreneurs, and as people—is to continue to push the boundaries of what we know and can do. Failure is a natural part of that process, but it's also the vehicle through which we uncover and develop the keys to success. Embrace failure as an ally in your quest to be all you can be.

OUR CAREER IS RARELY A STRAIGHT LINE

As looking into the deceptive nature of artist bios showed, it's easy to fall into the trap of thinking that Thing A will automatically and inexorably lead to Thing B. Sometimes that's true, but it can also work in the exact opposite way.

When I was still a graduate student, I had the opportunity to record my clarinet concerto (which I was writing for my final DMA project) with Richard Stoltzman and the Seattle Symphony. I needed money for the recording, so I went to a patron I'd been introduced to and asked her if she would support my project. My pitch was simple: this was an opportunity to have my work realized by world-class artists and would provide a jumpstart to my career that would open all manner of doors and performances at the highest levels. Invest in me, and I'll be off and running.

The gift came through, the recording was made, and then nothing really happened. We got some nice notices in the press, and somehow the recording made its way to Public Radio International and was occasionally broadcast on their member stations—which was cool, but didn't result in an agent from Columbia Artists Management happening to tune in one day and realize she'd just discovered her next superstar. Turns out the project was not the magic key that unlocked the door to a career of fame and fortune. (In fact, since the piece was recorded it has not been performed again!)

I was really devastated by this. I had fallen into the trap of believing that one accomplishment would lead in a direct and immediate way to the next, like simply connecting two dots in a larger design. Instead, I've learned that the dots are rarely connected in that way; in fact, sometimes the dots don't connect at all, or they end up connecting in ways that appear very strange to us at the time. Nobody can predict the future. Things usually unfold in ways we don't foresee, and often the destination is better than anything we envisioned initially: our career is anything but a straight line! Everything, including the entrepreneurial aspects of our careers, is a process, and a mysterious one at that. Entrepreneurship doesn't change this, but it does help us navigate the uncertainty with greater ease. It gives us tools to take advantage of changes and the unforeseen, to turn "bugs" into "features," and to make the most of the inherently twisty and unpredictable nature of our lives and careers.

ENTREPRENEURSHIP IS NO SUBSTITUTE FOR EXCELLENCE

"My teacher and I have been talking, and we agree that I'm not cut out for a performing career . . . so I figured I should come talk to you."

So not only am I the career vending machine, I'm also the last resort of those who can't make it as a performer.

Entrepreneurship is not some fallback thing for those who otherwise lack the talent to "make it" as performers. It's for all musicians, regardless of their path. Learning how to recognize and capitalize on opportunities, how to analyze and grow from setbacks, and how to stimulate demand for our products in the marketplace is a process that benefits the artistic director as much as the soloist, the educator as much as the administrator, the composer as much as the ensemble—and the superstar as much as the unknown. That's what's so great about the tools of entrepreneurship: they work for all situations, and how they are used in your particular set of circumstances is for you to decide.

The sticking point for many, though, is their unshakable belief that their talent will be enough to propel them forward, and that it's someone else's job to worry about the rest. That may have been partly true a century ago when the supply of musicians was a minute fraction of what it is today and a single introduction could significantly change the trajectory of one's career. But it hardly ever works that way now. For one thing, there are far too many musicians for such a system to continue to work, and they're all clamoring for attention; with the Internet, they can clamor far more effectively, too. Even those who are fortunate enough to secure management in the wake of winning a big competition, for instance, will discover that agents do far less for you than they used to and that you'll still need to exhibit a lot of initiative and opportunity recognition to keep your career moving forward. There's really no escaping the fact that, at the end of the day, the course of your career resides in two places: fate and your own hands. You can't control the fate part, but you absolutely can control the part that's in your own hands. Entrepreneurship gives you tools to do just that.

GARBAGE IN, GARBAGE OUT

When computers were starting to become more and more integrated into every aspect of our lives, folks began to learn something important about their limitations: the things that computers did for us were only useful when the input we'd given them was good to begin with. "Garbage in, garbage out" became an expression of the fact that computers were not some magical device to solve every problem, and at breakneck speed; they were only as good as the humans who designed them and the data we put into them.

Entrepreneurship is like that, too. An idea that seems great to us might turn out to be a big flop in the market. A beautifully written business plan might win a competition, but if the numbers used in it are based on unrealistic estimates or pure wishful thinking, it's worthless. Entrepreneurs can be polished in their pitches to potential investors, but the majority of ventures that receive venture funding still end up failing within two years.

Basing entrepreneurial plans on weak (or nonexistent) data is the number one reason why ventures fail, and the creativity, passion, and idealism of many musicians make them particularly susceptible to this pitfall. We get excited and caught up in the joy of creativity, and while that's not a bad thing in and of itself, it can lead us astray. There is simply no substitute for gathering as much information as possible, and nothing will increase your chances of success more than a clear-headed and objective assessment of your market, its needs, the existing competition, and all the other factors discussed in this book. Even then, with the best data and analysis possible, there's no guarantee, but the chances of success are exponentially higher. And without good data and analysis, failure is a lot more likely.

The story of Jack and the Beanstalk has always been a favorite of mine. Like most lasting fairy tales, it taps into a commonly-held aspect of human nature—in this case, the desire for wealth (or success) that comes without any significant effort on our part. Like my dad daydreaming about winning the lottery, we all like to think and hope that someday we'll stumble upon those magic beans that grow and take us to a goose who lays golden eggs. *And they lived happily ever after . . .*

We all want to believe that our own version of that story is out there somewhere, that our "happily ever after" is just one "big break" away. This of course can lead to disillusionment and frustration, even giving up altogether. It can also keep us from doing anything other than locking ourselves in the practice room, while opportunities walk by outside our closed door (with the paper pasted over the window, of course).

But let's consider an alternate ending to the tale. Let's consider that when Jack and his mom chopped down the beanstalk and the giant fell, the crash *killed* the goose. No more golden eggs forthcoming. Then the other two beans never germinated. And now they'd sold their cow, too. What would they do then?

I'd assert that this alternative ending to Jack's story is more akin to the way our careers tend to unfold. Even the most exciting "break" will not propel you forward indefinitely; sometimes things can be going great until they're suddenly derailed (an injury, the closure of your orchestra, the breakup of your chamber group). Life has a way of pulling the rug out from under our feet sometimes. What do we do then?

The point is, entrepreneurship isn't the goose that lays golden eggs. It's not the beanstalk that leads us to riches. It's not even the magic bean that, planted correctly, bursts forth.

It's the insight, ingenuity, tenacity, and strategic intelligence of Jack himself. It's his ability to find a way to turn tragedy into opportunity, to learn from his mistake and do better next time. It's his willingness to engage in a strategic process that will lead to a new way of farming; perhaps Jack develops his craft carving beanstalk remains into art or opens a store selling quilts made from Genuine Giant's Clothes™.

Entrepreneurship is no guarantee of success, nor is it a substitute for putting forward our very best. What it can do is equip us with tools to transform our ideas into products that have value in the marketplace, to analyze outcomes and try again; to see opportunities that others miss; to keep growing and moving forward, guided by a process of reevaluation and reiteration, even when apparent disaster crashes down on us. It's a process of discovery, refinement, and rediscovery, sometimes leading to the realization of a long-held dream, and sometimes leading to something more wonderful than we ever could have imagined when we started out.

We also need to remember that entrepreneurship is not an end in itself; it's just a means to realizing an end. In the organizational chart of our musical lives, the muse remains at the top.

But our muse can be unruly—that's part of its charm, its power. Its ideas can come out of left field; they can be impractical or ahead of their time. They can lack specificity as to how to realize them, or they can be merely the first seeds of something much larger. Sometimes our muse charges ahead like the proverbial bull in a china shop, and sometimes it needs to be prodded.

In short, our muse needs a partner. Not to rein it in or dispense discipline but to help give shape to its ideas, build a mechanism for their realization, and provide a process by which the idea can be refined, adapted, or transformed into something new and better.

That's the role of entrepreneurship: to be a partner for your muse. To help you move from a place of unrealized dreams to one of professional and artistic satisfaction. It's not magic, but the results can still be magical.

An Entrepreneurial Symphony

"Can I take you to lunch? I have an idea to run past you." It was September 2012 and just a day after I'd been to a presentation by the Geological Society of America on the geology of Colorado.

My mind hadn't stopped racing since.

So I had called up my friend Kevin Shuck, executive director of the Boulder Philharmonic, and asked him to lunch.

"Sure," Kevin replied. "What's your schedule like next week?"

"Umm . . . are you free today?"

We met at the Cuban sandwich place nearby, and after sitting down and exchanging some preparatory chitchat, my friend asked me what was on my mind.

"Well, I've got a crazy idea, but I think you're gonna love it."

"Okay . . ."

"Last night I went to one of the community seminars at the credit union. It was on the geology of Colorado—did you know I have a degree in geology as well as music?" He didn't. I went on. "The Geological Society is based here in Boulder, you know—in fact their office is right around the corner from where I live. So of course I had to go to this thing, geek out with the geologists, and get answers to some of the geological questions I've had since moving out here. And during their introduction they mentioned that 2013 will be their 125th anniversary and they're doing all sorts of things to celebrate, culminating in their annual meeting in Denver."

I paused for a moment, and then delivered my punchline: "So here's what we're going to do. The Boulder Phil is going to commission a symphony from me, inspired by the geology of the Rocky Mountains, and we're going to get the Geological Society to underwrite it in celebration of their anniversary."

I held my breath, wondering if he would love the idea or think I'd lost my mind.

"You're right," he replied. "That's a crazy idea. But I love it."

Fast-forward twelve months, nearly to the day, to the point where the final triumphant chord of the symphony rang through the hall and the audience leapt to its feet. It had been quite an intense year. Never before had a commission of mine fallen into place so easily. Never before had I tackled a project of this scope. And never before had I so publically shared the journey of creating a piece of music, from start to finish. Yet here we were: three curtain calls' worth of cheers, and a near-record opening night attendance for the Phil, despite a change of date mere weeks before the performance. How did we do it?

It starts with the Need—in this case, multiple needs, depending on which entity we're talking about. For the Boulder Philharmonic, a geologic symphony fit perfectly with the season they were already planning: a season of works inspired by the natural world. And why would the Phil think that theme would be particularly compelling for the Boulder community? The answer is that they had looked at the characteristics and sensibilities of their local market and identified Boulder's love of the outdoors, close connection to the earth and its resources, and appreciation of the stunning geology that shapes its backdrop. A geologic symphony would surely resonate with this community, and the Boulder Phil would be able to advance its mission of programming music that reflected the sensibilities and interests of its community.

Then there's the Geological Society of America. When we approached them with this idea, they were ecstatic. Geoff Feiss, president of the Geological Society of America Foundation at the time, said: "This is exactly the sort of thing we've been looking for. We've been trying to figure out some sort of keystone event to draw our anniversary celebration together, something that could headline our gala at our convention and celebrate our legacy . . . and not just a speech by some luminary. We wanted something totally outside the box, and this is it!"

So the project would meet the needs of the organizations involved—the Boulder Phil's season and mission, the Geological Society's anniversary—and as a result we had the project underwritten inside a month.

With the commission in place we had unlocked value for the Boulder Phil and the Geological Society, but that was only the first step: we still had to create value for our audience. Of course, we would market the concert just like any other—we couldn't dismiss the fact that people need to know that something is happening, where to go, how to buy tickets, and so forth. But marketing by itself does not create value; it doesn't even have much of an impact on sales if there isn't already a connection between the consumer and the product being offered. Before marketing can kick in, you have to create a connection with the audience you hope to reach. In the case of this project, we believed that we could bring people to the Phil who had never come before. But how would we engage them?

In pondering that question I realized that there were two incredibly valuable assets we needed to put to use with this project. The first was our close proximity to the very geology the music would be depicting. The second was my own unique story: my past as a would-be geologist and how that background would inform the composition of the symphony. I also realized that these assets had to be used in such a way as to demystify both the geology we would be exploring and the way I would translate that geology into musical ideas. Only then could we make this project relevant—and thus valuable—to the audience we hoped to reach.

The strategy that resulted was twofold. First, I would begin producing a video blog sharing my creative journey. Sometimes I would be in my studio talking about the creative process; other times I would be conducting "virtual field trips" to geologic sites throughout the region. And still other v-blog entries would talk about what all this has to do with entrepreneurship. All in all, I produced fifteen videos about the project, most of them between six and fifteen minutes long. The Boulder Phil and the Geological Society posted them on their respective pages as well; soon we had an avid following that cut across constituencies.

Then, as the date of the premiere approached, we conducted a number of events in the community, including talks about the symphony and guided hikes led by naturalists from Boulder Open Space and Mountain Parks and myself, armed with a portable MP3 player and snippets from the symphony to accompany our hike. The first hike, scheduled a week before the premiere, brought more than sixty people—only a small handful of whom were already Boulder Phil patrons. Many of these individuals had seen my v-blog and had been following me for months; others were on the Boulder Open Space and Mountain Parks email list and were intrigued. On the night of the premiere, I saw many of those faces again: the journey from information to engagement was complete. (The second hike, scheduled after the premiere so folks could experience the geology in retrospect, was unfortunately canceled due to the catastrophic floods that hit Boulder a week after our concert.)

Perhaps the most striking evidence of the success of this approach emerged when, less than a month from opening night, the University of Colorado announced that a football game would be taking place the same night. Since the Phil plays in the university's Macky Auditorium, and since a home football game not only closes the whole campus but paralyzes that entire section of town for hours before and after, the concert was going to have to be rescheduled.

Season brochures had already been sent out; ads had been printed. Schedules had been determined, and in the case of my family and friends coming in for the performance, plane tickets purchased. After assessing the various options, the concert was moved to the following night, a Sunday.

September in Boulder is still a time of transition for the locals: many are still spending their weekends hiking and biking in the mountains, while others are settling into the start of a new year on campus. Consequently, opening Night for the Phil has historically been more lightly attended than other concerts during their season. As you can imagine, our worst fear was that this dynamic, in conjunction with the schedule snafu, would result in a weak turnout. We did our best to spread the news and hope for the best: with only a few weeks left, there was not much else we could do. It was the ultimate test of whether or not our engagement efforts had yielded any fruit.

It is in this context that I'm particularly proud of the more than fifteen hundred people who were in Macky Auditorium on opening night, a near-record number for the Boulder Phil's season opener. The Phil's patrons had turned out in force; but perhaps more important, there were geologists, naturalists, and a whole range of other nonregulars who had read about the piece in the press, followed my v-blog, or come to a lecture. Their innate need to be moved by art was met once they were *in* the concert hall, but it was meeting their need to feel a connection to the work that *got them there in the first place*.

That's entrepreneurship at work: when needs get met, value is unlocked. In this case, value was unlocked for the Boulder Philharmonic—a successful season opener and inroads to parts of the community they would not have otherwise reached; and for the Geological Society—great press (including an interview with me in the international science journal *Nature*) and an exciting and unique event for their anniversary. The project has continued to generate value, especially for the Boulder Philharmonic: the commission was so successful that it really launched a whole new era for the orchestra of connecting to the Boulder community through nature and science as a key programming concept. The result of this and subsequent projects has, in turn, made the Boulder Philharmonic one of a handful of regional orchestras that are not just surviving but actually growing and thriving.

Lest we forget, value was unlocked for me, too, and not just value in terms of my commission fee: I finally got to bring together two great passions of my life in a way I had dreamed about for years and write the first of what I hope will be many more symphonies.

ENTREPRENEURIAL LESSONS

Was this just a "one-hit wonder"? Was it entrepreneurship that opened up this opportunity or just good fortune at being in the right place at the right time? I maintain that several entrepreneurial principles were at play here, as follows.

Opportunity Recognition

Given that I had been thinking about how to bring geology into my compositional work for some time, it's not surprising that listening to that seminar from the Geological Society got me thinking about a symphony. But it was the entrepreneur in me that immediately saw how to bring that thought into reality: who would perform it, who would fund it, and how we would promote it. Furthermore, the success of the symphony has injected tremendous energy into my creative life: several other projects have come to mind, none of them remotely related to geology but all based on the same idea of drawing together otherwise unrelated institutions to fund, promote, and perform a newly commissioned work. It's my entrepreneurial mindset that has produced these opportunities, and the entrepreneurial skill of opportunity recognition that will keep me looking for ways to bring these new compositional projects to life.

When Needs Are Met, Value Is Unlocked

When it came time to negotiate a fee for the commission, I consulted the handy "Guide for Commissioning Music" from Meet the Composer and promptly chose a dollar amount from the high end of their suggested scale. What gave me the hutzpah to ask for such a figure? Seeing the project from an entrepreneurial perspective gave me the confidence to recognize the value in the project and to therefore ask for what I thought my symphony was worth: I knew that the value the project brought to my partners would make the raising of those dollars feasible.

Value Must Extend to Your Audience

The most significant paradigm shift that creative artists must make in order to embrace an entrepreneurial career is to accept that their work extends beyond delivery of the artistic product itself. In fact, creation or performance of the work is only the beginning. In the case of the symphony, I recognized that I had to play a central role in reaching out to our prospective audience: the unique aspect of the project was the fusion of the regional geology with a new symphonic work, and as the geologist-composer only I could speak to the creative process as it unfolded. It's true that these efforts took considerable time and energy—the video blog, in particular, was a significant undertaking. But in addition to being a lot of fun, the process of disclosing my creative process and sharing the geology that had inspired me generated tremendous energy in the community and attracted considerable press. The process, in turn, inspired my creative work. On more than one occasion, when the notes were not flowing well, I would set off into the mountains to film some more footage for the v-blog or sit down at the computer to edit the next installment, and in these activities I reconnected to what I was trying to accomplish as an artist. The notes would inevitably start to flow again.

Ironically, I have found that many musicians are not comfortable talking about their artistic work. This is especially true of composers, for whom opening up their inmost thoughts is hard enough to do through their music; putting those impulses into words is even harder. But I maintain that speaking, blogging, or, in the case of this symphony, even hiking about music is simply another kind of performance: it requires preparation, practice, and delivery. And the more one does it, the easier it becomes and the better one gets at it. Audiences want to connect to the things they experience, and the more ways we can make that connection leading up to a performance, the more support we'll get when it's time for folks to buy a ticket. As creatives, it's in our best interest to be actively involved in shaping these connections. Claiming that it's "somebody's else's job" is not only self-defeating, it robs us of a rich range of experiences that help us see the impact of our work and can be creatively stimulating in and of themselves.

The abiding lessons for me from my experience with the symphony are twofold. The first was that thinking entrepreneurially can drive both the creation of new work and its presentation in the marketplace. That's probably not a terribly surprising statement. The second lesson, though, was perhaps more surprising: it wasn't until I embarked on the symphony project that I truly embraced the creative power of entrepreneurial thinking. The result has been a deluge of ideas for new projects, some I've been wondering how to produce for awhile, others emerging only when my entrepreneurial eyes started to see possibilities I had previously overlooked. The creative energy of identifying these opportunities has in turned energized my composition work, and it's this surprising lesson I most wish to pass on to you, my readers: entrepreneurial thinking is more than a way to promote your work; it can actually be a vehicle to fuel the creative process itself and open up new artistic possibilities you hadn't considered before. The entrepreneur in you can support your muse, but your muse can also be an entrepreneur. Allow them to work together, and you can unlock great things!

APPENDIX 2

Open Door Music: Lessons Learned from a Failed Venture

Open Door Music was my first real entrepreneurial venture. I had just finished my DMA at Rice and had elected to stay in Houston and launch my career as an independent freelance composer. As a singer I was often involved with church music in the area, and I had built a small but close-knit network of music directors. I began to think of how this network might help support me in ways beyond singing gigs, and that's what led to Open Door Music.

Open Door Music was a church music service designed to provide custom-made arrangements, instrumental accompaniments, and original compositions to church music programs in the greater Houston area. In my conversations with church music directors I repeatedly heard that the thing they needed most were things like good brass arrangements for Easter hymns and fresh service music for things like psalms and sung responsorial prayers. Anthems that were easy for their choirs to put together but still musically substantial were also sorely lacking. Since I enjoyed sacred music both as a performer and a composer, I saw an opportunity to create a steady income stream that would supplement the larger but more unpredictable sums that came from commissions for concert works.

Based on conversations with a few music director colleagues, I drew up a list of services I would offer and a price range for projects depending on their scope. I then created a nifty brochure in the shape of large, wooden church doors that opened to reveal the products and services of Open Door Music. A short bio spoke to my qualifications, and contact information was prominently displayed. I printed one thousand copies and *Voilà*: I was in business!

Next I started to think about how I would reach the Houston church music market. Like any large metropolitan area, especially in the South, Houston has a *lot* of churches of every stripe and size. In addition, I was involved with a monthly lunch group of about a hundred church musicians from around town. I figured this would be a good point of entry into the marketplace. I made an announcement at the next month's luncheon and passed around brochures to those who raised their hands (a dozen, perhaps). Later, I spent hours working my way through the phone book (don't laugh, it was 1994: we still had phone books back then!) and assembled a database of churches I decided were likely potential customers (though my criteria for culling the list were mainly based on whether the name sounded like an established sort of place that might have a robust music program). Several hundred more brochures were stamped and sent out.

And then I waited for the orders to come streaming in.

When that went nowhere, I started to follow up. I left a lot of voicemail messages. I nudged my friends in the field, who kindly kicked some work my way. But it was nowhere near enough to make much of a difference in my quest to support myself solely through composing. I was sitting right in the middle of this massive market, yet I could not figure out how to unlock value for my work in it. My market research (albeit modest) indicated that my prices were reasonable; a subscription plan offered even more savings but had no takers. What was I missing?

What was missing was a solid business model. My discussions with colleagues had revealed a genuine need, but my venture only went so far in meeting it. The problem resided in two interconnected issues. The first was that even the largest and best-funded churches still had limited budgets; they simply did not have the means to *regularly* purchase my services, even though my prices were reasonable. This led to the second problem: the only way to generate consistent orders would be to drop my prices far below the point at which the time I spent on each project would be reasonably compensated. Since the whole idea behind the business was to provide compositions and arrangements *made to order,* I could not find a solution to these issues that was financially viable and sustainable for any length of time. The last problem was one I hadn't fully encountered yet but was lurking just over the horizon: with desktop publishing of music only in its infancy and thus not an option, the costs of producing a professional-grade piece of sheet music would have further eroded what little income was coming in. In short, there was no way for any one unit of product (an arrangement or composition) to pay for itself, and there was no economy of scale to be had when each order was one of a kind. The math simply didn't work.

I shuttered Open Door Music not long after I'd opened it.

The failure of this venture was quite a blow, and it was a long time before I learned enough about the entrepreneurial process to understand what had gone wrong. For one, my market research was inadequate—and therefore misleading. I spoke to a few supportive friends, and while they had endorsed the price points in my menu of services, I neglected to ask them if they would purchase those services on a *regular and ongoing basis*. I also made the mistake of extrapolating the responses of a few individuals to the entire Houston market. (Those folks weren't even representative of the wider market, since they hailed from some of the city's largest and best-funded music programs. They also already knew me personally: beware of putting too much stock in the feedback of your friends if they're also your potential customers!) Thus, the heart of my business model—whether the income I could reasonably expect to receive would adequately cover my costs (including the value of my *time*)—was fatally flawed. Finally, I utterly failed the flexibility and adaptability test: I was so wedded to the notion of *custom-made* orders that I would not consider other alternative models more akin to a traditional publishing business. After all, my sources had indicated needs for several different types of music they could not find elsewhere: though my solution was flawed, the need was still there. I just wasn't able (or willing) to consider a different approach. On top of all these problems, hindsight indicates that the timing was simply wrong: ten years later I might have tried again, this time aided by inexpensive desktop publishing, digital distribution, and social media to personally engage a market far beyond Houston. (*Hmmm . . .*)

The Open Door Music story illustrates how important it is to have a solid business model—one that works at the outset *and* that is sustainable over the long haul. In the case of this venture, once the first few months' worth of work dried up, the flaw in my business model became apparent: even my music director friends were not going to give me work on a consistent and ongoing basis. The need was there, but identifying a need in the marketplace is just the first step to a successful—and sustainable—business venture.

TEN QUESTIONS FOR WHEN YOUR VENTURE IS IN TROUBLE

As you'll recall from many of the examples in this book, successful entrepreneurs often miss the mark with their first attempt at an entrepreneurial venture. If we accept it as a given that not every venture we try will find immediate success, what are some specific strategies we can employ to reveal the problem (which, in turn, will hopefully lead us to a solution)? Here are ten questions you should ask yourself if and when your venture encounters rough waters.

1. Is Your Market Research Flawed?

Scrutinize your assumptions. Are they informed by robust research and data? Is your viewing of the data skewed by your own bias? Are you confident that the feedback you've received from potential customers is unbiased? Are there gaps in your data that are proving to be problematic? Have you built an accurate picture of your ideal customers—and by accurate, I mean understanding their buying habits, financial capacities, sensibilities, and needs?

2. Does Your Business Model Require Repeated Purchases from Single Customers, and If It Does, Have You Overestimated the Frequency of Repeat Purchases?

As the Open Door Music case illustrates, relying on repeat purchases can be tricky unless you're sure of two things: (1) your customers are willing and able to afford your product on an ongoing basis, and (2) you are able to maintain a steady supply of your product, something that may be difficult if the product in question is always new/unique. Think about that for a moment: most products we consume on a repeated basis are mass-produced, making it a lot easier for the manufacturer to keep up with the market's demand. Keeping up with repeated purchases of something that is new every time is a very different proposition. Make sure you've thought this through carefully!

3. Are There Technological Tools You Can Employ to Deliver Your Product More Cheaply and Efficiently?

In the case of Open Door Music, the emergence of desktop publishing tools and Internet distribution would have been game changers in another five years. So in addition to assessing the current state of technology in your field, give some thought to emerging trends: what changes are over the horizon, and how might they impact your business? Alternatively, you may identify a new tool that emerging technologies can finally provide—perhaps the real entrepreneurial opportunity for you is in a tech venture!

4. Are You Overlooking Opportunities to Leverage Economies of Scale?

The magic of scaling is that once you've put in the time, effort, and money to make the first iteration of a product, producing more of the same thing costs you relatively little. For Open Door Music, a made-to-order arrangement of an Easter processional would still have likely appealed to any number of other churches with the same need. Incorporating this into Open Door Music's business model might have opened up sufficient sales to justify the time and opportunity cost of creating the arrangement in the first place. Not all ventures are designed to scale, especially in the arts: if the value of your product resides in its unique nature, then scaling is difficult (or impossible) and may undermine that value. That said, with some creative thinking you may still be able to identify aspects of your product/venture that can, indeed, benefit from scaling. Sometimes the revenue that scaling brings in can make the difference between an unsustainable venture and one that thrives.

5. Are All the Components of Your Value Proposition in Sync with Each Other?

As this book shows over and over again, the product that ultimately finds success in the marketplace may be substantially different from the original conception. This is because, regardless of how diligently you do your home-work, you can never completely predict how the market will respond to your product. So you launch your product or venture, and the response is not what you hoped or expected. What's gone wrong? Clearly, there's a disconnect of some sort: your product is not unlocking the value you hoped it would. To figure out what's gone wrong, go back and work through your value proposi-tion. Remember that the value proposition articulates what your product is (and its attributes), who it's for, and how they benefit. If your product isn't unlocking value in the marketplace, then one or more of those three elements is out of whack. Perhaps the attributes of your product are not the best way to deliver the benefits your customers want. (You need to change the user interface of your app, or the venue for your concert, or the channels you use to reach your customers.) Perhaps you're targeting the wrong customers. (You thought that consumers with attributes A, B, and C were the ones who would love your product, but, in fact, it's consumers with attributes A, C, and F.) Or perhaps the value in your product is actually different from what you realized or intended. (The app you intended to teach musical skills through gaming becomes popular as a tool for entertainment, not education.)

6. Is Your Product Sufficiently Different from the Competition to Lure Customers Away from Existing Offerings?

Remember that if you are trying to enter a market with existing products/ services, you need to be sure that what you're delivering is differentiated from your competition—and that this differentiation is sustainable. Entrepreneurs commonly try to differentiate themselves on price (i.e., "my product is cheaper than the competition"), but this is usually not sustainable: unless you have some sort of proprietary technology or intellectual property that protects your price advantage, there's probably not much keeping your competitor from responding with even lower prices. If you're in a price war, who is more likely to be the last one standing: the newbie without customers, consumer awareness, or deep pockets . . . or the well-established players with existing market share, a positive reputation, and some money saved in the bank? So, rather than focusing on differentiation based on price, make sure you're basing your differentiation on the product attributes you are most uniquely qualified to deliver. Deliver unique value through your personal, unique product, and your differentiation will be sustainable indefinitely.

7. **Have You Devised a Compelling "Story" Surrounding Your Product? That Is, Do Your Brand, Marketing, and Customer Interactions Demonstrate the Value of Your Product in a Clear and Compelling Way?**

It's easy to be so close to your product or venture that you make the mistake of assuming its value is self-evident. So you skip over the step of understanding and articulating the story behind what you do, why you do it, and why it matters. Your story is, in essence, a more human illustration of your value proposition: *this is my product, here are some of its attributes, and let me tell you why these things matter.* Artists have such powerful stories to tell, stories that delve deep down into the human experience and have the power to unite us, move us, and change us. Make sure you haven't glossed over the important step of fleshing out that story and then making sure it infuses every element in your brand and marketing.

8. **Does the Customer Experience of Your Product Allow Them to Completely Experience Its Value, or Are There Barriers Keeping Them from Fully Appreciating What You Have to Offer?**

Every product—even the most straightforward utilitarian one—has a wide range of elements that affect consumers' experience of it. As several chapters of this book discuss, in the arts those elements range far beyond the art itself. So perhaps you've put a great deal of effort into creating a concert that flows organically and successfully weaves a thread of meaning throughout . . . but the "feel" of the venue isn't the right setting for what you're trying to accomplish. Maybe you put on a great show, but you don't give your audience a chance to interact with the performers afterward—so you've laid the foundation for a relationship with your customers and then failed to finish what you've started. Perhaps your lessons are extraordinary, but your home studio space is disrupted by noisy neighbors or your dog who launches into a barking frenzy every time somebody walks down your busy street. The bottom line is that if you're convinced that your core product is as good as it can be and you're still not connecting with your customers as much as you hoped, you need to closely examine *every* aspect of the customer experience, from start to finish, and look for issues or barriers that diminish the value of your product in the eyes of your customers.

9. Are There Industry Trends Beyond Your Control That Render Your Venture Obsolete or Unsustainable?

I often ask students to imagine they're in the year 1908—the year the Model T Ford came to market. For the first time, an automobile was produced efficiently enough to make it affordable. Very soon, cars would be the primary mode of transportation for almost everyone. Now imagine that you're a maker of horse-drawn carriages. Up until now, cars were more or less novelties for the rich and eccentric; the market for carriages remained large and secure. But now something new has come along that's going to fundamentally shift the transportation paradigm. How will you react to that? We can actually look at real carriage manufacturers from the era to find out. Some of them simply started to make bodies for cars; others went even further and got into making their own automobiles. Still others went out of business when the market they knew and understood dried up. Markets rarely remain stable— especially nowadays. Smart entrepreneurs are constantly looking ahead for changes on the horizon. They're observing the habits of consumers and trying to anticipate changing or emerging needs and sensibilities. Of course, nobody can predict the future. But remaining oblivious to changes in technology, social trends, and market sensibilities will guarantee that you'll be caught flat-footed when the next paradigm shift comes to your field. Better to be looking ahead and avoid becoming just like those carriage makers in 1908 who refused to recognize the importance of Henry Ford's new product.

What's particularly interesting about the carriage-to-cars example is the contrast between those who applied their expertise in a new context versus those who took the full leap into manufacturing cars—a new industry altogether. The carriage makers Fred and Charles Fisher started making automobile bodies in 1908, using their expertise in fine carriages to build auto bodies that were comfortable and quiet. Soon they were the largest maker of automobile bodies in the world. They were later purchased by General Motors, and the Fisher trademark remains valuable to this day. On the other hand, carriage companies that attempted the full leap into automobile manufacturing almost universally failed. (The only exception was Studebaker, which remained in the car business until 1967.) These entrepreneurs, though brave, were entering a business they knew nothing about; the chasm between carriage making to automobile manufacturing was simply too large to clear in a single step. So when you identify changes to your market or field that have the potential to wipe out your existing business, you needn't jump ship into something else altogether. Instead, think about how your existing knowledge, expertise, and experience can be applied in a new way. Think about how the core of your artistry can be redirected or reshaped—rather than abandoned.

10. Are You Sure That Your Personal Investment in This Product Isn't Clouding Your Judgment or Causing You to Be Inflexible?

Whether they're artists or not, entrepreneurs tend to get attached to their products. They've invested a lot of time, effort, and, sometimes, money, in developing their idea, producing a prototype, and so forth. Yet this book emphasizes the tendency for products to undergo tweaks and revisions before they find success: entrepreneurs who embrace this process are more likely to find success. Conversely, behind every failed venture is a story, and often it's a story of stubborn refusal to respond to what the market is saying. A related story is one in which the entrepreneur recognizes that something needs to change but then lets her or his established worldview dictate assumptions or bias research. (Think of the symphony orchestra that spends a lot of time and money with initiatives to attract younger audiences but never hosts focus groups of younger audiences to find out what *they* say they want.) In both cases, the result is the same: hit-or-miss success, at best; abject failure at the worst. Being able to hear what the market is telling you, therefore, requires setting aside your ego and feelings. It requires careful research and as objective a reading of the results as possible. And it is best accomplished when your attitude is one of serving your customers first and foremost—rather than serving yourself.

APPENDIX 3

Exploring the Business Model Canvas

Chapter 5 introduces the Business Model Canvas, an incredibly useful tool for mapping out the various components of a venture and how they relate to each other. The Business Model Canvas is a visual representation of the main components in any business and illustrates how those components relate to each other. The Canvas also has the benefit of working for virtually any sort of venture: for profit, not-for-profit, a service, a hard product, you name it. It can illustrate a corporation with thousands of employees or the freelance activities of a solo musician. It can be an excellent visual summary of your venture's current state, or it can be a prelaunch worksheet to aid in developing a solid business model. And since it's an open-source document, you can print as many blank Canvases as you need!

The Business Model Canvas will be most useful in addressing questions 4 and 5 in the entrepreneurial process discussed in chapter 5. ("Is my solution financially and logistically feasible and sustainable?" and "How will I implement my solution?") By working through each segment of the Canvas, you can ensure that all the basic elements of a sound business model are present. The Canvas also helps you see how changing one component of your model can benefit (or undermine) others—meaning that you can "game out" various scenarios during your planning stages and can continue to do so as your venture grows and develops. Because you can visualize changes to your business model in the abstract, you are able to exercise greater flexibility and adaptability, too.

The Business Model Canvas is divided into three main regions: market (customer segments, relationships, and channels), operations (key activities, resources, and partners), and financial (income streams and expenses/costs). The value proposition is placed in the center of the Canvas and is the center of gravity around which everything else revolves. What results is a graphical representation of how the entrepreneur's maxim, explored in chapter 3, operates in the context of a specific venture. A brief outline of the function of each component of the Canvas follows; you can find additional resources for a more in-depth exploration of the Canvas and its many uses in the bibliography.

THE MARKET REGION

We'll begin on the market side of the Canvas, with customer segments, relationships, and channels.

Customer Segments

This area gives a description of the customers your product serves. Understanding our customers goes beyond describing *who* they are; it also involves things like their socioeconomic attributes and psychographics/sensibilities and, perhaps, things like geography or a host of other demographic categories. As always, be as specific as you can with defining these customers, and support your descriptions with as much evidence-based research as you can.

Customer Relationships and Customer Channels

I address these two areas together because they are inextricably linked to each other—and often confused. "Relationships" refers to the *nature* of the interaction between venture and customer; "channels" refers to the *mechanism* employed to maintain your customer relationships and deliver your value proposition. For instance, take an online retailer like Amazon. The customer relationship is virtual (you never actually speak to a person), and somewhat personalized ("People who bought this product also liked this"). The customer channels for maintaining that customer relationship include the website and the proprietary algorithms for helping to predict what other products you might like based on your and others' buying history. Other customer channels include Amazon's system for physically delivering your product (warehouses, independent vendors, the package delivery companies such as UPS, FedEx, and the US Postal Service). It's best to think about customer relationships first: what's the *best way* (or ways) to connect with your customers and embody your value proposition? The answer to that question will in turn dictate which customer channels are the best ones to maintain and support the customer relationships you wish to foster with your customers. See how these components are all interrelated?

THE OPERATIONAL REGION

Once the market side of the Canvas is complete, you'll use what you've worked out there to guide the operational side of your venture (key activities, resources, and partners).

Key Activities

This area is probably the most expansive of all components of the Business Model Canvas, since it includes literally every action required to smoothly and efficiently deliver your value proposition to your customers, via your customer relationships and channels. This includes everything from acquiring the supplies you need to spending time on marketing or seeking customers. To take a relatively simple example, "key activities" for your private teaching studio include more than just teaching lessons; they also include keeping on top of the latest method books and resources, maintaining your website and social media, hosting neighborhood meet-and-greets, conducting clinics at local schools, keeping up with bills and bookkeeping, and all the rest. Anything that you or an employee needs to *do* to make your business run is included here. As you assemble your list of key activities, it's a good idea to talk with a mentor or colleague who has been in business for awhile: they'll likely share some important tasks you might not have thought of initially. And if you're still in the planning stages, careful consideration of key activities is also helpful in identifying the opportunity cost of your venture.

Key Resources and Key Partners

These two areas are taken together because, just as with customer relationships and channels, they are in a close (and often symbiotic) relationship with each other. "Key resources" are everything you *need* to operate your venture. These can be tangible things like studio space, an instrument, software and equipment, and so on, or intangible things like your training and expertise. Partnerships are relationships with other entities that help you deliver your value proposition in a better, more efficient, and/or more cost-effective manner. For Amazon, their partnership with a host of independent vendors all over the world means they don't have to warehouse every product available through their website. They can focus on distribution and leave the vast majority of the actual physical products in somebody else's shop or warehouse. These partnerships are absolutely essential to Amazon's business model. For your venture, a "key partner" might be a shared workspace, the church basement you rent at a reduced rate for your class recitals, the copyist you employ for your manuscripts, or the publisher who distributes your work. Ideally, "partnerships" should accomplish two things: first, they should conduct a key activity or deliver a key resource better, cheaper, or faster than you could yourself, and second, the relationship should be *mutually* beneficial. If your "partners" aren't also benefiting from the relationship in some way, you're not going to be able to count on it over the long run. As you are thinking about the key activities and resources you need for your venture, make sure you spend considerable time thinking creatively about how they might be covered by a partnership: a good partnership can save you money, free you up to focus on the things you do best, and even open up doors to new pools of customers you might not have been able to reach on your own.

THE FINANCIAL REGION

Now, with market and operations fully fleshed out, you're ready to crunch some numbers! Often, when folks are trying to sketch out a business model for their venture, they will start with income and expenses. Unfortunately, as with so many other mistakes made by novice entrepreneurs, this is completely backward. Completing the "revenue streams" area of the Canvas is more than just identifying how you'll make money. You must determine the correct price for your product, how many customers you can project in a given period of time, and how often they will likely make a purchase—none of which can be determined without a thorough understanding of the market area of the Canvas. Likewise, you can't get an accurate handle on expenses until you've fully worked through all of your key activities, resources, and partnerships. It's tempting to skip all that hard work, pull up a spreadsheet, and start entering numbers. But unless those numbers are informed by careful working out of the other Canvas areas, they'll likely result in the proverbial "garbage in, garbage out" problem. And if, after all your hard work, you get to the financial region of the Canvas and the numbers just don't work, don't despair: go back and start seeing how you might change other areas of the Canvas to produce a more viable financial model. Is there a key partner you've overlooked who could reduce your expenses? Are there some key activities you can take care of yourself and save some money? Or, more fundamentally, do you need to go back to the market region of the Canvas and see if you've really identified the best product-market fit for your gifts and abilities? It's in these sorts of situations where the flexibility of the Business Model Canvas is so useful: it helps you experiment with a wide range of scenarios in a holistic way and readily identify how changes in one area of the Canvas influence others.

THE CENTER OF GRAVITY: YOUR VALUE PROPOSITION

Since it ties together all the other components in the Canvas, we end with the value proposition. The value proposition resides in the center of the Canvas because it is the foundation on which all other aspects of the entrepreneurial process rest. It's the concise summary of why your venture exists: what it is, who it's for, and how they benefit. What's new about the value proposition in terms of the Business Model Canvas is that you can now clearly see how it guides virtually every aspect of your venture. It's not a passive thing; it's a determinative force. Given your value proposition, what is the best way to relate to your customers (customer relationships)? What channels are the best ones to support your customer relationships? What activities, resources, and partnerships are required to deliver your value proposition effectively and efficiently, and do the numbers reflect a viable and sustainable business model? Also, because the Canvas should be a constant work in progress, you should not only start with a value proposition but also revisit it once you've worked your way through the rest of the Canvas: given all the other components, do you now see some ways in which your value proposition might be modified, strengthened, or clarified? What have you learned about your value proposition by completing the other elements of the Canvas? Every relationship in the Business Model Canvas, but especially the relationship between the value proposition and all other components, is a two-way street.

METHODS FOR EXPLORING THE CANVAS

To get to know and understand the Business Model Canvas better, we'll use the same approach as with the five questions of the entrepreneurial process: beginning with examples unrelated to your own venture before applying it to your own venture.

1. For your first interactions with the Business Model Canvas, it is useful to look at some examples from other industries. The book *Business Model Generation* has many of these, and it explores each aspect of the Canvas in detail. When you're ready, try some Canvases of your own based on known, existing companies. For instance, what would a Canvas for Pandora look like? Amazon? Facebook? What about your local symphony orchestra or community music school? It doesn't really matter what business you pick; the Canvas is applicable to virtually any sort of product, service, or business type. Just make sure you know enough about how that particular business operates so you can input good information. (And if you don't

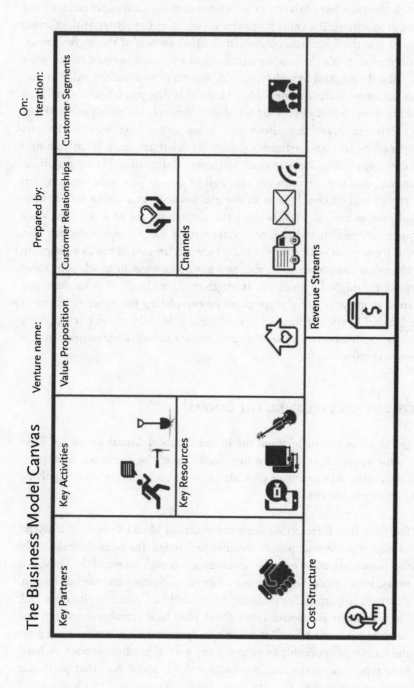

Figure App 3.1 The Business Model Canvas

know, do some research and find out.) Another good exercise would be to make a Canvas for any one of the examples in this book.

2. A more advanced exercise to do with the Canvas is to see what happens to each component when one thing about the business model changes. For instance, which components of Facebook's Canvas would change—and how—if they went to a paid subscription model? Have some fun seeing what kinds of wrenches you can throw into the business models of companies you know or admire. The results can sometimes be quite illuminating!

3. You can also use the Canvas for problem-solving. For instance, create a Canvas for Open Door Music and then ask yourself this question: what aspect(s) of the Canvas would need to change—and *how*—in order to make this venture a viable and sustainable enterprise?

4. Once you feel comfortable with the various components of the Canvas, how they interact with one another, and how different sorts of businesses have different Canvases, you're ready to create a Canvas for your own venture idea. (Again, it can be one that currently lives only in your brain or whatever you've already got up and running.) Remember that your Canvas, like a business plan, should be a living document. As you learn more and as circumstances change, you should be updating your Canvas in order to have a current and accurate picture of the dynamics of your venture. Think of it as kind of like a spreadsheet, where inputting new data generates new tallies. If you've got space in your studio, keep your Canvas constantly in view by putting up a whiteboard with your Canvas blocked out on it in tape. Then use those erasable markers to change and update the various components as your venture evolves!

5. Finally, because the Canvas is a visual tool that's easy to understand, it's a great way to get feedback from others. Ask friends and colleagues for their impressions of your model: what have you missed? Are you making any shaky assumptions? Do the various components truly reflect the value proposition?

For a comprehensive study of the Business Model Canvas and its many applications, I recommend the excellent book *Business Model Generation*. It's an open-source asset, so a wealth of information is also available online (including blank Canvases for you to download and copy as often as you like). Once you've spent some time refining your Canvas and solidifying your data, you can proceed to creating a business plan. If your Canvas work is done well, the business plan will simply be a more detailed, step-by-step plan for realizing the Canvas as an actual venture. Once again, the Internet is your friend, with many templates and guides for creating a business plan available. You'll soon discover that completing that plan will be infinitely less daunting if you've first completed a robust Canvas. So go forth, explore, and have some fun with this wonderful tool!

BIBLIOGRAPHY

This bibliography includes all the works referenced in this book, as well as other useful resources.

Americans for the Arts. Arts and Economic Prosperity Report. Washington, DC: Americans for the Arts, 2012.

Amussen, Gretchen, Angela Beeching, and Joan-Albert Serra. "New Approaches to Entrepreneurship in the Performing Arts." Special issue, *Arts and Humanities in Higher Education* 15, no. 3/4 (August 2016).

Beeching, Angela. *Beyond Talent: Creating a Successful Career in Music*. 2nd ed. New York: Oxford University Press, 2010.

Blaug, Mark. "Where Are We Now on Cultural Economics?" *Journal of Economic Surveys* 15, no. 2 (2001): 123–143.

Charters, Steve. "Aesthetic Products and Aesthetic Consumption: A Review." *Consumption, Markets and Culture* 9, no. 3 (2006): 235–255.

Cutler, David. *The Savvy Musician*. Pittsburgh: Helius Press, 2010.

Cutler, David. *The Savvy Music Teacher: Blueprint for Maximizing Income and Impact*. New York: Oxford University Press, 2015.

Essig, Linda. "Frameworks for Educating the Artist in the Future: Teaching Habits of Mind for Arts Entrepreneurship." *Artivate: A Journal of Entrepreneurship in the Arts* 1, no. 2 (2013): 65–77.

Florida, Richard. *The Rise of the Creative Class: And How It's Transforming Work, Leisure, Community and Everyday Life*. New York: Basic Books, 2002.

Geroski, Paul A. *The Evolution of New Markets*. Oxford: Oxford University Press, 2003.

Grantmakers in the Arts. "Arts Funding Snapshot: GIA's Annual Research on Support for Arts and Culture." *GIA Reader* 25, no. 3 (2014): 1–10.

Hirschman, Elizabeth. "Aesthetic Ideologies and the Limits of the Marketing Concept." *Journal of Marketing* 47 (Summer 1983): 45–55.

Hirschman, Elizabeth, and Morris Holbrook. "The Experiential Aspects of Consumption: Consumer Fantasies, Feelings, and Fun." *Journal of Consumer Research* 9 (September 1982): 132–140.

Hirschman, Elizabeth, and Morris Holbrook. "Hedonic Consumption: Emerging Concepts, Methods and Propositions." *Journal of Marketing* 46 (Summer 1982): 92–101.

Holbrook, Morris. "Mapping the Retail Market for Esthetic Products: The Case of Jazz Records." *Journal of Retailing* 58, no. 1 (1982): 114–131.

Inter-University Consortium for Political and Social Research. *Survey of Public Participation in the Arts*, U.S. Department of Commerce. Bureau of Census, U.S.

Department of Labor. Bureau of Labor Statistics, National Endowment for the Arts. Ann Arbor: 2013.

Kennicott, Philip. "America's Orchestras Are in Crisis: How an Effort to Popularize Classical Music Undermines What Makes Orchestras Great." *New Republic*, August 25, 2013. https://newrepublic.com/article/114221/orchestras-crisis-outreach-ruining-them.

Klein, Gary. "Performing a Project Premortem." *Harvard Business Review* (September 2007).

Klickstein, Gerald. *The Musician's Way: A Guide to Practice, Performance, and Wellness.* New York: Oxford University Press, 2009.

Lacher, Kathleen T. "Hedonic Consumption: Music as Product." *Advances in Consumer Research* 16 (1989): 367–373.

Lacher, Kathleen T., and Richard Mizerski. "An Exploratory Study of the Response and Relationships Involved in the Evaluation of, and in the Intention to Purchase New Rock Music." *Journal of Consumer Research* 21 (1994): 366–380.

Levy, Sidney J. "Symbols for Sale." *Harvard Business Review* 37 (July–August 1959): 117–119.

National Endowment for the Arts. *Beyond Attendance: A Multi-modal Understanding of Arts Participation.* Washington, DC: 2008.

National Endowment for the Arts. *How a Nation Engages with Art: Highlights from the 2012 Survey of Public Participation in the Arts.* NEA Research Report no. 57. Washington, DC: 2012.

National Endowment for the Arts. *When Going Gets Tough: Barriers and Motivations Affecting Arts Attendance.* NEA Research Report no. 59. Washington, DC: 2015.

National Endowment for the Arts. *Spring 2016 Imagine Your Parks Projects.* Washington, DC: 2016.

Nytch, Jeffrey. "The Aesthetic Product as Entrepreneurial Driver: An Arts Perspective on Entrepreneurial Innovation." *Journal of Management Policy & Practice* 13, no. 5 (2012): 11–18.

Nytch, Jeffrey. "Beyond Marketing: Entrepreneurship, Consumption, and the Quest to Rebuild Audiences for the Performing Arts." *Journal of Marketing Development and Competitiveness* 7, no. 4 (2013): 87–93.

Nytch, Jeffrey. "The Case of the Pittsburgh New Music Ensemble: An Illustration of Entrepreneurial Theory in an Artistic Setting." *Artivate: A Journal of Entrepreneurship in the Arts* 1, no. 2 (2012): 25–34.

Osterwalder, Alexander, and Yves Pigneur. *Business Model Generation: A Handbook for Visionaries, Game Changers, and Challengers.* Hoboken: Wiley, 2010.

Rabideau, Mark, ed. *The 21CM Introduction to Music Entrepreneurship.* Lanham, Md.: Rowman and Littlefield, 2018.

Ries, Eric. *The Lean Startup: How Today's Entrepreneurs Use Continuous Innovation to Create Radically Successful Businesses.* New York: Crown, 2011.

Sarasvathy, Saras D. "Causation and Effectuation: Toward a Theoretical Shift from Economic Inevitability to Entrepreneurial Contingency." *Academy of Management Review* 26, no. 2 (2001): 243–263.

Sarasvathy, Saras D. *Effectuation: Elements of Entrepreneurial Expertise. New Horizons in Entrepreneurship.* Northampton, MA: Edward Elgar, 2008.

Slywotzky, Adrian. "How Symphonies Grew Strong Audiences by Killing the Myth of the Average Consumer." *FastCompany.com*, October 13, 2011. https://www.fastcompany.com/1785985/how-symphonies-grew-strong-audiences-killing-myth-average-consumer.

Slywotzky, Adrian, and Karl Weber. *Demand: Creating What People Love before They Know They Want It*. London: Headline, 2011.

Tendler, Adam. *88 x 50: A Memoir of Sexual Discovery, Modern Music and the United States of America*. New York: Adam Tendler, 2012.

Ward, Thomas. "Cognition, Creativity, and Entrepreneurship." *Journal of Business Venturing* 19 (2004): 173–188.

York, Jeffrey, Saras D. Sarasvathy, and Andrea Larson. "The Thread of Inchoate Demand in Social Entrepreneurship." In *Values and Opportunities in Social Entrepreneurship*, edited by Kai Hockers, Johanna Mair, and Jeffrey Robinson. New York: Palgrave Macmillan, 2010, 141–162.

INDEX

Murray, Brooke, 40–41
muse, 24, 43, 77, 125, 127, 185
  entrepreneurship as partner, 186, 192
music
  classical (*see* classical music)
  education of, 14, 44, 61, 155, 164
  emotional/spiritual aspect of, 10
  needs fulfilled by, 72, 74
  as a product (*see* product, musical)
  See also market
musicians
  conservatory-trained, 14
  need for (*see* market, need)
  speaking
    about compositions, 192
    onstage, 147, 171
  success and failure, 14, 77, 158
  toolbox, 16, 21, 33, 58, 77, 99, 183

National Endowment for the Arts, 91, 106,
    153, 156–57, 161, 166
National Park Service, 165
need. *See* market, need
Netflix, 104–5
"Net-MC-Dohs." *See* Network of Music
    Career Development Officers
Network of Music Career Development
    Officers, 1
neuroscience, 72
New World Symphony, 109–13, 173
New York Chamber Symphony, 7
Noe, Kevin, 169
Nytch, David, 132
Nytch, Jeffrey
  Concerto for Clarinet and Orchestra,
    xv, 182–83
  investment advisor, 55–58
  Open Door Music, 193–94
  piano study, 27–28
  slogan campaign, 176–78
  students, interaction with, 1–2, 35,
    40–41, 181, 183
  Symphony No. 1, "Formations," 187–92

observation
  entrepreneurial, 6, 24, 29
  strategic, 16–17, 30, 96, 99,
    116, 120–21
opportunity
  cost, 35, 137

through differentiation, 74
  recognition, 6–8, 21, 23, 30, 165, 184
  See also classical music; digital
    revolution; entrepreneurial,
    mindset, three components of

PARMA Recordings, 7–8, 34
patronage, 37. *See also* classical music,
    business models
Pittsburgh, 82, 169
Pittsburgh New Music Ensemble, 47,
    125–27, 169–70, 173–74, 177
  First Limer program, 126–27, 143,
    170, 174
  Theatre of Music, 46, 126,
    169–70, 173–74
prairie dog eradication, 64. *See also*
    market, "niche"
"premortem," 33
price. *See* ticket, price
product, 60–62, 70
  art as, 60
  artistic, 2, 44, 100
  artistic (hedonic)/utilitarian, 89–90
  defined, 60–61
  differentiation, 68, 73–74, 76
  industry/market
    distinctions, 70–71
    examples of, 70
  linked with market, 70
  musical
    examples of, 60–61
    purpose of, 67
  need for (*see* market, need)
  symbolic associations, 89
programming philosophy,
    self-defeating, 70
proposition, value. *See* value, proposition
psychographics. *See* market, psychographics
Puts, Kevin
  The Manchurian Candidate, 171
pyramid. *See* market, music

repertoire, 11–12
research, scope and value of, 19–20
resourcefulness, 31, 35–39, 116, 139
Rice University, 193
risk
  assessment, 31–35
  tolerance, 31